D1534937

# Uva's Rigging Guide
# for Studio and Location

# Uva's Rigging Guide for Studio and Location

**Michael G. Uva and Sabrina Uva**

*with illustrations by Christi Friesen*

**Focal Press**

Boston   Oxford   Auckland   Johannesburg   Melbourne   New Delhi

Focal Press™ is an imprint of Butterworth–Heinemann.
Copyright © 2000 Butterworth–Heinemann

 A member of the Reed Elsevier group

∞ Recognizing the importance of preserving what has been written,
Butterworth–Heinemann prints its books on acid-free paper whenever possible.

 Butterworth–Heinemann supports the efforts of American Forests and the Global
ReLeaf program in its campaign for the betterment of trees, forests, and our
environment.

**Library of Congress Cataloging-in-Publication Data**
Uva, Michael.
    Uva's rigging guide for studio & location / Michael G. Uva, Sabrina Uva.
      p.  cm.
    ISBN 0-240-80392-2 ( pbk. : alk. paper)
    1. Cinematography—Handbooks, manuals, etc. I. Title: Rigging guide for studio
and location. II. Uva, Sabrina.
TR899.U97 2000
778.5'3—dc21                            99-089953
                                         CIP

**British Library Cataloguing-in-Publication Data**
A catalogue record for this book is available from the British Library.

The publisher offers special discounts on bulk orders of this book.
For information, please contact:
Manager of Special Sales
Butterworth-Heinemann
225 Wildwood Avenue
Woburn, MA 01801-2041
Tel: 781-904-2500
Fax: 781-904-2620

For information on all Butterworth–Heinemann publications available, contact our World
Wide Web home page at: http://www.focalpress.com

10 9 8 7 6 5 4 3 2 1
Printed in the United States of America

This book is dedicated to all the manufacturers, inventors, and others who have contributed so much of their time and expertise to the film industry. They all have tried to make it a safer place to work. Great rigs, good job, folks.

It is also dedicated to my lovely wife, Sabrina. Besides Saint Peter, she is my rock.

This book is also dedicated to my son, David. I spent many hard years training him. He endured them and not always with a smile. After years of training, he did learn how to smile and nod a lot. He has virtually taken the torch from the master's hand. He has turned out to be an excellent grip, a fine best boy, and a very good key grip on several occasions. At this writing, David is an old man of 26 years. From father to son, good luck in your career. David, I am very, very proud of you.

*Love,*
*Dad*

# Contents

# Contributing Companies

## Manufacturers and Suppliers

Able Equipment Rental
8242 Orangethorpe Blvd.
Buena Park, CA 90621
(714) 521-5602
Fax (818) 997-0478

ADCO Equipment, Inc.
P.O. Box 2100
City of Industry, CA 91746
(562) 695-0748

Advanced Camera Systems, Inc.
16117 Cohasset St.
Van Nuys, CA 91406
(818) 989-5222
www.advancedcamera.com

Aero Cam Productions
6920 Hayvenhurst Ave., Suite 202
Van Nuys, CA 91406
(818) 997-0512

Aerocrane USA, Inc.
16139 Wyandotte St.
Van Nuys, CA 91406
(818) 705-5681 or (888) 766-0650
Fax (818) 705-5683
aerocraneusa@aol.com

Anytime Production Rentals
755 N. Lillian Way
Hollywood, CA 90038
(323) 461-8483
Fax (323) 461-2338

Cablecam Systems, Ltd.
17070 Simonds St.
Granada Hills, CA 91344
(818) 601-6333
Fax (818) 363-2570
jr@cablecam.com

Cinema Products
3211 S. La Cienega Blvd.
Los Angeles, CA 90016-3112
(310) 836-7991
Fax (310) 836-9512
www.steadicam.com

Ron Dexter
320 Calle Elegante
Santa Barbara, CA 93108-1809
(805) 565-3156

Eagle High Reach
14241 Alondra Blvd.
La Mirada, CA 90638
(800) 363-6590 or (714) 522-6590
Fax (714) 522-6591

Egripment U.S.A., Inc.
7240 Valjean Ave.
Van Nuys, CA 91406
(818) 989-5222

Equipment Express
11862 Balboa Blvd., Suite 398
Granada Hills, CA 91344-2789
(818) 360-8002

Bill Ferrell Co.
14744 Oxnard St.
Van Nuys, CA 91411
(818) 994-1952
Fax (818) 994-9670

J.L. Fisher, Inc.
1000 Isabel St.
Burbank, CA 91506
(818) 846-8366
Fax (818) 846-8699
jlfisher@worldnet.att.net

Genie Industries
18340 NE 76th St., P.O. Box 97030
Redmond, WA 98073-9730
(425) 556-8620
Fax (425) 556-6535
www.genielift.com

Geo Film Group
7625 Hayvenhurst, Ste. 46
Van Nuys, CA 91406
(818) 376-6680
Fax (818) 376-6686
www.geofilm.com

Gyron Systems International, Ltd.
39 E. Walnut St.
Pasadena, CA 91103
(626) 584-8722
Fax (626) 584-4069
www.danwolfe.com

Hachapi Tees
(Custom graphics and illustrations by Christi Friesen)
20407 Brian Way
Tehachapi, CA 93581
(661) 822-6999

Hollaender Manufacturing Co.
10285 Wayne Ave.
Cincinnati, OH 45215-6399
(800) 772-8800 or (513) 772-8800
Fax (800) 772-8806 or (513) 772-8806
www.hollaender.com

HydroFlex
5335 McConnell Ave.
Los Angeles, CA 90066
(310) 301-8187
Fax (310) 821-9886
www.hydroflex.com

Isaia and Company
4650 Lankersheim Blvd.
N. Hollywood, CA 91602
(818) 752-3104
Fax (818) 752-3105
www.isaia.com

Matthews Studio Electronics, Inc.
6910 Tujunga Ave.
North Hollywood, CA 91605
(818) 623-1661
Fax (818) 623-1671
www.camerasystems.com

Matthews Studio Equipment, Inc.
2405 Empire Ave.
Burbank, CA 91504
(818) 843-6715

Modern Studio Equipment
7428 Bellaire
North Hollywood, CA 91605
(818) 764-8574
Fax (818) 764-2958

Nebekers Motion Picture Video
1240 E. 2100 South, Ste. 300
Salt Lake City, UT 84106
(801) 467-1920
Fax (801) 467-0307

NES Studio Equipment
11043 Olinda St.
Sun Valley, CA 91352
(818) 771-9351
Fax (818) 252-7711
www.n-e-s.com

Ragtime
10905 Chandler Blvd.
North Hollywood, CA 91601
(818) 761-8463
Fax (818) 761-8483

Reel EFX
5539 Riverton Ave.
North Hollywood, CA 91601
(818) 762-1710
www.reelefx.com

Jack Rubin & Sons, Inc.
523 Flower St.
Burbank, CA 91502
(818) 562-5100
Fax (818) 562-5101
jrubin@wirerope.net

The Shotmaker® Co.
10909 Van Owen
North Hollywood, CA 91605
(818) 623-1700
Fax (818) 623-1710

ShowRig, A Division of SGPS, Inc.
1744 Abalone Ave.
Torrance, CA 90501
(310) 328-9844
Fax (310) 328-9843

SpaceCam Systems, Inc.
31111 Via Colinas
Westlake Village, CA 91362
(818) 889-6060
Fax (818) 889-6062
www.spacecam.com

Timco
10314 Farralone Ave.
Chatsworth, CA 91311
(818) 700-9005
timco@aol.com

Tyler Camera System
14218 Aetna St.
Van Nuys, CA 91401
(818) 989-4420
Fax (818) 989-0423
www.tylermount.com

VER Sales, Inc.
2509 N. Naomi St.
Burbank, CA 91504
(818) 567-3000
Fax (818) 567-3018
www.versales.com

Weaver Steadman
1646 20th St.
Santa Monica, CA 90404
(310) 829-3296

Wescam
7150 Hayvenhurst Ave.
Van Nuys, CA 91406
(818) 785-9282
Fax (818) 785-9282
www.wescam.com

## About the Author

This is Mike Uva's second book. The first, *The Grip Book,* the second edition of which was published in 1997, contains all the basic knowledge one would need to get into and function well in the film industry. The new book is about state-of-the-art studio equipment. This book branches out in a new direction. It includes helicopter, boat, motorcycle, jet ski, and auto mounts; manual and remote camera heads (the latest to date); special effect rigging trusses and cables; and all the hardware needed. Mike delves into mounting the camera in all kinds of precarious places—the belly of a Douglas DC3 aircraft, a jet ski, even the front of a train! Believe me folks, this newest book is written in depth. Look through it—you probably will see something that pertains to your department.

Mike has spent the better part of twenty years working with the finest directors and camera operators, great grips, and manufacturers of the best equipment invented for the movie and television industry. Mike teaches and shares the knowledge he has acquired in the form of books as well as his annual one-week class at the famous UCLA extension courses and seminars in different cities. Read this book, and join him in class. He promises, "You will learn." Mike keeps his word. I know this first hand. Thanks, pal!

*Jose A. Santiago*
Key Grip
IATSE #80

## Acknowledgments

### *Tribute to "The Deb"*

I had been doing my job for about 21 years when I wrote this book. I met Deb Schneider when I was still a grip driver, in about 1983. I had worked for many production managers before meeting her and have worked for several since then. I give tribute to Deb for the mere fact that I have traveled to several parts of the world with her in charge of production. Every time, and I mean every time, Deb had it together. From the moment I got the call for a booking, everything was, or so it always seemed, on automatic. There were storyboards (drawings of what has to be filmed), scouting, equipment, the shoot, the wrap, . . . the paycheck. Everything on time, every single time. On domestic and international jobs, from tickets, to airport, to hotel, to per diem, to scouting, to shoot, to wrap, to travel, . . . to paycheck. Please don't get me wrong—there are many super production managers. I have just been blessed with working with Deb a lot over the years. We all have our favorites. Me, I am just so old now, I feel I can put it in writing. Oh sure, I'll get a lot of ribbing and kidding from now on, but hey, I figure at my age, "The only way they can hurt me now is to roll up my paycheck and poke me in the eye with it."

## What This Book Is About

OK, folks, let me explain why I've written another book. I started with *The Grip Book*. That book, an excellent one I might add, describes the tools of the trade. Along with the tools are the tricks of the trade, then the nomenclature of dollies, cranes, jibs, and arms, basic and advanced mounts, not to mention expendables and gels, color temperatures and sprays. The book ends with a host of terms in a great glossary. The book was put together with the gentle hands of the publisher, Focal Press.

After *The Grip Book* was written and published, my good friend Marie Lee, publisher at Focal Press, said, "Mike, you should write another book. There was so much information in your first manuscript that you could compile the unpublished material into a second book." Well, being me, and having my ego fed about writing another book, I did what any red-blooded grip with a huge sense of self-worth would do. I compiled more of my education and experience along with the newest, latest equipment and technology. You will be so up-to-date with this book that you will find yourself explaining things to others.

Thank you in advance for looking at this book. I hope that you will find the following words educating and entertaining. If you are the kind of person who believes in "just show me how to do something, and then get out of my way," this may be the right book for you. When I was writing this book I thought about titles such as, *One Idiot's Complete Guide to One Way to Get into the Movie Business,* then *The ABCs of Gripping,* then I asked, what's in a name? This book will teach you enough to get a foot in the door. Once you have someone's attention, you can show them your desire, determination, and experience. Yes, your experience. You already have daily life experience that you use, well, daily.

You, he, she, young, or old (like me) can be a grip in the film, television, stage, or video industry. Yes, $E = mc^2$, but you won't be using any of that stuff. You will be using all your life experience no matter how much life you have lived. I bet that right now you can do at least three things that I do in my grip job. I am going to show you *every thing, every trick,* and *every way* that I have learned (and can remember). Here is one basic thought for getting into and staying in this business: Believe that you can be here. Your frame of mind will propel you. Now stop. Just for a second. Think about someone, anyone you have met who had or has a very positive attitude. It is like the flu—very contagious. Develop a "can do" attitude. Then smile! Almost everyone likes people who smile. That's your first lesson. Dress well!

Have you ever used your hand to shade (flag) your eyes so that you can see something? Well, my friend, you now have some grip experience. About 25 to 50 percent of your job as a grip is flagging (shading) the camera lens (eye) from light going down the barrel of the camera (directly into your eyes). You will just be using different equipment as a grip. That's the second lesson. Have you ever put on a pair of sunglasses or seen someone put a tint material on a car window? You now have more grip experience. The tint put on a car's window is nothing more than a large pair of sunglasses (filters). We use different types of filters, sometimes colored filters and sometimes almost clear ones. Each filter gives a different effect. You just have to learn how, where, and when to apply them. As you do, you will learn the why. That's the third lesson.

You have progressed to the next level of learning. Good for you! Now you can really earn your money, because you are going to learn a little about a lot. I am going to suppose that you are trying to get work in the movies or television/video industry. You don't have to be a grip to use this book. This book was written to help all departments.

I hope you see in truth what we use, when we use it, how it is used, why we use it, and where to get it. This book is written for directors, camera operators, special effects teams, set companies, and all the way to the top of the heap, production assistants, who will be procuring this equipment for the others.

All joking aside, browse through this book. You will probably find something to help you in your job. I have listed the company names and phone numbers to help you the same way they have helped me. These folks are the experts. Ask them. They will help.

This book contains a little about a lot. We use many items in television, film, and video. Let me take it one step farther. Suppose you want to work at a local convention center or circus or that a carnival comes to town and you want a job. The materials described in this book are used in these areas as well as in film and video. You can use your everyday experience with help from this book and create your own rigs.

In this book I list a number of other fine books. This book summarizes the material I have gathered in my careers. Yes, *careers.* I have worked mostly in film but spent several years as an airframe and power plant mechanic. I also was a Marine flight crew member (CH46s). What I am trying to say without trying to brag is, "You can do it." Just try and try and try again! If a 17-year-old high school dropout like I was can turn his life around, you can too. Just do it! (I borrowed that from Nike.)

This book provides lots of specifications and drawings of equipment and tells you where to order it. It also contains suggestions from me and folks I have worked with. But this book is not the perfect answer. I am trying to give you a feel for real moments and specific situations. Perfectly loaded grip trucks, equipment working flawlessly—it ain't gonna happen! I have used a towel for white bounce, aluminum foil for a shiny board, and a bifold table top for dolly track. I have used and will continue to use any substitute when the proper piece of equipment is not available. If something is unsafe, however, don't even think about using it. It will bite you in the butt every time. I have never been fired for saying something is wrong or for doing something safely. I am not perfect—far from it—and God willing I hope not to make any huge mistakes. Think about what you do. That is what you are being paid for. This reminds me of an old saying I heard when I was a young aircraft mechanic learning to fly in my off time: "There are old pilots, and there are bold pilots, but there are very few old, bold pilots." The translation is don't be dangerous, do it safely.

The way I show you how to do something in this book is not the gospel. It is one of many ways to do one job. It can give you a running chance at figuring out what you need for each shot. I do not explain all there is to know about hardware, mounts, remotes, and so on. I give you enough information to get a feel for what is needed. You will learn some of the language I use almost every day in my line of work. I list several great books I have read, owned, and heard of. With my book and the others, you should be able to make it happen for you. Remember, if you don't knock, they won't answer the door! Start knocking!

## UVA F.A.C.T.s
### (Film Advice and Camera Tricks)

The dictionary describes the word *fact* as a thing known to be true or to have really happened. I use a UVA F.A.C.T. to offer some field advice from my experience as well as the expert experience of others in the film industry. I also offer some camera tricks. These F.A.C.T.s are just some of the many ways to help you on your shooting days. I hope you will be able to use them daily. If you find a different way of doing a job using my field experience and your experiences and life's knowledge, it might help you and others. My guess is that you bought my book hoping to pick my brain. Dinner is served.

The first section of this book comes from an acclaimed director-cameraman for whom I have had the pleasure of working since the start of my career. Consider this master's word of advice to be almost the gospel. He knows the complete ins and outs of the commercial studio business. It gives me great pleasure to pass on some of his knowledge. Meet director Ron Dexter. He is a cameraman and inventor, and real Yoda-like in knowledge. May his force be with you. Read on.

## Warning/Disclaimer

This book is written to provide only pictorial information on the subject matter that is covered. It is not intended to give legal or professional service. If you need a legal expert for assistance, find one. Before you try to work as a grip in the film or television/video industry, find someone who is well qualified to train you properly. This book is a great aid, but it is in no way the final word on gripping or working in any other film or television/video department.

As they say on television, "Kids, don't try this at home." What I'm trying to explain is that reading this book will not make you a grip or anything else. It shows you the tools of the trade, not how to work them. Work only with a professional. Thanks!

This book does not contain all the information available to the publisher or author on any one subject. It has been written to complement and supplement other texts. This book is meant to be a guide to help the reader identify a piece of equipment on sight and learn the manufacturer's proper name. It is written to be as complete as possible without trying to train you to do this sort of work. I take responsibility for any mistakes, whether they be typographic errors or problems with the content.

The author and publisher will not accept any liability for damage caused by use of the information contained in this book. Again, it is highly recommended that the reader first work with a highly skilled technician. The sole purpose of this book is to educate and entertain.

REMEMBER, SAFETY FIRST AND FOREMOST.

## The Big Break, by Ron Dexter

MIKE'S NOTE: *Ron Dexter has been a camera operator since 1962. He is a member of the National Association of Broadcast Employees and Technicians Election Board, a union negotiator, director of television commercials since 1972, a member of the Directors Guild of America, and owner of a TV commercial production company since 1977. He is an equipment designer, a mechanic, and a teacher. He has shot commercials in 20 foreign countries and 35 U.S. states. Ron's business philosophy: Give people more than they bargained for and they will be so relieved about not being robbed that they will gladly pay the bill and not question it the next time. It works much of the time.*

Most people prepare and wait for the chance to move up the ladder. Often that next chance is only a trial to see whether you are ready. The chance usually is given when the opportunity-giver believes you are almost ready, not when *you* think you are ready. Your talk of moving up can be taken as normal ambition or a swelled head.

Once given a chance, don't assume too soon that you have made it. You may have to step back down to your old job for a little longer because you are not quite ready or because you are not needed in the new position at the moment. Breaks often are given on less demanding jobs so that you will have a better chance of succeeding.

Too often a break goes to one's head. You cannot become an old pro in three weeks. Knowing the mechanical skills of a job is only a part of the job. Every advance requires additional communication skills. This is where people often have trouble at the next level. Sometimes both the mechanical and the personal skills suffer for a while. Running a crew is a skill that takes time to learn. How you give orders is important.

It is wise to take on small challenges before tackling the big ones. Getting the best help is wise, as is asking for help from a more seasoned crew.

1

Often the opportunity for the next step up the ladder comes not from the boss for whom you have tried to make a good showing but from a coworker who has noticed your honest effort and hard work. A recommendation from a coworker with credibility is worth more than the observations of bosses who don't have time to notice much of the working situation.

### New on the Set

If you are new on a job or production, it's best to let your knowledge be discovered slowly as you work with people. They will be more impressed if you don't try to show them everything you know right away. Some outspoken people really do know a lot, but it's the big mouths who make the truly knowledgeable ones suspect. For every outspoken knowledgeable worker, ten are full of baloney.

### Offering Expert Advice

If you have experience in a special skill, offering advice can be tricky, especially if you are new on a set. Humbly offer your advice to your immediate superior and let him offer it to the group. It is more likely to be heeded. If your superior gives you credit, good. If the boss takes the credit, she will remember that you made her look good. Try (*very softly*), "I worked construction for a few years, and we tried this. It might work here."

### Offering a Hand

Question: When can you offer to help workers outside your department? Answer: When it doesn't threaten their jobs and your helping can't do more damage than good. Helping someone carry equipment cases often is allowed *if permission is given*. Dropping or spilling things is not help. Setting a flag for a grip usually is not appreciated. A camera assistant who builds a good relationship with the grips may be allowed to adjust a flag as the sun moves *if* the grips know the assistant is not trying to make them look bad or eliminate their jobs and if the assistant knows what he is doing. Getting a feel for what is appreciated and what is not appreciated is the key. Don't assume that people want help, and respect their refusal. Maybe they just don't have time to explain the task just then.

### Don't Be a Hero

For every mistake "a hero" discovers, there is someone who made the mistake. Don't let that person be blamed publicly. If you see something that appears to you to be a mistake, say something quietly and humbly to your immediate superior: "This may sound stupid, but is the 'stupid' on that sign spelled wrong?" Let your boss go to her boss so she can quietly say something to the next person up the ladder. The sign might be out of frame or be so small it won't make a difference, or it may have been decided that the sign is not a problem.

If you run out and yell something in order to be a hero, you are taking a big risk. The person at fault will remember for a long time the public embarrassment caused by the young hero on the set. The worst thing would be to go over your immediate superior's head to the director, assistant director (AD), or a different department. You won't hear, "Who is that smart kid?"

### Set Etiquette

Most people in the entertainment business at one time or another have a problem with set etiquette. For a newcomer on a set it's like being dumped in a foreign country. The language alone is a struggle. For people moving up the ladder, there are problems, and even old timers can lose their bearings. The rules often are different, and the glamour factor can distort one's views.

This is a compilation of issues as viewed by various professionals in the industry. These are not elaborate theories but are observations and opinions gleaned from many years of working in the business. Things are done differently on different sizes and types of shoots. Without a carefully defined structure, a large shoot would be chaos. On small shoots departmental lines can become blurred, but certain rules of etiquette still apply. Newcomers should consider all the rules until they are sure which ones apply. Here are a dozen universal rules for any set:

1. Show up a bit early for the call.
2. Be polite. Say please and thanks.
3. Let people do their jobs.
4. Be humble.
5. Ask questions about assignments if in doubt.
6. Watch what's going on in *your* department.
7. Make your superior look good.
8. Don't embarrass anyone.
9. Don't be a hero.
10. Listen very carefully before a leap.
11. Learn and use coworkers' names.
12. Work hard and willingly.

### Location Etiquette—Getting Along with Locals

Don't think that just because you are in the TV or movie business that you are something special. To a local person, you may be a once in a lifetime opportunity to fame or an emissary from hell. Your success on a location and the success of future crews on that location depend on your behavior. Everywhere you are treading on someone's turf. Tread lightly. The locals' opinion of you will determine how cooperative they will be. The first impression is often the most important.

The first contact should be made by the crew member who is the most diplomatic and has the most in common with the people who live in the area being considered for the shoot. Say, "Hello, how are you? You might be able to help us.

We're trying to find out who owns . . . ." Don't say, "We're here from Hollywood and we're going to . . . . " They may see Hollywood, TV and movies, and the city as the reasons that their children are tempted by drugs and sin. Or you might be the first convenient person to whom they can vent anger about something that you have nothing to do with. To a shopkeeper, you can be a customer or a shoplifter. Clothes appropriate to the area make you stand out less.

Start any conversation with a perturbed local with, "I'm sorry, let me get these people out of your way." Don't say, "We'll be a minute . . . ." Being there legally or having permission from a higher authority may not apply locally. The local people may have a battle going on with the higher authority.

Drivers should park out of people's driveways and parking spaces. Get permission. Don't block traffic. When it's time to leave, get directions to the next location, get oriented, and be ready to roll.

Treat motels and lodgings with respect. Use heating, cooling, and lights as needed. Don't "borrow" towels for your own or company needs. Close the door and turn off the lights when you leave. Be quiet, especially early and late. Park in stalls. Keep a low profile with the camera gear. Don't tempt. Word gets around a small town about your behavior.

An obvious effort to protect people's property will soften the blow when unavoidable damage does occur. Make a vocal effort to remind your crew to be careful. Cover floors, and have people store their valuables. Your crew is probably honest, but bystanders may not be.

### Teachers and Students

Like almost every seasoned person in the business, I am happy and feel obligated to pass on what I know to the younger generation. When there is time, I like to explain not only the method but also the principles. Sometimes people are insulted when told something that they already know. That's unfortunate. I may not recall that I told them the same thing before, and I have no way of knowing what they already know. The intent is to pass along useful information. Prefacing something with "you probably already know" will help avoid the insult. I start a job with a new crew with, "Forgive me if I repeat myself or tell you things that you already know."

On the other hand, I never expect people to know more than I know they should know. Asking me how to do something or how to approach a problem or situation only makes me, the teacher, feel better in passing along my infinite wisdom. I am never bothered by being asked again how to do something, even if I have already explained it. If, however, someone doesn't ask the second time and does something wrong, I am perturbed. I know that people can't absorb all the information thrown at them. When things are not understood, I give people the benefit of the doubt and assume that I was the one who failed to make myself clear.

There is so much to learn about our business that few on-the-job situations can teach us all we have to know. One has to eat, sleep, and live the film business to keep ahead of the competition. The grip must learn mechanics; the electrician, the theory of light; the camera operator, photography; and they must operate all the equipment besides. Our business always has someone waiting in the wings for us to falter if we do not keep up with the times. When we feel secure that we have it made is when the competition catches up.

## Can We Help?

Our business is not an exact science, and there often are many ways to do things. A wise boss listens, but some bosses, especially directors, are not secure enough to solicit help when they should. They are afraid to look dumb and can blunder ahead trying to be "the director." Crews have to be careful how they offer help. Asking "what are you trying to do, and can we help?" sometimes breaks the ice and opens up a dialogue when things have stalled. Or sometimes it is taken as doubting the director's ability.

## Examples of Bad Bosses

Their "improvements" will assure their taking credit for "saving" the project.
Their contributions must look good in the eyes of their superiors no matter what the effect on the project is.
They use "I" and "mine," not "we" or "our."
Their mistakes have to be covered up to avoid embarrassment, even if the results hurt a project.
They don't give examples of what they want and avoid commitment by saying they will know when it is right "when they see it."
They never arrive on time to a meeting of subordinates. They must appear always busy to justify their positions.
They schedule extra and inconvenient meetings to make their staffs work harder.
They are never available to approve work in progress that might save some work.
They never inform others about possible problems.
They save problems as ammunition.
They never blame outsiders for problems. By saying "you should know better," they keep the blame at home.
They never give praise, raises, or titles; doing so builds too much confidence.
They use the threat of firing to keep people in line.

## My, My, My

A "my crew," "my set," "my shoot" attitude on the part of a production manager or production coordinator rubs most people the wrong way. Along with the "my crew" attitude is often an attitude that future jobs depend on making that production coordinator happy. "Do things *my* way, treat *me* right, and I will see that you work in this town again."

People are very uncomfortable working under such conditions. Directors, producers, directors of photography (DPs), key grips, and gaffers can call their crews "my crew," but not the AD or production coordinator, who only puts out the work calls. The crew usually is selected by the director, DP, and so on. The coordinator only makes the calls.

Often accompanying the me-my-I attitude is never admitting to a mistake. A scapegoat for any mistake must be found and admonished, often along with a threat to job security. "If you want to work for me, you must make me look good in the boss's eyes."

On the other hand, DPs or department heads may talk affectionately about "my crew." They are saying "you had better take care of them," "don't abuse them," and "talk to me before you try to take advantage of them."

## Titles

People often are concerned about their job titles. A title is an objective measure of success. Respect people's titles. People who are the most secure with what they are doing usually care less about titles. It costs nothing to call someone a prop master. Take a cue from what people call themselves. You may give coworkers a boost by using a title when introducing them, even if they don't seem to care about the title. Examples are as follows:

| Rather Than | Use |
|---|---|
| Cameraperson | Cinematographer |
| Prop person | Prop master |
| Gaffer | Lighting director |
| Script clerk | Script supervisor |
| Wardrobe | Stylist |
| Someone's friend | Associate producer |

If people congratulate your doing a good job, give your crew credit for making it possible. Credit every good idea and effort so that people hear it. It costs nothing.

## From Production

1. All orders go through production!
2. Get start slips, W2 forms, and time cards.
3. Order all special tools and equipment through production, including pickup trucks, all-terrain vehicles, cranes, insert cars, jibs.

## From Other Departments

Check with all departments that may need support from the grip department.

## The Morning of the Shoot

1. Arrive before call time and assist the AD or transportation captain in placing the grips' electrical generator away from the location yet close enough not to impede fast setup and departure.
2. Have a shot list and confer with the AD to see whether there are any last-minute changes.
3. Inform the best boy what equipment is needed first and what may be needed later. Try to get a jump on the next shot.
4. Key grips should have their ears keenly tuned to at least three voices—the director, the DP, and the first AD. This minor eavesdropping will allow the key grip to keep abreast of the trio's desires and changes during the course of the shoot.

## Etiquette for Leaders

Say "hello." Introduce yourself, and get to know people a bit before you give orders. Ask about the families of those you know.

Use names. Make a list.

Thank people. "Yes, sir" and "Thank you, sir" or ma'am implies respect. Try it. (Works when you have forgotten a name.)

Appreciate people's efforts even if they make mistakes. If they are trying, give them credit for trying. Maybe your instructions were inadequate or confusing.

Assume that people are trying to do a good job and that they are trying to please you. Even if you think your instructions were clear, it is wise for you to take the blame for not communicating. The person who messed up will not feel bad and grumble the rest of the day.

In any conversation, listen first. Try to understand the other side first. It will give you time to plan your own approach. Your ideas will be better accepted if people are given a chance to contribute.

Let's say a director has very carefully researched and planned how to do something mechanical. Rather than telling the crew exactly what to do, he might start with, "I'm sure that you have a better way of doing this, but I had to plan this before you were on the job" or "I didn't get a chance to ask you about this, let's get through it and see if my idea will work." You can reduce their resistance to your offering expert information by being humble. Even if your way is best, a crew may be able to add shortcuts and ensure safety. Listen and let them do their jobs.

Make sure runners and assistants understand instructions. Instruct them to call back if they can't find something or if things cost much more than expected. Sometimes limited availability necessitates finding a substitute. Tell the assistant to call in as things change. Take the time to explain what you want so that the runner will have an idea whether something will work. Warn runners, however, not to make major changes unless they call first. Giving a priority to items can help. Simple things can seem insignificant but can be crucial for the first shot.

Ask for forgiveness if you have to repeat things or explain things workers may already know. Some egos are easily insulted. "I'm sure that you already know . . . . Forgive me for repeating myself."

## Personality Problems

We are never the cause of unpleasant events on the job. It's always the other guy who has personality problems. In most disagreements, both parties usually are right to some extent. The rightness or wrongness usually has little to do with the job and a lot to do with egos. Winning an argument can lead to losing a war. If two people who don't get along have to be kept separate, one or both will lose work. If one of the persons has anything to do with hiring, it can be a disaster for the other.

Don't risk your future over making a personal statement. Tempers cool off after a job and pressures are gone. Then it's wise to be humble and apologize, even if you are sure that you were right. Sometimes two people will fall all over each other claiming who has more fault.

Good friends do not blindly support everything we do. They should whisper in our ears that maybe we are out of line. Advice on the spot in the heat of anger is sure to be rejected. If you see that a coworker is losing perspective, think it over and even write down what you think. Making it clear on paper may make it more understandable. Even if you don't show the coworker the paper, look at it after the job to see whether you still agree with your observation. If your perception was correct, you may show it to the other person or talk about it.

Cautiously approach discussions about behavior. Listen first. You will be much more able to tailor your questions or comments to what the other person says. Often just their telling you about something, with a few questions from you, will help them understand a problem.

We all sometimes have personal problems that are difficult to leave at home. Both production and crew members should take this into consideration. There is an intimate relation between work and personal life. If someone is unhappy on the job it's difficult not to take the problem home and vice versa.

## Always Out of Line for Crews

Inappropriate sexual jokes and talk.

Political, religious, or racial jokes and slurs.

Having such a good time at night on location that safety and performance are compromised the next day.

Alcohol or drug abuse.

Negative criticism of anything or anybody within the hearing of clients, producers, visitors, cast, and locals. Keep your opinions to yourself.

Bad mouthing other production companies, equipment houses, and crews.

Loud talking on the set.

Radical wardrobe on location. Make your personal statements in your own
 neighborhood.
Accepting conflicting jobs.
Replacing yourself on a job without warning.
Not saying anything when you see a dangerous situation evolving.

Even if people are dumb enough to take unnecessary risks, if you see danger
evolving, you are morally obligated to say something. People often rely on others
to determine whether something is safe. Your concern may make people think
twice. In our business there are many ways to make things look exciting that are not
as dangerous.

### Out of Line for Production

Booking crews when a job is not yet firm.
Not sharing cancellation fees with canceled crews.
Holding checks or time cards.

### Always in Line for Production

Uniform deals for the entire crew.
Per diem paid promptly.
Paying for a wrap dinner.
Prompt equipment rental checks.
Keeping crews informed about job scheduling.

### How Not to Get Hired Next Time

Demand Hertz rental rates for your 10-year-old car.
Demand full equipment rental rates for your sideline rentals.
 (Negotiate and ask "what's fair?")
Put more on your time card than the rest of the crew without approval.
Increase your rate after being booked.
Obviously come off another job at call time.
Spend too much time on the telephone.
Don't watch what's going on in your department.
Talk too loudly.
Fraternize above or out of your category.

### How to Get Hired Again

Show up early for the call and ready to work.
Give 110% effort.
Be honest and straightforward.
Treat people as honest unless they prove to you that they are not.
 (You may have heard only one side of derogatory gossip.)

Cheerfully help others if asked.
Cover your immediate superior's interests.

## Company Vehicles

Don't abuse a company or rental vehicle just because it's not yours.
If you hear strange sounds, find out what they are. Turn the radio down so that you can listen for knocks and grinds.
Don't drive the vehicle until it dies. If you suspect a problem, tell someone in production or transportation so things can be fixed. If you are on the road, stop and have the vehicle checked. Call production immediately.
When you get gas, check the oil and radiator fluid. Engines die for the lack of either one. Check the tires for proper inflation.
If the radiator needs a lot of water, check the antifreeze mixture. Engines rust when there is not enough antifreeze. Let someone know.
Watch gauges and warning lights.
If a vehicle steers strange and shimmies, drive below the shimmy speed and tell production or transportation about the problem.
Don't trash a good vehicle with props and equipment. Protect floor, roof, and upholstery.
If a vehicle clicks when you try to start it, check or have someone check the battery cables. Push or jump start only if you know what you are doing.
Lock the vehicle if you are not in it.
Remove props, tools, and equipment from the vehicle if your driveway is not perfectly safe. Lost articles can mean disaster on the next day's shoot.

## Filling Out Time Cards

"Don't ever hire Fred again!" "Why?" "He pads his time card."
What really happened: The crew went into meal penalty by 420 minutes. The production manager went to three "almost staff" people and asked them to waive meal penalty. With that concession the manager went to the rest of the crew saying, "Everyone is waiving meal penalty" and got concessions from everyone except Fred, who was in the darkroom. Fred feels that rules are rules; he was the only one who put in for meal penalty and was blackballed for it.
This happens too often. Filling out time cards if the rules are being bent in any way has to be a group effort so that no one has hours different from the rest. Production uses all kinds of reasons to keep hours down. If the department works as a group, talk to the contact with the producer to reach a fair settlement. Fewer problems will arise.
Some producers have no idea how many extra hours camera assistants, prop masters, and production assistants (PAs) put in. (That's why PAs with no clout often have to work for a flat rate.) Warning your contact with production that there will be extra hours will take the burden off your back. If you don't clear putting in extra

hours, it might be wise to "eat" some of those extra hours. For example, let's say you find out that it's going to require that you go into turnaround to complete a job for tomorrow's shoot. You had best get permission to do so. Putting on another person to finish the job might solve the problem. You should have some idea how long it should take to complete a job. Turnaround is not a device to pad a time card. It's a device to prevent producers from working people so long that it becomes dangerous. You need your sleep. It's your responsibility to get enough rest and to plan your work to avoid too many hours.

### Crews and Their Own Equipment

Buying equipment to supplement one's income can be wise, but don't assume that it will help you get work. Would your employers be glad to rent from you *and* would you then become competition to your own regular suppliers? A camera assistant who buys filters and batteries to rent cuts into one of the money makers for the camera rental house. Rental houses lose money on camera body rentals but make it up on accessories such as batteries and filters. You might jeopardize your own standing with the rental houses by renting out your own equipment.

It's tough deciding how to charge for equipment that you happen to bring to a job. If something is requested, a rental price should be agreed upon. If you happened to bring along something that saved the day, be careful about how to collect for it. Some producers are fair and some are not, no matter how much time and money you might have saved them. Sometimes your future job may be at risk. It can be assumed that because you are not in the rental equipment business, what you bring along are tools of the trade.

Asking for a small payment is better than demanding it. First save the day, then humbly ask for compensation. Try asking, "What's fair?" I know, production rarely scrimps on their own comforts. It's your job to make good film; their job is to save money. In collecting for your equipment, don't "nickel and dime." Let people feel they are getting a bargain. "Pay me the regular price for X and Y, and I will throw in Z." "As use" deals (where an employee gets paid for equipment only if it is used) generally are welcome, if you can live with them.

Remember that your garage operation is in competition with established businesses that have more overhead, such as insurance, rent, and payroll. Be cautious with your sideline business. Don't let it interfere with the job that is your main source of income. It's better to give something away than to lose work. If they make you a better technician, your toys are worth the cost even if you don't make a lot of money with them.

Your job performance should in no way be compromised by your equipment rentals. You should deliver your equipment as any other rental house would and not be paid to deliver it. You can't spend all your efforts on the set watching out for your equipment. It's there just like anyone else's stuff. Everyone's equipment should be taken care of. If you show concern for everyone's equipment, maybe others will respect yours. Don't bother a company about payment for equipment. Many rental companies have to wait for money, as do producers of commercials.

## The Professional Look

There is a good reason to use professional-looking tools and equipment—to protect yourself if things go wrong. You can always blame the equipment if you have standard equipment. If things look homemade, problems can become your fault for not ordering the right thing. Although saving the day with a tool jury-rigged on the set can look heroic, bringing the same tools to the set can look unprofessional.

I have watched crews with chrome-plated tools in fancy cases make expensive mistakes and then charge the client an arm and a leg with a smile. I have also seen some bare-bones riggers do wonders with surplus junk for peanuts and watched them have to argue about a few real extra dollars after saving the client thousands. Yes, impression is important. A coat of paint and some painted boxes might be a compromise. Knowing how to make your rigs work covers for lack of flash, but consider the impression. People are fooled by fancy-looking equipment even if it doesn't work well. The world is impressed with technology and fancy wrapping even when it doesn't work well.

## Leaders: Facilitator or Dictator

### The Facilitator

A facilitator does the following:

Appreciates all workers' efforts because she assumes the workers are trying to do the job right.

Shows appreciation for hard work no matter how far off track it may be.

Even if workers are off track, doesn't say so until he listens to the entire presentation.

Doesn't point out flaws as she sees them but asks for clarifications with noncritical questions to help workers find the flaws themselves.

Readily admits failure to see the merits of a great idea; also avoids looking like a fool for not seeing the merits.

Gives workers public credit for good work.

Uses *we* and *our* not *me* and *mine,* except to admit a mistake.

Gives workers enough time to work on a project and keeps them updated to avoid unnecessary work.

Tries to let workers finish one project before adding another.

Makes himself available.

Make allowances for personal ups and downs and evaluates people on longterm performance.

Uses praise, raises, and titles as rewards for good work.

### The Dictator

A dictator does the following:

Never finds anyone's work satisfactory.

Approves nothing because she might be held responsible if the project doesn't turn out well.

Must improve everyone's work with his corrections, whether the work is perfect or flawed.

Starts making improvements in someone's work as soon as she starts reading it.

### Crew Issues to Address

Film students and relatives on the set

Renting every new toy to try it out

Always "making do"

Old pros who ration their efforts, teaching younger people not to hustle and thus make everyone look bad. There is a balance between abuse by management and featherbedding by crews.

Who is responsible for safety

Turnaround, meal penalty, overtime (OT), kit rentals, travel pay

Who looks out for the crew

Flat rates

Keys' picking seconds, including producers, coordinators, PAs. Ensure that they are qualified.

Loyalty—"You paid me peanuts when you didn't have money. Now that you have a big budget you are hiring all expensive professionals."

Crews who test new directors and DPs

Crews who always want more help

Unqualified assistants hired by production

Seeing different ways of doing things (by director or DP)

Crew invited to dailies

The time and place for appropriate conversation. A PA who is asked about his aspirations by a director he is driving home one night is ignored the rest of the shoot. Loose lips sink ships, maybe yours.

"It's not in the budget."

Definitions—call time, wrap, kit rental, booking a job, replacing yourself, flat rate, union, P and W, OT, turnaround, meal penalty, and so on. A new person on the set needs to know these terms (see Glossary).

"All producers care about is money."

"We'll take care of you next time."

### "Juices"

We talk of creative juices in our business. Here are some (very unscientific) thoughts. The best juice is adrenaline. It flows into our systems when we skydive, bungee jump, ski downhill, or finish a great shoot day. It flows when we see good dailies or the ultimate, a great cut. Adrenaline keeps us young with an upturned mouth from a continuous smile. Every smile releases a little adrenaline, a laugh even more—it keeps us well. Have you heard about laugh therapy? It works. We become ill only after a hard shoot when our adrenaline releases are down.

Adrenaline accelerates the creative process and facilitates the mind to think clearly and see things that we normally wouldn't. It puts us on a roll. We pump more adrenaline on shoot days. Our efficiency is three times that of a prep day. At the end of a shoot day, it takes a couple of hours to come down from the adrenaline pumped up. At dinner we can fall asleep over the soup. At the end of a shoot it takes a few days to rebuild our stores. Relaxing too much is dangerous. Without a cut to see or a new hob to start, we relax and don't pump adrenaline, then we catch the cold we had suppressed during the shoot. We also become addicted to adrenaline. We need to do something exciting or creative. Is that why we become workaholics?

The worst juice is bile. We pump it when no one listens. A good idea dies. Bile flows when last minute changes occur or the rig doesn't work. When we have bile in our systems, our brains grind to a halt. Solutions don't pop up like they did when the adrenaline was flowing. All we want to do is get the job over with. We give up. "If you insist on garbage, I'll give you garbage." Bile turns our mouths down and makes us old.

What about other juices? It's said that not many creative juices flow during a $200 lunch. True, but we can find that others can be reasonable about baseball, babies, movies, and food. Maybe after lunch they can be reasonable about a story board and others' ideas. The juices needed to digest lunch may also buffer the ego juices, and the delivery of ideas may be less charged with emotion. The need to defend one's precious ideas may become dulled. For more of this kind of thinking, try reading the works of Kurt Vonnegut.

## Résumés

Unfortunately some people exaggerate their experience on their résumés. That makes all résumés suspect. I throw most of them away. Most of my hiring is based on personal recommendations. It's much easier to bring in a person known by at least part of the crew. Most of my crews are hired by the department keys and the rest by the AD, producer, or coordinator on the basis of availability.

## Call Time

*Call time* means go to work or be ready to travel. It's not time to pour a cup of coffee and catch up on the gossip. If you want to socialize, arrive at work a bit early. Coffee and doughnuts usually are there early.

## Wrap Time

*Wrap time* mean just what it says. Wrap it up. It is not time to break out the beer and slow down. The pay is the same (more if into overtime), and the performance should be the same. Although beer is a nice touch, alcohol or drug use invalidates most company insurance policies on the set and on the way home.

### An Eager Attitude

Acting eager to work not only is a sign that someone is a kid fresh out of film school but also shows that work is a two-way deal. Eagerness shows that one is willing to make an effort for a day's pay. Sometimes, however, old-timers think it's not cool to look eager. It really makes a positive difference when a crew seems eager: "What can we do for you?" "Yes, sir!" "We're on it!" "You got it!"

### Peer Evaluation

Many jobs come from recommendations from established crew members. They know when someone is ready to move up. They also know when a certain project is over one's head and when someone else with a bit more experience is needed.

### Health on the Set

To survive in a world full of bacteria and viruses we have to build an immunity to them. If we were raised in a sterile environment, we would die at contact with the first germ. Less sanitized societies have strong resistance to germs. Our overpurification of food and water may increase our susceptibility to sickness. We are a society obsessed with cleanliness, but with the spread of powerful diseases, health should be everyone's concern. Some situations are as follows:

**Soft Drinks**   All actors should have their own bottles. During shoots with "hero" bottles or glasses (the bottle or glass being filmed), each actor's bottle or glass should be refilled or washed in a sanitary washing system. Restaurant supply houses sell disinfectant washes.

**Coffee**   Steaming coffee is always a problem. Liquid hot enough to steam is too hot to drink. A-B smoke (made with two chemicals by a special effects team) is pretty strong to sniff. Adding steam in postproduction is not difficult nowadays.

**Kissing**   How do you cast and shoot a close-up toothpaste commercial? The Screen Actors Guild (SAG) should be consulted about rules. Don't push actors to do something they aren't comfortable with.

**Cold and Flu**   Infecting a crew is somewhere between careless and criminal. In Japan people with colds wear masks. The mask is a badge of concern for even a stranger's health. We have medicines to hide cold symptoms, but we are no less contagious. Keep your distance if you have a bug or think you might be getting one.

**Smoke Masks**   There is much debate about smoke on the set. If masks are used, everyone should be provided with one if they request. Problems arise when one grip has a Darth Vader–type industrial-strength mask and makes a big deal about health risks. It looks like everyone else is less protected. We have been lied to so much about health safety that it's difficult to draw a line. Some crew members are more fatalistic about their safety and ignore the concerns of the more sensitive.

**Spray Paint**   The smell of spray paint is strong, and efforts should be taken to protect cast and crew from having to breathe it. Outside with a little breeze an actor can hold her breath if only a little dulling is necessary. Ask whether it's OK. Don't *tell* her it's OK.

**Camera Eyepiece**   We do catch infections through the eyes. Some people have very sensitive eyes. Assistants should be protective of the operator or DP who says he has a problem. A separate cup or cover should be standard equipment if requested. Eye problems can put people out of work.

**Hot Weather**   People often don't drink enough water. Lots of slightly cool or air temperature water should be provided. Personal plastic jugs with a name on each should be available for the crew. Everyone should be encouraged to drink water.

**Cold Weather**   Any day can turn cold and wet. It's smart to bring clothes for a wet, cold, or even a hot day. Get in the habit of carrying a small bag with rain gear and a change of clothes.

**Bee Stings**   Many people are allergic to bee venom. Parks are particularly bad. The food table can attract bees and wasps. Especially cover the meat. A can of stinky cat food some distance away may lure them away.

**Makeup and Hair Products**   The DGA and SAG have rules covering many of the makeup and hair products for any pyrotechnical procedures.

## The Answering Machine

People often don't want their answering machines to alert callers that no one is home. However, a cryptic or incomplete message is not helpful to a caller who needs to leave an important message. Have I reached the correct person? The correct number? Should I look for another number? Is the person I need out of town? Will he or she show up on the set at call time? Is that a nickname? Is that his or her child, wife or husband, or dog?

Try this: "You have reached 555-123-4567. This is William, known as Will. I will return your call if you leave your name and number. If you need me immediately, page me at 555-234-5678. Dial in your phone number after the machine beeps. Thanks." (Or, "I am not available until the 16th. Call 555-456-7890 for my availability thereafter." This avoids revealing that you are out of town, while still alerting the caller that you may be unavailable for any jobs.) Either way, you must always return the call with a "yea" or "nay."

### Success and the Ego

Success in the entertainment business can be rocket propelled. But DPs and directors often don't know how to handle success any better than a rock star, a politician, or a whiz kid. Making big bucks and having everyone desiring one's services can go to one's head. Ghandi kept himself humble by doing humble things every day. We often don't have the time or inclination to practice being humble. It's human nature—power corrupts. A formerly humble worker can become a tyrant in a new job that has a little power. One of the casualties of the demise of the studio training system was gradual advancement through the ranks. Now people can move too fast, sometimes from bottom to top in one or two steps. Be humble. Don't be a threat to people. Let them feel worthwhile. Let them succeed. Give them plenty of credit for their efforts.

### Financial Responsibility

One measure of success is the ability to buy things we couldn't afford on the way up. All the goodies can strap a technician, camera assistant, or budding director with payments that can be a huge burden when the real break arrives. One often has to work for a lot less money or none at all when taking the next big step up the ladder. Lots of vans, boats, and even houses are lost for nonpayment when the economy slows. Losing hard-earned things is a blow to one's self-esteem. You can blame the economy, a union out on strike, or changes in the business, but how far you extend yourself financially is your own decision.

### Ron Dexter's Suggested Book Source List

**Sources**
Both Birns and Sawyer, (213) 466-8211, and Gordon Enterprises, (213) 466-3561, carry a good stock of motion picture and TV technical books. Still camera stores such as Sammy's, (213) 938-2420, and Pan Pacific, (213) 933-5888, carry many books on still photography, but the stock varies. Books on TV and motion pictures carried by general bookstores often are "coffee table" books that have no focus, organization, or value as a text. Opamp Books, (213) 464-4322, orders and ships anything in print with a credit card order, as does Book Soup, (213) 659-3110. For used books, try Book City, (213) 466-2525, and Larry Edmunds, (213) 463-3273. Samuel French on Sunset Blvd. in Hollywood also has used books. SuperCrown and Bookstar special order and offer discounts. Try Barnes and Noble and Amazon.com on the Internet.

**Publishers**
Focal Press publishes a very informative collection of books on photography, film, and video. The books are quite well-edited for focus on a subject and are aimed at a specific level of reader. They are gold mines of material but can be over one's head.

Amphoto publishes a very good line of books on still photography. Many have sections and techniques applicable to TV and motion picture work. The books, with the exception of their camcorder book, are well-edited and focused on a subject.

MIKE'S NOTE: *This list is some of the many sources out there in the world. If you want to learn, start asking questions. Go to your local library. Call bookstores. Visit bookstores, ask colleges, and just keep trying until you are satisfied.*

## A Professional's Point of View

Here's a point of view to think about. Be a professional. Keep in mind the writers who have spent several hours, weeks, months, or years to put the project together. Think of the talented actors and actresses who are doing their best to make the thoughts on paper come to life. A great deal of time, effort, and money have been expended to set up the show on which you are working and for which you are being paid. It should be given every chance at success. Don't screw it up by talking and lollygagging while the others are doing their jobs. Be a professional.

If I don't show you a piece of equipment, I hope I have explained it in the glossary. This book is not the end-all of books; it's a thrust. I hope you gain enough knowledge to justify the cost. If you learn one thing and use it to improve your skills, others will notice, and it might get you called back. That's one of the many things I have aimed for.

Here's my advice about fraternization. Think of yourself as a home owner. You are looking for a great general contractor. You get a name, call the contractor, and conduct an interview by phone. It appears this person may be the one. The general contractor and the crew show up. They build exactly what you want and leave. This goes on for several jobs. The contractor is fantastic and does great work, as does the crew. All this time you have never invited the contractor over for supper. Then you do. Afterward, you sit around the table and swap stories. This happens a few times. You're still the boss, the contractor is still the employee. Then you hire the contractor again for a big job. Well, the contractor, who is now your buddy, is in high demand. Because you are the contractor's new best friend, you understand why he is not available for you. When he does show up, he is in a hurry because of his busy schedule. The work is not as good, but you understand, don't you? What I am implying is something I learned in the military. "Familiarity breeds contempt." Or to borrow a line from the movie *Moonstruck,* delivered by the character played by Olympia Dukakis, "You don't s___ where you eat." There is an invisible line in all business. Try not to cross it, unless you plan on staying on the other side. That's OK too.

## Hotel Awareness

1. Stand in the hallway and get a sense of how far it is to an exit. Count your steps to the exit, stop, and make a mental note whether the hallway makes a shape left or right to the exit.

2. Determine whether you can jump to safety from your floor.
3. Determine whether you can open the window in your room or smash it and find what you might use to smash it.

This is not paranoia. These are steps you actually should think about. Have a plan for the worst and pray for the best. I was on the eighteenth floor of a hotel when a fierce electrical storm knocked out all normal electrical systems. It set off a false alarm at 1 A.M., shocking me awake. I ran to the stairs from the dark of my room to a very dimly lit hall. On reaching the exit, I found myself being almost claustrophobic at the surge of humanity rapidly filling the staircase. Fortunately, a cadence was set, and we all found the ground level safely. Then the real tragedy began. Picture a huge casino and hotel complex on a holiday weekend.

The emergency was declared to be a false alarm caused by a tripping of the emergency system in the storm. Normalcy returned in a few hours. But I had a feeling. Have you ever gone against your inner feeling, wishing later on that you had not? Fortunately, I did not yield to just letting it pass. I found myself very aware of "what might have happened." I decided to walk off an approximate distance to several different exits in case one were damaged or closed. My wife, Sabrina, who just happened to be on this location to visit our children in the city where I was filming, came along. Although tired, she was keyed up from our rude awakening. She thought it a pretty good idea "just in case."

After walking the distances a few times, we decided to return to God's hands. After returning to our room on one of the now-working elevators, we discovered that the main electric power was still off. The room was cold and comfortable enough to allow us to return to our bed until full power could be returned to the hotel. Power, it seemed, was quite quickly returned to the gaming area (I assume it was closer to the electric control room). We finally fell into a light sleep.

6:45 A.M. Wham! The suction of the air conditioner returned. The lights came on (the switches had been left on from the ordeal earlier in the night). What, another rude awakening? How many more could I stand? Didn't these folks understand? I was there to make a commercial. The nerve. Well, my lovely wife, Sabrina, being the sweet woman that she is, said "You stay in bed, hon. I'll catch the lights and we'll get a little rest before your unholy call time of 11 A.M. for a scout." As she turned off the last switch, Sabrina noticed that the heavy blackout-style curtain was awry. Part of it had been sucked over the wall vent, it appeared. As she approached the curtain, Sabrina noticed the faint smell of smoke, so she thought, possibly dust that had been heated to the point of . . . well . . . smelling like fire. As she strongly pulled at the drape, filtered light from outside entered our almost pitch black room. Preparing to open and close the heavy material, Sabrina froze. "Mike, the hotel is on fire!"

Springing like a cat (something I don't do often at 49 years of age), I saw a huge plume of smoke. Deep, dark, black smoke, stretching for what seemed like miles. Then as if all hell were making a room service call, a burning shard fell on our window sill. It was as if someone were above our room throwing burning pieces of eight-and-a-half by eleven paper in front of our eyes. The pieces rested for their final moments before being consumed rapidly by the eager fire.

As we made our way down, I noticed that there appeared to be smoke in the exit stairwell. I knew I could not stop and return as if I were a salmon. Should I bolt out the next door into a hallway? What if I couldn't open it? Was it the self-locking type, a one-way egress? I peeked over the rail just in time and noticed to my horror and delight that a motorized fan was blowing outside air into the staircase. I was delighted because I knew we could pass through this area without much inhaling.

Here's my advice. Sometimes I say advice usually is worth what it cost you. Except in this case. Be afraid, be very afraid of fire. I travel with a small, battery-operated smoke detector. They are inexpensive at home and building supply stores and any hardware store.

### Travel Advice

1. Carry a battery-operated smoke detector.
2. Carry a small, double AA flashlight.
3. Keep a clear path for the door.
4. Eject, eject, eject!

## Fluid and Remote Heads

The fluid head in a camera gives hands-on control. The heads are designed with springs and lubricants that give the camera operator pan and tilt movement. The device usually has adjustment levers or collars that can restrict or lighten the friction of each head; the system is similar to that of an adjustable power-steering unit. Each operator likes a certain feel to enhance the movement of the camera. There are several designs. I describe some that are used daily.

Remote heads are electronic heads that attach to cranes, dollies, or rigs. Use of these heads is becoming preferred to having a person ride a crane and operate the camera. Remote heads have control wheels, a joystick, or even a fluid-type head with sensors to operate the remotely controlled head. Remote heads can be placed up to one hundred feet from the operator.

### *Fluid Heads*

#### Weaver Steadman Fluid Head

The Weaver Steadman balanced fluid head has a modular design and unique tube frame versatility to deliver 360 degrees of tilt with only light finger pressure.

**Features**    A tube is inherently rigid. The design offers maximum stiffness for all cameras up to 80 pounds (36 kg). Four lengths of tube are supplied with the head to allow for extreme tilt angle or minimum profile. The camera can be supported conventionally from below to be suspended from above. Extremely low camera angles can be obtained.

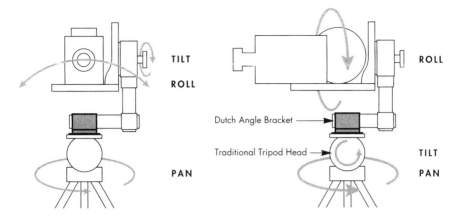

**Figure 1a** Balanced fluid head. Dutch angle bracket configurations.

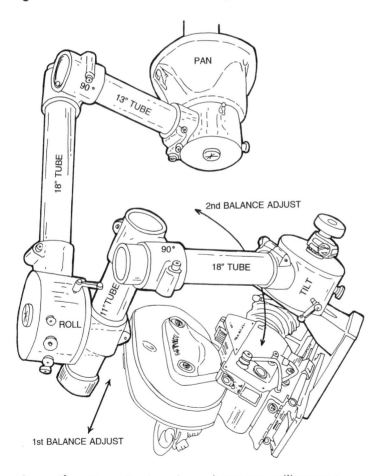

**Figure 1b** Weaver Steadman three-axis system on ceiling mount.

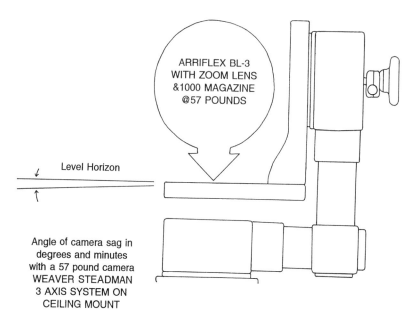

ARRIFLEX BL-3
WITH ZOOM LENS
&1000 MAGAZINE
@57 POUNDS

Level Horizon

Angle of camera sag in
degrees and minutes
with a 57 pound camera
WEAVER STEADMAN
3 AXIS SYSTEM ON
CEILING MOUNT

**Figure 1c** Arriflex BL-3.

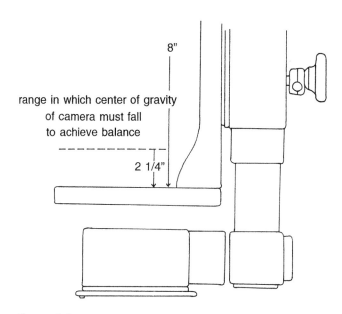

8"

range in which center of gravity
of camera must fall
to achieve balance

2 1/4"

**Figure 1d** Standard mounting.

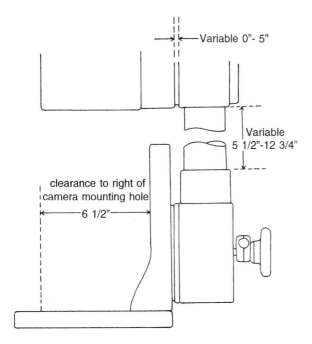

**Figure 1e**    Inverted mounting.

## NEW FEATURES

Lead screw leveler that simplifies camera balancing
Heavy duty axles, drop safety collar
Dutch angle bracket that allows mounting a Weaver Steadman tilt mechanism
on a traditional head for a roll axis

### Specifications and Components

| | |
|---|---|
| Weight | 18 lb (8 kg) |
| Maximum camera weight | 80 lb (36 kg) |
| Mounting | Mitchell base standard |
| Tubes | 4 supplied |
| Camera plates | 3 supplied for Panavision, Arriflex, and video cameras |
| Contact for sales and rental information | Weaver Steadman Camera Support Systems, 1646 20th St., Santa Monica, CA 90404, (210) 829-3296, fax (310) 828-5935 |

MIKE'S ADVICE: *Although ordering the camera equipment is not normally a grip's job, I have ordered this piece of equipment after speaking with a DP. It solves several unforeseen problems.*

### Balanced Fluid Heads

Comparison of Three-Axis Systems on Ceiling Mounts

| Feature | Weaver Steadman | Ronford 7 |
|---|---|---|
| Center of gravity design | Yes | Yes |
| Weight | 18 lb (8 kg) | 24 lb (11 kg) |
| Camera sag with 57 lb (26 kg) Arriflex | 0°21' | 1°26' |
| No. of dampening increments | 5 | 4 |
| Arri BL-3 compatible | Yes | Yes |
| Panaflex® compatible | Yes | No |
| Variable geometry | Yes | No |
| Camera to deck clearance | 1$^1/_{16}$" | 1$^9/_{16}$" |
| Level for inverted mounting | Yes | No |
| Dual brakes on pan and tilt | Yes | No |

### Pearson Balanced Fluid Heads

All Pearson balanced fluid heads are designed for professional film and video camera operators who demand the ultimate in smoothness and versatility in a camera head. The A4000 Pearson Head is supplied complete with the basic sealed fluid units, handle, and controls and is ready for mounting on Pro Jr. Tripod top plate. The A4000 requires the addition of a camera mounting assembly to complete the fluid head.

### Features

Model A camera mount assembly for Arri 35IIC
Model E-V camera mount assembly for lightweight video, Arri, and Eclair 16 mm cameras
Model BL-V camera mount assembly for larger video cameras and Arri 35BL and Arri III

### Specifications: Model A4000

| | |
|---|---|
| Body casting | Lightweight magnesium |
| Other hardware | Stainless steel or chrome plated for corrosion resistance |

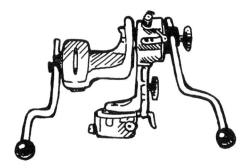

**Figure 2**   Pearson A4000 balanced fluid head.

| Handles | One 22″ stainless steel control handle supplied |
| | Two control handles can be used; the second handle and mounting bracket are optional |
| | Adjust to 360° rotation |
| Weight | 20 lb (9 kg) |
| Mounting | Any Pro Jr. tripod |
| | With optional adapter on Mitchell tripod or high hat |
| | No additional accessories necessary to mount upside down on crane or jib-boom arm |
| Operational range | +140° to −40° |
| Maximum distance between control handles | 22″ |
| Pivots | Ball bearings for pan and tilt action pivots |
| Control | All-adjustable fluid tension control allows three stages of control |
| Leveling | Spirit level |
| Tilt | Capable of full tilt with many models of cameras |

The Pearson Dual A4000 fluid head is supplied complete with three sealed fluid units, two control handles, and is ready for mounting on any Pro Jr. top plate. The design of the Dual A4000 eliminates the need for a separate camera mounting assembly and easily accommodates a wide range of camera sizes. The Dual A4000 is designed for very large video and film cameras with two control handles for mounting zoom and focus controls. It can be mounted upside down and maintains perfect balance.

**UVA F.A.C.T.**
Use celo material to make rain hats; use with grip clips.

### Specifications: Model Dual A4000

| Body casting | Lightweight magnesium |
| Other hardware | Stainless steel or chrome plated for corrosion resistance |
| Handles | Two 22″ stainless steel control handles |
| | Adjust to 360° rotation |
| Weight | 35 lb (16 kg) |
| Mounting | Any Pro Jr. tripod |
| | With optional adapter on Mitchell tripod or high hat |
| | No additional accessories necessary to mount upside down on crane or jib-boom arm |

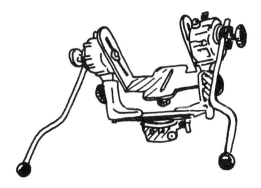

**Figure 3**   Pearson Dual A4000 balanced fluid head.

| | |
|---|---|
| Operational range | +140° to −40° |
| Maximum distance between control handles | 22″ |
| Pivots | Ball bearings for pan and tilt action pivots |
| Control | All-adjustable fluid tension control allows three stages of control |
| Leveling | Spirit level |

### OTHER CAMERA MOUNTS

**Model A Camera Mount**

Assembly for Arri 35IIC with ³⁄₈-inch × 16 pitch captive tie down screw

**Model E-V Camera Mount**

Assembly for lightweight video, Arri, and Eclair 16 mm cameras with ³⁄₈-inch × 16 pitch captive tie-down screw

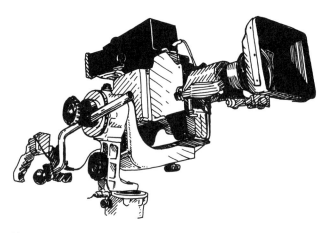

**Figure 4**   Pearson A4000 with video camera.

## Model BL-V Camera Mount

Assembly for larger video cameras and Arri 35BL and Arri III with ³/₈-inch × 16 pitch captive tie-down screw

These mounts are for video, 35 mm, and 16 mm cameras. The Pro Jr. to Mitchell adapter assembly has a shaft, washer, and lock-off knob.

The unique design of the Pearson head allows it to be mounted upside down (underslung) on a boom or crane that provides a low optical axis for ground level and table top filming.

MIKE'S ADVICE: *The Pearson head is great for low-angle shots. I suggest you look at the story board and talk to the DP to determine whether such a head can be used. The camera department usually orders this piece of equipment.*

### UVA F.A.C.T.

For remote heads, measure doors, and watch out for the hinged side of a door. It decreases the size of the doorway. For example: Bank of America's 70-inch-wide door actually is only 54 inches wide. Let air out of tires to decrease height. For installation, put the head on the ground and loosen level head screws, which are now upside down. Install the head being careful not to damage the thread. During installation of a remote head on a jib arm, or crane arm in an underslung position, it is easier to loosen all four leveling bolts to allow the leveling head movement and four-way tilting freedom. Set the remote head on the ground (deck) with the threaded portion upward if the head allows. With the arm balance out, lower it to the threaded end of the remote and gently slide the receiver hole over the threads of the remote, making sure not to damage the threads. Align the keyway, then install the wing gland nut on the threads and rough level it in place. Add weight to the bucket end of the jib or crane to re-balance the pivot point of the arm. Raise arm to a working height. A six-step ladder under the arm does nicely. Install the camera and safety. Rebalance the arm for the camera weight.

## Remote Heads

On a set I am often asked what remote heads I want to use. The production personnel want to place an order to hold a particular piece of equipment. I give them my standard answer: As soon as I talk to the DP and find out what kind of camera is being used and how high the crane or jib is to be. The weight of each camera usually is not the main factor. It is one of a few factors. Another factor is the length (or how high the camera is to go). The longer the arm of a crane, the less weight can be put on the receiving end. You have to know the weight of the remote head and the weight of the camera. Always use your worst-case scenario—the heaviest remote with riggers and extensions, the heaviest camera with zoom, and the largest film magazine. Plan for the worst and design for the best. Some cranes may take a lot of weight. But they must have added cable strength. This is wonderful for safety, but it calls for a wider crane. This can be a problem in a tight spot. You may not get the desired movement on the crane shot. Remotes can be squeezed down (the unit adjusted to a smaller size) for use on a shot. Say you want a high shot that drops as the actor approaches the walkway to a door, opens the door, and walks into the building. The remote head can enter through an adjoining window and go inside with the actor.

You can see why there is no easy answer. You have to know the other factor—the shot. After you have planned the shot, you have to find out what equipment is available. Sometimes because of lack of availability of equipment or money, shots may have to be reconsidered. I have worked with very together production companies and had equipment not show up, through no fault of the production company. The company is told, "By the way, we do have this other equipment in stock." You are faced with ensuring that the equipment will work and that it is safe.

I have always liked the Power Pod head system. It is pretty close to grip proof. It has one attaching nut, as do most remotes. It has very few cables, and the ones it has are bundled together in one jacket. Each connection is color coded, differently sized, and differently pinned. The Power Pod head comes with a small remote control box called a *zapper*. It is almost mistake proof. It either works or it does not. A technician usually is not needed.

Another good head system is the Cam-Remote by Matthews. This remote unit can be built to a smaller overall size. It can go through a small opening, such as the side window of a car. This unit usually comes with a technician. This is an added cost, and you have to watch your budgets. I say this as a company man. That's because I am one. If I put the production company out of business because of cost overruns, we both lose. So watch it. Discuss it. Figure out what's best for all. There usually is a happy medium.

When working with remote heads you are usually on a crane, jib, or arm. This takes you away from the camera operator; you are not in close contact as you are on a dolly. You can find yourself anywhere from 25 to 100 feet away. Have the sound technician set up a one-way communication system for the operator and you and for your helper grip on the crane or arm. Have the sound department wire an omnidirectional microphone and transmitter. You and your helper should be wired with a receiver and headset.

**UVA F.A.C.T.**

Listen like a field mouse, but be ready to spring like a leopard when needed. This proves two things:

1. You're paying attention (good for points).
2. You can anticipate what's needed (better for call backs). This practice works for any profession.

MIKE'S NOTE: *The following specifications were up to date at printing. Things change.* Always *check with the manufacturer or vendor to ensure you are getting the latest specifications. I can only show you some of the equipment available. New products are always being introduced, and old products are always being changed.*

### MicroShot Head

### Specifications

| | |
|---|---|
| Height | 3.5″ (8.8 cm) |
| Width | 3.0″ (7.6 cm) |
| Depth | 2.5″ (6.3 cm) |
| Weight | 1.3 lb (0.6 kg) |
| Maximum load | 3.3 lb (1.5 kg) |
| Maximum speed | 360° in 2.5 s |
| Minimum speed | 360° in 17 min |
| Voltage | 12 V DC |
| Temperature range | −59°F to 131°F (−51°C to +55°C) |
| Drive shaft | 0.35″ (0.9 cm) |
| Control cable length (tested) | 1000 ft (300 m) |

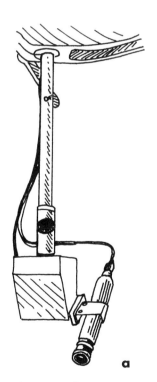

**a**    **b**

**Figure 5a, b**    MicroShot head.

### *Hot Shot*

**Features**

Nodal camera position allows the camera to pan and tilt on the center axis of the lens.

Pan slip rings allow continuous rotation of the Hot Shot.

Tilt limit switches ensure that there is no snagging of cables.

New electronics offers the sensitivity and control obtained with the Hot Head.

Fully adjustable speed controls allow 360-degree control of pan and tilt in speeds ranging from 2.5 s to 17 minutes.

Choice of control systems—standard joystick console or the tracer pan bar system—allows flexibility.

Reversing switches ensures that the operator has total and user-friendly control of the head and the camera.

**UVA F.A.C.T.**
If you have a scuba certification card, photocopy it. You have to fax a copy to production now and then so they can rent equipment.

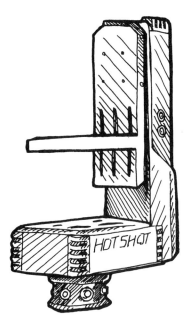

**Figure 6** Hot Shot.

## Specifications

| | |
|---|---|
| Height | 22″ (56 cm) |
| Load capacity | 50 lb (23 kg) |
| Width | 7″ (18 cm) |
| Voltage | 24 V DC, 100–240 V AC |
| Upright Width | 5″ (13 cm) |
| Maximum speed | 2.5 s/360° |
| Depth | 14″ (36 cm) |
| Weight | 38 lb (17 kg) |

## *Mini Hot Head*

### Specifications

| | |
|---|---|
| Height | 17″ (43 cm) |
| Width | 12″ (30 cm) |
| Depth | 6″ (15 cm) |
| Weight | 11 lb (5 kg) |
| Load capacity | 33 lb (15 kg) |
| Voltage | 24 V DC, 100, 110, 220, 240 V AC |
| Maximum speed | 2.5 s/360° |
| Minimum speed | 17 min/360° |
| Number of slip rings | 24 |
| Number of limit switches | 2 |
| Riser height | 4″ (10 cm) |

**Figure 7**   Mini Hot Head.

## Hot Head II

The Hot Head II can handle almost any 35 mm, 16 mm, or video camera. The system comes with the Preston lens control system and Microforce and Micro-servo controls with Heden Motors for zoom, focus, and iris. The camera has full triaxial capability without danger of dropout through broadcast quality slip rings.

### UVA F.A.C.T.
If asked to work dolly, don't roll over any cables. It may throw off the pin registry (the interior movement of the camera). It can also damage the dolly.

### Features
360-degree simultaneous pan and tilt
Full slip-ring control of all functions of film and video cameras
Broadcast-quality video pictures through slip rings
Adjustable height arm that accepts all film magazines up to 1,000 ft (300 m)
Speed range of 2.5 s to 15 minutes for 360°
Worral-type handle controls
Video console that provides one-person operation of head, zoom, and focus
Fully adjustable electronic limit switches
Power supply: 110 V, 220 V, or 24 V battery
Multicore, digital, or radio link gives complete cable-free operation up to
    1 mile (1.6 km)
Shot box facility allows all functions to be memorized and repeated in up
    to 99 user-defined positions

### Hot Head II Package
Hot Head II
Preston complete lens control system
Lens Witness camera
Pan and tilt wheels
125 feet (37.5 m) Hot Head main cable
Monitors
Triaxial adapters for video cameras
Experienced technician

### Specifications
| | |
|---|---|
| Height | 27″ (69 cm) |
| Width | 15″ (38 cm) |
| Depth | 11″ (28 cm) |
| Riser height | 4.4″ (11 cm) |
| Weight | 44 lb (20 kg) |
| Load capacity | 154 lb (70 kg) |
| Maximum speed | 2.5 s/360° |

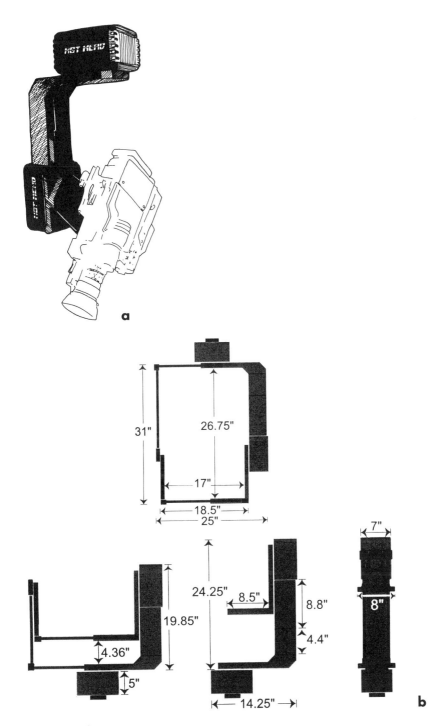

**Figure 8a, b** Hot Head II.

Minimum speed            17 min/360°
Voltage                  24 V DC, 100, 110, 220, 240 V AC
Type of mount            Mitchell
Number of limit switches 2

## Hot Head II Plus

### Specifications

Height              31" (79 cm)
Width               25" (64 cm)
Depth               19.85" (50 cm)
Riser height        8.8" (22 cm)
Weight              45 lb (20 kg)
Load capacity       120 lb (54 kg)
Maximum speed       3 s/360°
Minimum speed       16 min/360°
Diameter of tilt plane 19" (48 cm)

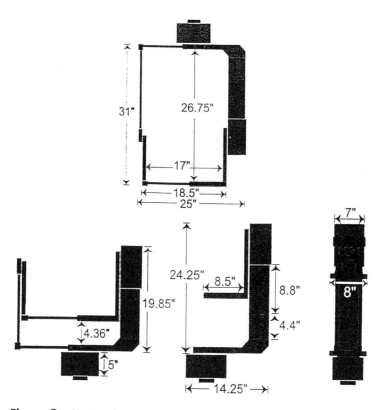

**Figure 9**   Hot Head II Plus.

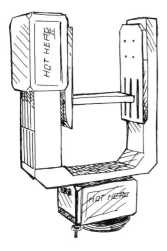

**Figure 10**    HD Hot Head.

## HD Hot Head

### Specifications

| | |
|---|---|
| Height | 27″ (69 cm) |
| Width | 19″ (48 cm) |
| Depth | 11″ (28 cm) |
| Weight | 48 lb (22 kg) |
| Load capacity | 176 lb (79 kg) |
| Voltages | 24 V DC, 100, 110, 220, 240 V AC |
| Maximum speed | 2.5 s/360° |
| Minimum speed | 17 min/360° |
| Number of slip rings | 34 |
| Number of limit switches | 2 |
| Riser height | 4.4″ (11 cm) |

## Hot Head S/NTS

### Specifications

| | |
|---|---|
| Height | 27″ (69 cm) |
| Width | 15″ (38 cm) |
| Depth | 11″ (28 cm) |
| Weight | 44 lb (20 kg) |
| Load capacity | 154 lb (69 kg) |
| Voltage | 24 V DC, 100, 110, 220, 240 V AC |
| Maximum speed | 2.5 s/360° |
| Minimum speed | 17 min/360° |
| Number of slip rings | 34 |
| Number of limit switches | 2 |
| Riser height | 4.4″ (11 cm) |

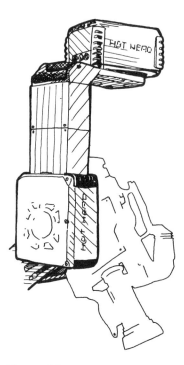

**Figure 11a**    Hot Head S.

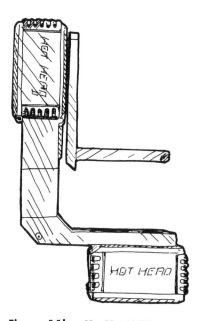

**Figure 11b**    Hot Head NTS.

## Pee-Pod 1000 Video Remote Head

### Features

Lightweight construction
Multiple slip rings with triaxial channel
Precise smooth control at slow and high speeds
Low noise levels
Simple cabling

a

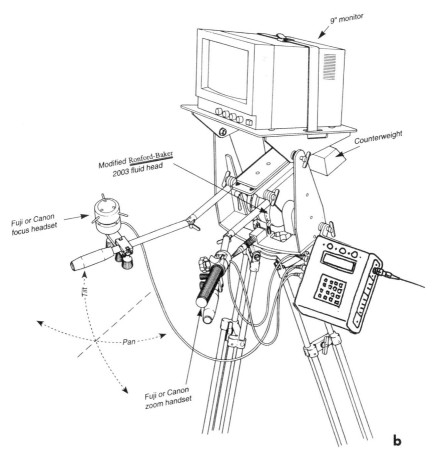

b

**Figure 12a, b**   Pee-Pod 1000.

Capability for programming
Capability for linkage to a personal computer by means of RS 232
On-board intelligence
Direct interface for zoom or focus with most broadcast lenses
Operator link via cable, telephone, radiofrequency (RF), microwave,
   or satellite

**UVA F.A.C.T.**
Copy your passport, driver's license, and social security card. Make sure you
have an up-to-date passport. I had mine for 10 years and never used it. Then
wham! I filled it up in a short time and had to get a second one. Jobs just
pop up sometimes. Production loves to see that you have your stuff together.
It makes for a lasting impression. I play a little game; it's called anticipation.
Everyone is impressed with a person who is together.

### Power Pod System

The Power Pod is a sophisticated electronic pan and tilt head, much like the Hot
Head II. Both Power Pod and Hot Head II are designed to capture dangerous shots
that would not be obtained if the camera operator and crew were to be kept at a safe

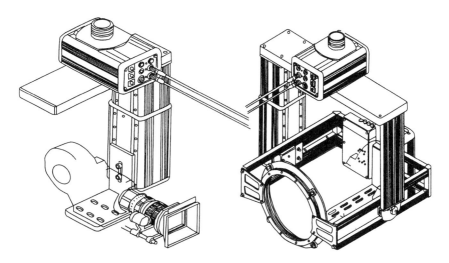

**Figure 13a**   Power Pod 2000.

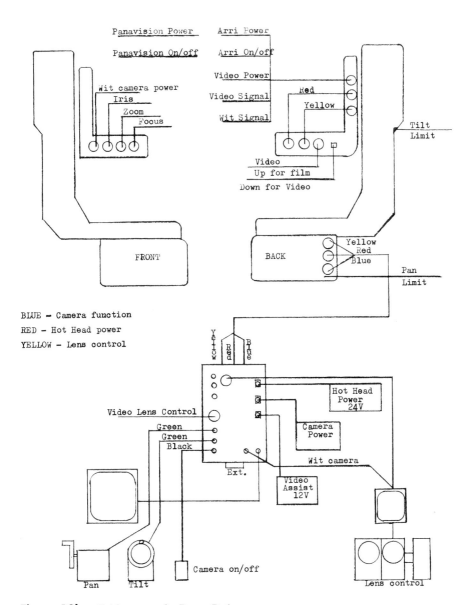

**Figure 13b** Cable system for Power Pod.

distance. With these remote heads one can capture moments of danger and excitement without compromising or losing artistic inspirations. The Power Pod and Hot Head II also give the camera operator an extra edge by allowing placement of the camera in unusual and precarious setups. Both heads are especially useful for sporting events and special effects.

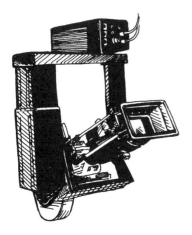

**Figure 13c**    Power Pod 2000, two axis.

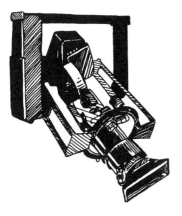

**Figure 13d**    Power Pod 2000, three axis.

### Specifications

| | |
|---|---|
| Height | 19″ (48 cm) |
| Width | 11″ (28 cm) |
| Depth | 17″ (43 cm) |
| Weight | 40 lb (18 kg) |
| Load capacity | 80 lb (36 kg) |
| Voltage | 12, 24, 30 V DC |
| Maximum speed | 3 s/360° |
| Minimum speed | 16 min/360° |
| Number of slip rings | 4 |
| Number of limit switches | 2 |
| Riser height | 12″ (30 cm) |

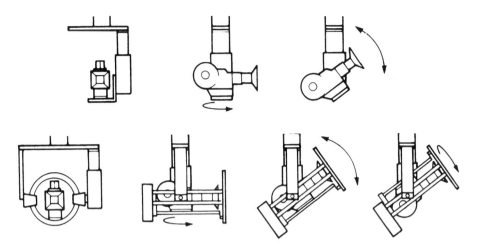

**Figure 13e**    Power Pod 2000. *Top,* two axis format. *Bottom,* three axis format.

**UVA F.A.C.T.**
Duvatyne poncho: Peel off about 4 to 5 feet of Duvatyne. Cut a hole approximately 18 inches from the end, and use it as a large black bib for reflectors.

The Power Pod is a remote head system that offers the director and the camera operator a variable format that can easily be changed in minutes. The Power Pod can handle loads up to 60 pounds (27 kilograms), giving smooth pan and tilt with very low noise levels. In its lowest profile the Power Pod offers a minimum distance of 8.5 inches (22 centimeters) from the top of the leveler to the base of the camera, giving a low profile and rigid unit with plenty of torque. In its tallest profile the Power Pod can rotate the Golden Panaflex®, Arriflex BL® cameras, and Movie-cam®, all with 1,000-foot (300 m) magazines and long focal length lenses. The Power Pod is useful for all video cameras.

### Specifications: Power Pod 2000

| | |
|---|---|
| Weight of two-axis format | 70 lb (32 kg) |
| Weight of three-axis format | 125 lb (56 kg) |
| Maximum recommended load | 200 lb (90 kg) for two-axis format |
| | 150 lb (68 kg) for three-axis format |
| Pan, tilt, and roll movement | 360° continuous |
| Electronic limit switches | Tilt and roll |
| Speed range of pan, tilt, and roll | 2.5 s to 37 h |
| Mounting base | Standard Mitchell |

A simplified control system reduces the number of cables needed to run the head without any loss of response or sensitivity. Control handles are only one option offered; these are Worral-type handles with adjustable fluid damping that gives smooth drag to the handles. A joystick control is another standard option. As with all Power Pod electronics, this unit is based on its own plug-in personal computer board, which can easily be mounted into other control panels. Both systems comprise three basic units, as follows:

### The Head
The head consists of two basic modules that when used together or with the other Power Pod accessories can be rearranged in minutes to produce many different geometric formats.

### The Electronic Control Module
The electronic control module (ECM) is a single unit that runs the head.

### The Command System
For the command system there is a choice of ways to control the head. These command systems are plugged into the ECM and tell the ECM the movement the operator wants from the Power Pod. The most commonly used command systems are Worral-type handles or a joystick. These and other options are available for the Power Pod.

## Cam-Remote Systems

### Mini-Mote Head Configurations

### Specifications

| | |
|---|---|
| Camera cradle capacity | 60 lb (27 kg) |
| Weight (empty) | 44 lb (20 kg) |
| Voltage | 18–27 V DC, 110–220 V AC |
| Pan speed (maximum) | 1 rev/2.4 s |
| Tilt speed (maximum) | 1 rev/2.6 s |

### UVA F.A.C.T.
Use whatever is available to get the shot. I needed a long dolly shot in front of a pirogue small swamp boat in the Louisiana swamps. The actor was to stand in a small craft and push off with a long pole into the swamp floor. It was a slow-paced movement. The director wanted long, slow movement down the center of this bayou. We couldn't place the camera in a boat because the boat would rock, causing unwanted camera action. I used two floating platforms that were square and flat bottomed. The camera, camera operator, and camera assistant rode on one platform. This was tied behind the other platform, which carried excess camera gear and two grips. A 600-foot rope on the front platform was tied to a tree down the bayou. I pulled the rope to set the pace requested by the camera operator.

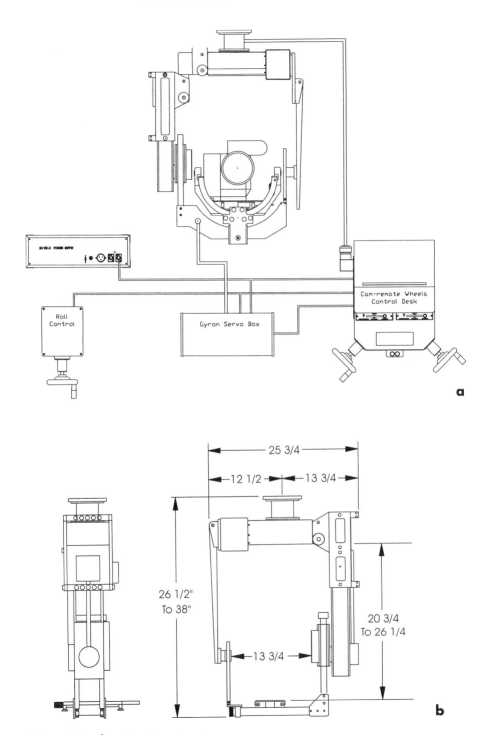

**Figure 14a, b**   Cam-Remote system.

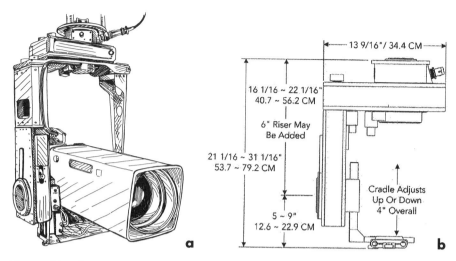

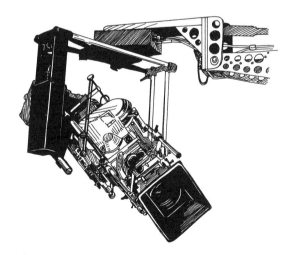

**Figure 15a, b**   Mini-Mote system.

### Scorpio II Three-axis Remote Head

Three hundred sixty degree continuous rolls are possible with the new Scorpio II remote head. The digitally controlled Scorpio performs flawlessly with camera loads up to 176 pounds (79 kilograms). All axes (pan, tilt, and roll) can be programmed and repeated. Hand wheel, joystick, and pan-bar control systems are available, and the video monitor displays all camera data.

**Figure 16a**   Scorpio II three-axis remote head.

**Figure 16b**   Scorpio II three-axis standard handwheels.

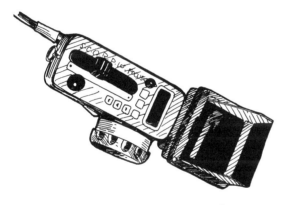

**Figure 16c**   Scorpio II lens motor control.

## Specifications

| | |
|---|---|
| Maximum weight at the head | 176 lb (79 kg) |
| Two-axis head weight | 62 lb (28 kg) |
| Three-axis head weight | 86 lb (39 kg) |
| Pan, tilt, and roll | 360° continuous rotation |

**UVA F.A.C.T.**

Place neutral density gel inside a lampshade or wall sconce glass to reduce light if no dimmer is used.

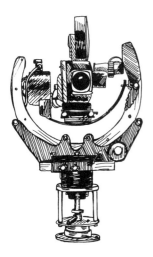

**Figure 17a**   Libra III.

## Libra III

The Libra III is a new-generation three-axis remote camera mount. It is unique in that it can be operated in either direct mode (digital) or stabilized in one, two, or all three axes at the flick of a switch. Custom-designed motors give the Libra III the precision of a well-tuned geared head that is complemented by the world of possibilities offered by stabilization.

**Figure 17b**   Libra III, three-axis handwheel.

Extremely stable, wet and muddy conditions are well tolerated. The Libra III excels in action on a boat, off road, on a camera car, or on a long crane. In stabilized mode, automatic back panning on an arcing crane or dolly move is an added bonus. At the other end of the scale, precision moves are taken in stride. The Libra fits all industry standard cranes and gripping equipment and can be suspended or mounted upright. The onboard memory card can store moves of up to 40 seconds. Recording of longer moves or motion capture is available as an option.

### Specifications

| | |
|---|---|
| Pan rate | 130°/s |
| Tilt rate | 130°/s |
| Roll rate | 100°/s |
| Voltage | 24 to 35 V DC/V AC |
| Weight | 50 lb (23 kg) |
| Width | 20″ (51 cm) |
| Height | 20″ (51 cm) |
| Power static | 3 A |
| Power dynamic | 8 A |
| Memory | RAM card |
| Pan travel | 350° |
| Tilt travel | 270° |
| Roll travel | 90° |
| Mounting bracket | Mitchell |

## Cablecam

### General Information

Cablecam can be suspended above any terrain, including mountains, forests, rivers, waterfalls, lakes, playing fields, roadways, stadiums, city streets, off-road terrain, and skiing courses. Cablecam is not temperature or moisture sensitive and runs smoothly in a wide range of conditions. Setup and breakdown of the system usually takes 1 or 2 days, depending on the location.

Running spans of up to 2,000 feet (600 meters) are readily achievable with the standard 60-foot (18 meters) towers. Longer spans are possible with higher attachment points, such as larger towers, cranes, or the tops of building or stadiums. Dollies with or without operators can boom up or down during a shot to match a landscape or to ascend or descend in relation to obstacles in the path of the dollies. This is accomplished by means of paying in or paying out high-line cable on or off a hydraulic winch. The dolly that carries an operator is 3 feet (0.9 meters) wide. The dolly that does not hold an operator is 2 feet (0.6 meters) wide, which allows rigging through tight areas, such as between trees, through windows and doorways, and under lighting grids and scoreboards. The remote dolly can be safely flown close to pyrotechnical effects. Note: Cablecam now uses remote camera operation for greater safety. Check with Cablecam *before* you decide on which system to use. They are fantastic and will help you design the safest way to get your shot.

## Suspension / drive system

Aluminum towers are transported in 8' sections and assembled on site.

Earth, rock, barrier, block, or bladder anchor.

Hydraulic winch

Hydraulic propulsion unit (electric or gas)

(Microwave visual receiver)
(Spread spectrum camera control transmitter)
(R.F. paint transmitter)

(Microwave visual transmitter)
(Camera control receiver)
(R F paint receiver)

Drive line counterweight

Suspension cable take-up drum

Cablecam

Dolly and tower sections are transported via trailer, or entire system can be flown to location

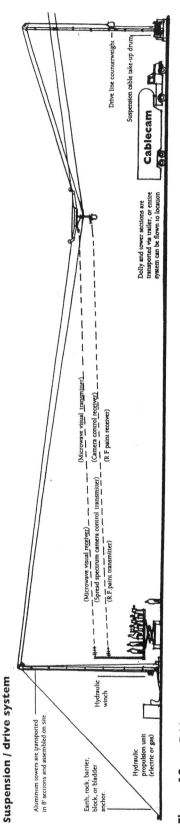

**Figure 18a**   Cable camera system.

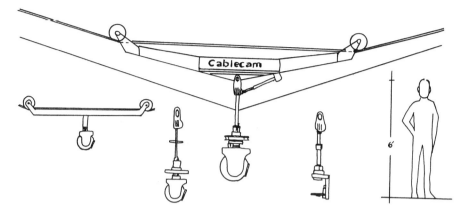

**Figure 18b**    Cable camera system, remote.

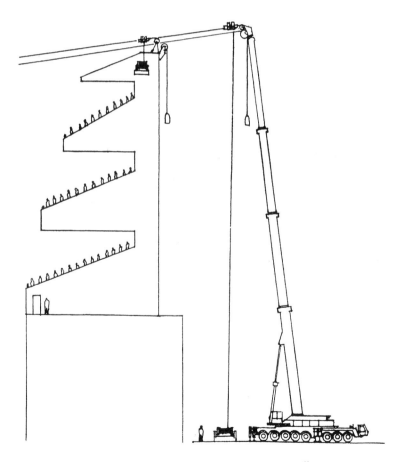

**Figure 18c**    Cable camera system on truck tower at a stadium.

## The Accompanying Crew

Cablecam has several crews specially trained to handle the electronic, hydraulic, and rigging technologies. The crew consists of a crew chief, lead rigger, dolly operator, camera operator, and microwave-RF technician. The staffed Cablecam setups generally require four or five technicians; remote setups require five or six technicians. Additional technicians may be needed if the location is especially difficult to rig.

### Cablecam Motion Control System

The dolly and camera move is programmed to repeat itself during each take. The computer can memorize dolly height, speed acceleration, deceleration, and direction. The computer also can memorize camera pan, tilt, roll, speed and aperture, zoom, and focus. The system can be set up to simultaneously trigger synchronized special effects sequences. These features eliminate the variables a filmmaker faces when combining camera tracking, stunt action, and pyrotechnical effects.

### Camera Payloads

The platform can carry 70 mm, 65 mm, 35 mm, and 16 mm film cameras, most video formats, maximum imager (IMAX™), Omni™, Showscan™, three-dimensional 65 mm, and any combination up to payloads of 2,000 pounds (900 kg) with crew.

#### Specifications

| | |
|---|---|
| Remote system | 60 mph over 2,000 feet (96 km/h over 600 m) |
| Standard remote dolly | 12′ long × 6′ high (4 × 2 m) |
| Standard minisystem | 6′ long × 3′ high (2 × 0.9 m) |

---

## Helmet Camera System 35 mm Point of View

The total system as shown in Figure 19 weighs only 13 pounds (6 kilograms), including the camera, the lens, 100 feet (30 meters) of 35 mm film, the helmet, and a 24-volt battery pack.

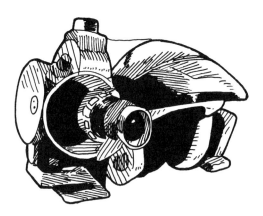

**Figure 19**   Helmet camera.

## Steadi-Cam

**Figure 20**   Steady camera system.

## The PogoCam System

### Specifications

| | |
|---|---|
| Construction | Aluminum |
| Batteries | 12 V nickel-cadmium system |
| Charger | Dual 110 V/220 charger |
| PogoCam camera | Nine-speed crystal control motor out of sync light, LED readouts (frame and footage), interchangeable lens mounts, inching knob |
| Video assist | Sony low light level, auto iris |
| Operator's monitor | Sharp 3″ (8 cm) LCD |
| Director's monitor | Sharp 5″ (12.7 cm) black and white |
| Weight | 19 lb (9 kg) |

**Figure 21**   PogoCam system.

## Aircraft Helicopter Remote Heads

The Gyron, the SpaceCam®, Wescam®, and any other mount outside a helicopter usually is mounted by a technician skilled at or working for the provider of the equipment.

### Wescam®

Wescam® systems are the original gyrostabilized film cameras built with more than 20 years of experience in stabilization and research and development engineering. All systems are manufactured to strict military specifications at a

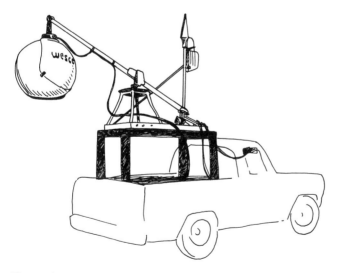

**Figure 22**   Wescam® in camera car.

quality-controlled plant in Flamborough, Ontario, Canada. Wescam® manufactures 35 mm, video, high-definition video, and infrared systems for rental and sale to entertainment, sports, electronic news gathering, airborne law enforcement, and military organizations.

### FILM SYSTEMS
**Standard Package**

Wescam® three-axis gyrostabilized camera mount
Mitchell S35 Mark II camera
10:1, 25 to 250 mm zoom lens
Two 1,000-foot (300 meter) film magazines
Speed aperture control
Crystal frame speed (1 to 120 feet per second [fps]; 0.3 to 36 meters per second [mps])
Filters (85s, neutral density [ND], and polarizers)

**Additional or Optional Equipment**

Helicopter nose mount bracket
1,000-foot magazines
Cargo van
Microwave-RF assist
Wireless remote control Sony video combo (8 mm)
Extra filters
Super 35 format
VistaVision™
Photosonics high speed
Panavision lenses
Specialty lenses

**Figure 23**   Wescam® on helicopter.

### SPECIFICATIONS

| | |
|---|---|
| Weight | 200–250 lb (90–113 kg) rigged |
| Shipped package | 14–15 pieces; 1,000–1,500 lb (450–675 kg) boxed |
| Electric requirements | 28 V DC input, 20 A current demand on gyro start-up, 7 A with gyros up to speed |
| Pitch and roll | ±30°, not rate sensitive |
| Yaw | 360° continuous, not rate sensitive |

### Image Stability

Images containing angular resolution elements of less than 3 microradian can be acquired with a Wescam® mount attached to aerial, aquatic, and terrestrial moving vehicles. Hands-off pointing accuracy can be obtained with respect to direction in space from a moving vehicle. Drift rates are less than 10 microradians per second. Line-of-sight isolation from vehicle motion is obtained.

### Capabilities

Under normal operating conditions, a level horizon is maintained. This can be modified for a rolled horizon (Dutch shot). Continuous pan is 360 degrees in either direction; tilt is up 30 degrees or down 90 degrees from the horizon. The variable frame rate is 1 to 120 fps continuous and remotely selectable crystal sync for any speed, including TV sync. The speed aperture control system yields constant exposure with variation in frame rate while retaining a rock solid image.

All camera, lens, and steering functions are remotely controlled and monitored from the operator's console. Function status and the frame line generator are displayed on the monitor. The monitor view is actual ground glass. The monitor display shows speed aperture control, focus (range in meters or feet), iris (f-stop), zoom (focal length in millimeters), filter (types), navigation coordinates (graphic display indicating pan and tilt angles), date, time, and elapsed time, and other readouts.

A separate operator's remote box is available for the assistant or Wescam® technician to manipulate all Wescam® controls, including focus and iris. This allows the operator to concentrate solely on pan, tilt, and zoom. The Wescam® system can be tuned to meet the operator's personal requirements through an RS-232 cable connection from the Wescam® laptop computer.

Steering is accomplished with a joystick on the control console or a hand controller (compatible with wheels on request). Steering aids are available, such as a zoom multiplier that automatically decreases the steering sensitivity during a zoom in for more precise control at narrow fields of view. Other steering aids that help tracking are standard equipment.

A dome enclosure with an optically perfect, antireflective glass porthole provides environmental protection and clear imaging. The windowless enclosure can be used to more than 80 knots. Side and nose mounts are available on most helicopters.

### Installation and Equipment Applications

Wescam® has extensive experience in sports, film, commercials, and music videos. The company has worked with innumerable directors, DPs, and producers to design custom mounts for specialized shots. Wescam® accommodates the creative needs of its customers. Experienced and trained technicians work with clients to find the best way to make the client's vision a reality. Examples of Wescam® custom work can be seen in a variety of commercials for Eric Saarinen and Plum Productions. Renny Harlin's *Deep Blue Sea,* James Cameron's *Titanic,* and John Frankenheimer's *The Island of Dr. Moreau.*

### Air: Helicopter

**Bell 106B Jet Ranger**   This is an excellent machine for low-altitude flying when no prolonged hovering or fast pull-aways are needed. Brackets can be adjusted to allow the rear doors to remain in place. Maximum aircraft speed is 135 miles per hour (216 kilometers per hour).

**Bell 206L Long Ranger**   The Long Ranger series is a larger and more powerful version of the Jet Ranger with extended cabin space. This is an excellent machine for many applications and better for high altitude and high temperature than the Jet Ranger. Maximum aircraft speed is 135 miles per hour (216 kilometers per hour).

**Aerospatiale AS350 A-Star/AS355 Twin-Star**   The Twin-Star is a dual-engine helicopter, and the A-Star is a single-engine helicopter. The Twin-Star is useful when the added safety of the extra engine is required, especially over open water or congested urban or city areas. These aircraft also provide a more comfortable cabin environment for filming operations. The B1 and B2 models of the A-Star provide extra power for high altitude and high temperature operations and when extra personnel are needed in the aircraft. Maximum aircraft speed is 135 miles per hour (216 kilometers per hour).

**Aerospatiale SA315B Lama**   The Lama is used primarily in high-altitude filming operations in which extra power is necessary. Although it cannot sustain high airspeeds, the Lama can climb like no other helicopter. It holds the world record for highest altitude for helicopters. Maximum aircraft speed is 85 miles per hour (136 kilometers per hour).

**Hughes/MD 500**   This series of helicopters is extremely small and has excellent speed and maneuverability. The small rotor diameter makes these aircraft useful for narrow streets, river gorges, and other narrow flight paths. However, cabin space is at a premium. Maximum aircraft speed is 133 miles per hour (213 kilometers per hour).

### Air: Fixed-wing Airplane

**Diamond MPX, Cesna 337, Cesna 172, Cesna 182, Aero Commander**   The fixed wing provides an economical approach to aerial filming. These planes can fly quite slowly, but approach a helicopter in terms of versatility and airspeed at substantially less cost. The system is mounted on the wing. Aircraft speed ranges from 50 to 160 miles per hour (80 to 256 kilometers per hour).

**Air: Airship, Blimp**

As used by Fuji, Goodyear, and Budweiser, these airships provide a nearly silent and very stable aerial platform when paired with a Wescam®. Although quite slow, the airship has very good endurance and is typically used for sponsorships. Wescam® has been providing aerial images for years for sporting events and live television airships. Maximum aircraft speed is 60 miles per hour (96 kilometers per hour).

**Air: Tether Balloon**

This small version of a blimp is attached to a ground cable and typically suspended above stadiums, golf courses, and motor races to provide aerial shots for sponsorship applications.

**Land**

**Camera Cars**   The Wescam® can be mounted to any camera car, insert car, or Shotmaker® rig by means of a hard mount to any part of the car or from a crane arm from the rear of the car. A long control cable allows remote operation of the Wescam® regardless of the length of the arm. A Super Technocrane can be mounted to a camera car to allow telescoping of the crane arm.

**Cable**   The Wescam® has been used in a variety of cable applications for specialized moving shots in which a wireless remote is needed. Descending rigs are used to lower the Wescam® hundreds of feet from tops of buildings, cliff edges, or anywhere else a camera drop is required. Cable rigs and mountings can be custom designed to fit almost any specialized filming situation that requires stability. The Wescam® was used on a cable rig for a Chevy Blazer commercial in which no other means was available to get close to the vehicle. Through the use of cable suspended between two anchored towers, this dolly setup allows moving shots where other systems such as helicopters and camera cars cannot maneuver.

**Cranes**   The Wescam® can be used on nearly any crane capable of supporting the weight of the system. Cranes commonly used are the Lenny Arm©, Pegasus® crane, Enlouva®, and the Akela™ crane. Any vibration, wind movement, or bumps during dolly moves are not seen by the camera regardless of the length of the camera arm.

**Tracks**   Track systems can be used when a traditional dolly shot will not work. A track system can provide a very long, uninterrupted shot or camera move from ground level up to several stories above the ground. Wescam® revolutionized the way the Olympics are televised by using track systems in multiple locations and events. The company has used tracks by Camera Tracking Company and Cam Trak, among others.

**All-terrain Vehicles**   The Wescam® is perfect for any all-terrain vehicle (ATV) shooting application. It provides smooth shots for ground-based shooting, field events, and sideline coverage. Wescam® can be mounted to Chapman vehicles and most ATVs.

## Sea

Wescam® has a long-standing history of marine cinematography. We can use our exclusive stabilized boat mount for work in demanding conditions such as high speed or rough seas or mount to a crane arm and extend over the side of the boat for close-up and boom shots. None of the wave action or vibrations from the boat motors are seen in the image. The Wescam® has been the only stabilized camera system used for major sporting events such as the America's Cup, Olympics, and off-shore power boat racing.

## Cameras and Lenses

Wescam® gets the shot with reliable Mitchell Mark II™ cameras that are fully integrated into each Wescam® system. Smooth, stabilized images can be captured at frame rates of 1 to 120 fps. The Wescam® speed aperture computer allows programmable speed ramping while exposure is kept constant for exciting in-camera effects such as time compression. Although the Wescam® comes standard with the Mitchell Mark II™, the system can be modified for a variety of other cameras, including the following:

Industrial Light and Magic's Empire VistaVision™ camera
Beaumont's Minicam VistaVision™
Photosonics high-speed camera
Sony high-definition camera

The Wescam® accepts Panavision® mount lenses. Each Wescam® comes with a 25 to 250 millimeter zoom lens. The following lenses have been tested for use with the Wescam®, and almost any other lens can be adapted as required.

| *Lens* | *Range (mm)* | *Stop* |
|---|---|---|
| Zoom Lenses | | |
|   Panavision Primo 4:1 Zoom | 17.5 ± 75 | T2.3 |
|   Panavision Primo 11:1 Zoom | 24–275 | T2.8 |
|   Cooke/Panavision 5:1 Zoom | 20–100 | T3.1 |
|   Cooke/Panavision 4:1 Zoom | 150–600 | T6.3 |
| Anamorphic Zoom Lenses | | |
|   Panazoom Anamorphic 10:1 | 50–500 | T5.6 |
|   Panazoom Anamorphic 5:1 | 40–200 | T4.5 |
|   Primo Anamorphic 11:1 Zoom | 48–550 | T4.5 |
| Spherical Prime Lenses | | |
|   Primo Primes | 14.5–150 | T1.9 |
|   Ultra Speed "Z" Series | 14–180 | T1.3–T2.0 |
|   Super Speed "Z" Series | 14–180 | T1.9–T2.0 |
|   MKII Primes | 14–150 | T1.0–T2.8 |
| Anamorphic Prime Lenses | | |
|   Primo series | 35–100 | T2.0 |
|   E series Auto Panatar | 35–180 | T2.0–T2.8 |
|   C series lenses | 35–80 | T2.3–T3.5 |
|   Super Speed series | 35–100 | T1.1–T1.8 |

*(continues)*

| Lens | Range (mm) | Stop |
|------|-----------|------|
| Special Purpose Lenses | | |
|   Frazier lens system | | |
|   Inclining prism | | |
|   Century Precision Periscope | | |
|   Kenworthy Snorkel | | |
|   Optex Periscope | | |

**Uses**

Films

    Aerials and ground, moving-platform shots for the following:
      Special effects and plates
      Opening and closing sequences
      Establishing shots
      Action sequences
      Beauty shots
Commercials
Music videos
Live sports broadcasting
Olympics and other global events coverage
Concerts and special events
Documentaries
News coverage
Military uses
      Day and night observations
      Patrol, military police, and security
      Surveillance and identification
      Damage inspection
      Disaster inspection from distance
      Search and rescue, day and night
      Coastal, border, and crowd surveillance
      Antiterrorist surveillance
      Long-range tracking
      Transmission line inspection
      VIP protection
      Tactical defense
      Maritime patrol

**Video Systems**

Wescam® offers four video systems for the entertainment industry—10, 16, 24, and 36 inches (25, 41, 61, and 91 centimeters). The 10-inch Weecam® system is the latest addition to the video family. It was used for the 1998 Goodwill Games and

Commonwealth Games to cover gymnastics and figure skating and is quickly finding new applications. This miniature gyrostabilized system allows the operator to capture unusual points of view without disrupting the sport environment.

The 16-inch system is a small, light system available in a variety of lens options, including a 10:1, 20:1, 33:1, and 38:1. It is built for diversity, ranging from superwide to long focal length shots. In the 1996 Olympics, it was popular for shooting on tracks and boats.

The 24-inch system is a full three-axis stabilized system that is rock steady. It is most commonly used on helicopters, although the Wescam® 24-inch provided spectacular footage on boats and track systems in the Barcelona and Atlanta Olympics. Considered the workhorse for sports coverage, it is also used extensively for TV specials, commercials, and music and corporate videos. It mounts to airships, boats, cranes, and ground vehicles.

The 36-inch system is the largest and most powerful of the Wescam® systems. The integration of the Canon 45× studio lens and Wescam® gyrostabilization has made it the premier unit for video applications. Combining high optical performance with broadcast-quality cameras allows extremely long focal lengths of up to 855 millimeters. This unit is used extensively for major sporting events. Most aerial shots are taken from airships to allow epic pullbacks from close action to city vistas in one long, continuous zoom.

### Video Packages

Wescam® three-axis gyrostabilized mount
Sony BVP-570 digital camera or BVP-T7/70 camera
Standard lens (options available)
10-inch Weecam® system lens: Fujinon 14× lens, focal length range
of 5.5 to 102 mm
16-inch video system lens: Fujinon 20× lens, maximum focal length
of 320 mm
24-inch video system lens: Fujinon 24× lens, maximum focal length
of 550 mm
36-inch video system lens: Canon 45× lens, maximum focal length
of 855 mm
Cargo van
Radios (intercom)
RF microwave link
Monitor, 8-inch Sony
Waveform monitor
Recorder and transmission equipment
Data acquisition system (global positioning system [GPS] logging)

Capabilities and equipment applications for film are roughly the same as for video with minor variations and additional features.

## Gyron Stabilized Gimbal, Model 935

### GIMBAL SPECIFICATIONS

| | |
|---|---|
| Pan rotation (azimuth) | 360° continuous |
| Power | 32 V DC |
| | 3 A standby |
| | 5 A maximum active |
| Tilt rotation (elevation) | ±75° from horizontal |
| Steerable roll rotation | ±88° from horizontal |
| Gimbal rate | Up to 70°/s |
| Gimbal weight | 135 lb (61 kg) |
| Stabilization | More than 5 microradians |
| Off-Gimbal electronics case | $17.4 \times 6.5 \times 7.7''$ ($44 \times 17 \times 20$ cm) |
| Laptop control desk | $16 \times 10 \times 2.5''$ ($41 \times 25 \times 6$ cm) |

### CAMERA SPECIFICATIONS

| | |
|---|---|
| Camera | Sony models: BVP-T70 or BVP-T7A as an option |
| Sensitivity | f8.0 @ 2000 lux (3,200K 89.9% reflectance) |
| Minimum illumination | 7.5 lux @ f1.4, +18 dB gain |
| | 2/3v format ($8.8 \times 6.6$ mm) |
| Gain selection | O dB, +9 dB, +18 dB (+24 dB option) |
| Picture elements | $768 \times 494$ NTSC ($752 \times 582$ PAL) |
| Horizontal resolution | >700 Lines |
| Optical filters | 1:3,200K, 2:5,600K +1/16 ND, 3:5,600K, 4:5,600K +1/4 ND |
| Video signal to noise (S/N) ratio | 62 ndB NTSC (60 dB PAL) |

**Figure 24a**  Stabilized Gimbal model 935.

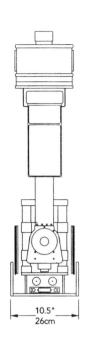

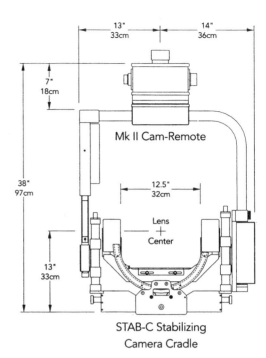

Mk II Cam-Remote

STAB-C Stabilizing
Camera Cradle

**Figure 24b**   Gyron STAB-C.

## LENS SPECIFICATIONS
Fujinon A-36 × 10.5
BERD-R28, f2.0
36 to 1 zoom ratio
Built-in extender

## CASE DIMENSIONS AND WEIGHT
### Camera

| Case | $D \times W \times H$ | Contents |
|------|------------------------|----------|
| 1 | $43 \times 40 \times 27$ | Dome |
| 2 | $41 \times 22 \times 38$ | Camera, gyro door |
| 3 | $32 \times 32 \times 18$ | Console |
| 4 | $21 \times 20 \times 30$ | Accessories, spare parts |
| 5 | $10 \times 20 \times 26$ | Tools, accessories |
| 6 | $20 \times 32 \times 18$ | Counterweight, inverter |
| 7 | $24 \times 12 \times 11$ | Gyrostabilizer |
| 8 | $10 \times 20 \times 26$ | Spare electronics components |
| 9 | $30 \times 18 \times 54$ | Aluminum stand |

Dimensions are in inches. Approximate weight for nine pieces: 1,084 lb (488 kg).

### Helicopter Bracket

| Case | $D \times W \times H$ | Model | Approximate Weight |
|------|-----------------------|-------|--------------------|
| 10a | $13 \times 49 \times 45$ | Jet Ranger | 190 lb (87 kg) for two pieces |
| 11a | $12 \times 23 \times 82$ | Jet Ranger | |
| or | | | |
| 10b | $61 \times 15 \times 19$ | A-Star/Twin Star | 310 lb (140 kg) for two pieces |
| 11b | $76 \times 13 \times 27$ | A-Star/Twin Star | |
| or | | | |
| 10c | $7 \times 14 \times 73$ | Lama 150 lb (68 kg) | |

Dimensions are in inches.

## Gyrosphere

### Specifications

| | |
|---|---|
| Camera | Modified Mitchell Mark II ™ with 1,000′ magazines (only 1,000′ loads may be used) |
| Standard lens | Cooke 10× zoom is available with 2× extender, and anamorphic adapter |
| Optional | Cooke 5× zoom, BNC mount, Canon high-speed prime lenses |
| Speed aperture computer | Standard |
| Camera speed range | 1–36 fps |
| VCR format | VHS |
| Power requirements | 28 V DC, 20 A maximum, 110/220 V AC, 750 V AC |

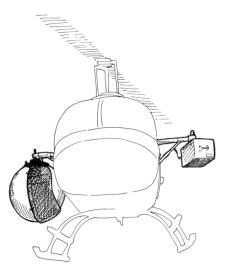

**Figure 25**   Gyrosphere.

## *SpaceCam®*

### Camera Formats

The SpaceCam® gyrostabilized camera systems are equipped with in-house 35 mm–4 perforations and 35 mm–8 perf. VistaVision™ or 65 mm–5 perf. cameras, all with 1,000-foot loads and a wide variety of lens options. SpaceCam® also can accommodate 65 mm–8 perf., 65 mm–15 perf., IMAX™, and high-definition television (HDTV) configurations.

### Applications

SpaceCam® provides exclusive Federal Aviation Administration (FAA)–approved nose mount brackets for helicopter applications. These brackets can be mounted on a variety of other structures or conveyances, including horizontal and vertical cable rigs, camera cars, boats, and cranes.

### Contact

Ron Goodman, President; Rich Winogard, Marketing Manager
SpaceCam Systems, Inc.
31111 Via Colinas
Westlake Village, CA 91362
(818) 889-6060
Fax (818) 889-6062
www.spacecam.com

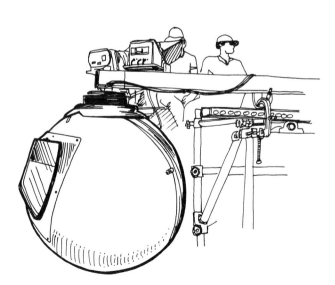

**Figure 26**   SpaceCam® on back of insert car.

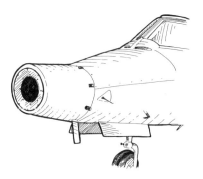

**Figure 27** Arri 535 Lear nose mount.

## Arri 535

### Lear Nose Mount

The standard nose mount has been modified to accept the Arri 535 camera with a 1,000-foot coaxial magazine. A new snout for the Lear nose mount provides room for almost any camera, including IMAX™ format. IMAX™ now can be shot from a completely redesigned belly port. The images are stunning.

### Belly Mount

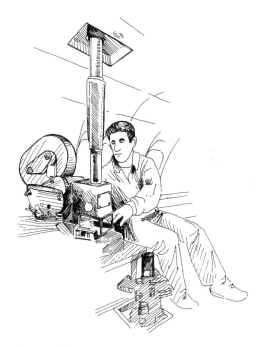

**Figure 28** Belly port.

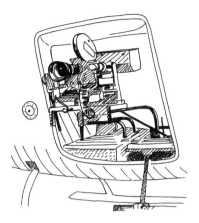

**Figure 29**   Magnum mount.

## Continental Camera Systems, Inc.

### Magnum Mount
A magnum mount is a side-looking helicopter camera system for smooth and spectacular aerial action sequences. Continental can provide a camera and operator, or you can use your own.

### Outside Mount
The outside mount allows extremely smooth and dynamic shots with excellent stability. The camera operator has unrestricted photographic access to subjects. Points of view (POVs) can be obtained that never before were available from a helicopter. This mount is available only as a complete package (pilot/DP, helicopter, operator, and mount).

**Figure 30**   Outside mount.

## Belly Mount

The belly mount is an under the helicopter camera system remotely controlled from the cockpit. It tilts from horizon to straight down. Continental can provide a complete package, or you can use your camera and operator. Any camera up to 40 pounds can be used.

### Technical Specifications

| | |
|---|---|
| Format | 35 mm full aperture |
| Frame rate | 1–40 fps |
| Registration | Pin registration |
| Shutter | Variable 11°–130° |
| Power | 24 V DC, nicad pack |
| Lens mount | Arri |
| Magazine | 100′ daylight load |
| Weight | 5 lb less lens and film |
| Viewing | Boresight |

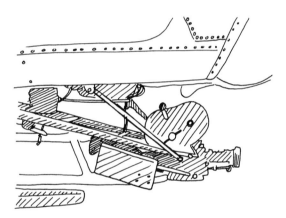

**Figure 31**   Belly mount.

## Tyler Camera Systems

### Tyler System Supplemental Type Certificate

FAA APPROVED ROTOR CRAFT FLIGHT MANUAL SUPPLEMENT TO BELL MODELS 206, 206A, 206A-1, 206B, 206B-1 (JET RANGER II AND III), 206 L-1, AND 206 L-3 ROTOR CRAFT FLIGHT MANUALS

The information in this document is FAA approved material which, together with the basic Flight Manual, is applicable and must be carried in the basic manual when the helicopter is modified by the installation of the Tyler Model 806 Major Mount in accordance with STC SH3234NM.

The information in this document supersedes the basic manual only where covered in the items contained herein. For Limitations, Procedures, and Performance not contained in this supplement, consult the manual proper.

### I. Limitations

1. VNE = 100 mph (87 KCAS) power ON or OFF with mount, with or without camera assembly and Lexan Wind Guard, with ONE or BOTH aft cabin doors OFF, sea level to 3000 ft. density altitude.
2. VNE = 80 mph (69KCAS) power ON or OFF with mount, with or without camera assembly and Lexan Wind Guard, with ONE or BOTH Forward, All, or Any Combination of Forward and Aft Doors Off, sea level to 3000 ft. density altitude.
3. Decrease VNE one mph per 1000 ft. above 3000 ft. density altitude.
4. Protracted Rearward and Sideward Flight Prohibited with any combination of Doors Off, with or without camera assembly and Lexan Wind Guard.
5. Model 206B longitudinal C.G. limited between 106.0 in. and 110.0 in. with one or both Forward doors OFF or any combination of Forward and Aft cabin doors OFF with mount, with or without camera assembly and Lexan Wind Guard.

### II. Normal Operations

The basic Tyler Camera Systems 806 Major Mount configuration is with Camera Assembly (Camera, mount, film magazine) installed. Operation, installation and removal of the Camera Assembly and Camera Ballast are to be conducted in accordance with Tyler Camera Systems Installation Manual No. TCS4-85, "Tyler 806 Major Mount for Bell Jet Ranger Helicopters."

The Camera Assembly may be installed or removed by a certified mechanic. Caution: Handle mount with care as it is heavy and unwieldy.

For right side installation during takeoff, landing and ferrying, the camera operator will loosen his safety belt, turn so that his back is against the camera mount backrest-headrest, secure camera installation from movement and tighten safety belts.

For left side installation during takeoff, landing and ferrying, the camera operator will sit with his back against the helicopter firewall and use the standard far left passenger safety belt as well as camera mount safety belt. See report TCS4-85 "Installation Manual for Tyler 806 Major Mount for Bell Jet Ranger Helicopters."

### III. Performance Data

1. Hover performance not affected.
2. Reduce Rate of Climb Chart Data 350 ft/min when operating with one or both aft cabin door(s) off.

FAA APPROVED: Frank J. Hoerman
Supervisor, Flight Test Section
FAA Western Aircraft Certification Office
Northwest Mountain Region
DATE: March 18, 1986

### Tyler Middle Mount

I have mounted this equipment for years on the prescribed helicopter. Today most pieces are mounted before the aircraft arrives. There may be times, however, when you need to know how to mount something. I strongly suggest that you have the vendor or supplier or a Tyler representative show you how to perform the installation. The Tyler website (www.tylermount.com) is extremely helpful. Find the

**Figure 32** Tyler Model 403 helicopter camera middle mount. Maximum camera weight is 80 pounds.

mounts you need, and print the step-by-step instructions, which are up to date. Then call the vendor-supplier or Tyler.

Safety is a huge concern with all rigs, not just Tyler mounts. The illustrations herein are provided only to give you an idea of what each rig entails. *They are not instructions.* Almost everyone who works with this equipment is very talented. I have been walked through a problem over the phone by representatives from Tyler. I have even met Mr. Tyler himself. He is a delightful genius. His company has the same philosophy. They are there to help you from A to Z. A visit to the Tyler shop will give more than you need for the most tricky shots.

### Installation of the Tyler Middle Mount

Remove the PI pins (aka, quick release or safety release pins) or screws from the doors and remove the doors. Replace the PI pins or screws. Remove all seat and back cushions or other obstacles from the seat and floor.

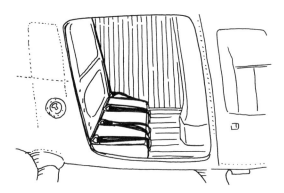

**Figure 33** Preparation for Tyler middle mount.

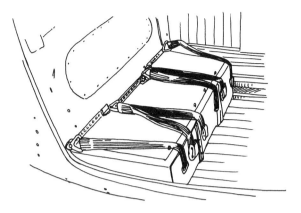

**Figure 34**    Preparation for Tyler middle mount, continued.

Place the camera mount seat assembly on the rear seat of the helicopter (right side) and unfold the camera operator's seat.

**Figure 35**    Camera mount seat assembly.

Pivot the seat up 45 degrees and slide the backrest on from the rear of the operator's seat. The headrest installs on the right side only.

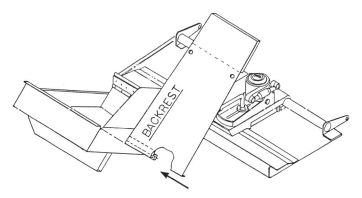

**Figure 36**  Rear view.

Hook the two bungee cords into the holes in the backrest. Pull the bungee cords over the pilot's backrest and hook them into the pilot's seat belt D rings (one on each side).

**Figure 37**  Bungee cord hooked.

Slip the tie-down bar through the right-hand camera mount restraint strap then through the existing helicopter seat belt D ring and through the seat base assembly mounting bracket. Continue by sliding the tie-down bar through camera operator's seat belt safety strap and then through the second existing helicopter seat belt D ring and then through the center camera mount restraint strap. Continue sliding the tie-down bar through the third and fourth existing helicopter seat belt D rings, and then through the left hand camera mount restraint strap. Secure with a bolt and nut through the end of the tie-down bar.

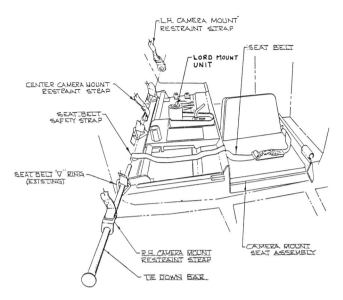

**Figure 38a**    Seat base seat belt (right side installation). Backrest is not shown.

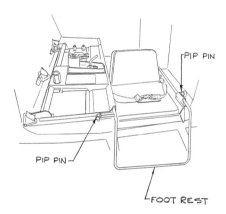

**Figure 38b**    Installation of optional footrest.

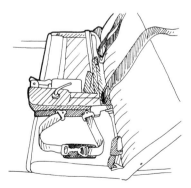

**Figure 38c**    Seat base seat belt (left side installation).

Move mount slider to the left side of the seat base and secure with lock knob.
Loosen the Allen bolt on the tilter and rotate so that the Lord mount faces the front of the helicopter, and then tighten the Allen bolt.
Remove the camera operator's seat belt from the right-side seat and clip it on to the attached rings on the left side of the seat base.
When flying, use the existing helicopter seat belt and the middle mount seat belt.
Install the camera mount mast post into the Lord mount assembly. Rotate until the mast post drops into the detent slot.

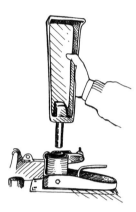

**Figure 39**   Installation of camera mount.

Install the camera mount arm into the mast post, sandwiching the restraint strap bracket facing aft. Secure with the large wing nut. Attach the straps to restrain camera movement.

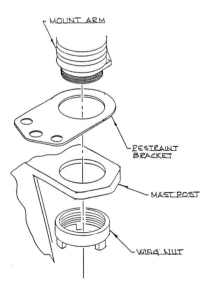

**Figure 40**   Installation of camera mount, continued.

Attach the balance weight to the rear of the camera mount arm and secure with a PI pin.

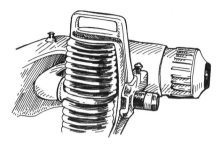

**Figure 41**   Attachment of balance weight.

Position the camera package onto the front of the camera mount arm, close the receiver lever, and twist the safety knob to the upright position. Plug in the camera and lens cables to the center of the handles.

**Figure 42**   Installation of camera mount, continued.

**Figure 43**   Completed camera mount installation.

Install the Lexan windscreen to the existing door hinges. Secure with PI pins or the bolts and nuts that normally hold the door in place. Install on the right or the left side, depending on the direction of the camera mount installation. This completes the camera mount installation for right side filming. Reinstall the left rear helicopter door.

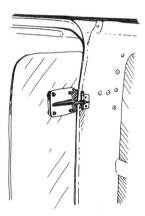

**Figure 44**  Installation of wind guard.

**Figure 45**  Camera operator's position during takeoff and landing when filming from the right side.

To film out the left side, follow these steps:

1. Remove left rear door.
2. Remove the camera and the counterweight, in that order.
3. Pivot the camera mount balance arm to the left side by loosening the retaining bolt on the Lord mount unit, then retighten the retaining bolt.
4. Replace the counterweight and the camera, in that order.
5. Remove the windscreen from the right side and install on the left side.
6. Install the right rear helicopter door.

During takeoff and landing the camera operator sits facing forward and uses the left passenger seat belt and the camera mount seat belt.

### Tyler Nose Mount

This camera installation with the Tyler nose mount applies only to Bell Jet Ranger Models 206, 206A, 206A-1, 206B, 206B-1, and 206B-3 and Long Ranger 206L, 206L-1, 206L-3, 206L-4 series helicopters. These helicopters also must be equipped with a high gear Bell kit no. 206-706-031-1, no. 206-706-010-21, no. 206-706-210-103, no. 206-706-064-101, or no. 206-706-064-003. Maximum camera weight is 39 pounds.

### Installing the Tyler Nose Mount

Remove the sixteen existing 10-32 bolts from the underside of the helicopter fuselage between stations 17.5 and 38.0. Save the bolts to reinstall them after the nose mount is removed from the helicopter.

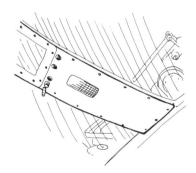

**Figure 46**   Screw removal.

Install the Tyler nose mount attach frame (narrow end forward) with the sixteen 10-32 bolts and washers provided and a $5/32$-inch (4 mm) Allen driver at approximately 2 foot-pounds torque. Use sixteen of bolt no. MS 16996-15 cut down to 1 inch long to form the Tyler attach frame bolt. See Tyler drawing no. TYL-206-001, sheet 1 dash no. 45.

**Figure 47**    Installation of frame.

Insert nose mount into attach frame with air vents forward. Insert all four expando pins into holes on side of the attach frame. Do not lock expando pins until all four pins are in place.

**Figure 48**    Position of nose mount.

Swing all cam handles on expando pins toward rear of helicopter until the green safety-lock lever on the exapando pin locks into position. Expando pins should be snug in holes just before they are locked. If an expando pin feels loose in the hole, make the necessary adjustments according to the instructions.

**Figure 49**    Position of expando pins.

Fasten the quick-release plate to the camera (at the fore-to-aft balance point) with the $^3/_8$-inch × 16 pitch hex head nylock bolt provided. Using a $^9/_{16}$-inch wrench, apply approximately 9 foot-pounds of torque. All cameras are authorized that accept the Tyler quick release plate (part no. TYL-206-007). The weight of the camera, including the magazine, film, or video tape is not to exceed 39 pounds. Maximum frontal area of these parts is not to exceed 9 square feet.

**Figure 50**    Fastening the bolt of the quick-release plate.

With the red cam arm open on the quick release plate, slip the camera onto the dovetail plate of the nose mount. Position the camera so that the fore-to-aft balance point is near the center of the dovetail plate. Secure the camera by locking (closing) the red cam-arm, and inserting two PI pins into the dovetail plate, one at either end.

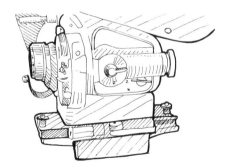

**Figure 51**    Securing the camera.

Loosen two $^5/_{16}$ hex head bolts on the underside of the tilt base and slide the camera inboard toward the mount as far as the camera will allow and lock it into position. Using a $^1/_2$-inch box wrench, apply approximately 7 foot-pounds of torque.

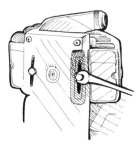

**Figure 52**   Securing the camera, continued.

Adjust the camera lock-down bar against the film camera magazine or video camera handle. Center the upright arm over the magazine (or handle) and lock it in place by tightening the red lever. With the red knob loose, push and hold the lock-down bar against the magazine or handle and tighten the red knob.

**Figure 53**   Camera lock-down bar.

Plug in the cables. To install the rear panel of the nose mount, securely fasten the control and coaxial cables. Twist the shell on the connector clockwise to lock it. To install the tilt arm of the nose mount, securely fasten the camera, coaxial, and any other cables necessary. Twist the shell on the connector clockwise to lock it.

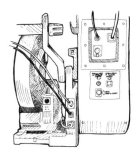

**Figure 54**   Cables plugged in.

Route the cable from the nose mount into the cockpit and connect them to the nose mount control console. Cables usually are routed through a hole in the left chin bubble. Otherwise, route them through the left side window. Remove the left seat cyclic and collective helicopter control handles and stow them. Tape down excess cable in the cockpit to prevent interference with helicopter controls.

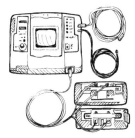

**Figure 55** Cable connections.

Connect the nose mount power cable from the control console to the 24 to 28 V DC power source.

Mode 1: Tyler (or equivalent ) 24 V/12 AH battery pack.

Mode 2: Helicopter auxiliary 28 V DC power connector, using Tyler ship power cable, if provided.

Mode 3: Helicopter auxiliary power connector and a battery pack, using Tyler ship and battery power cable, if provided.

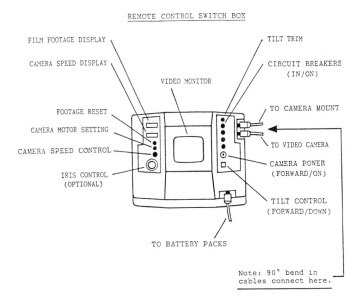

**Figure 56** Tyler system video and control box.

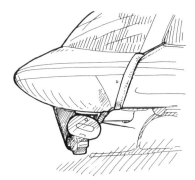

**Figure 57**   Completed nose mount assembly.

**Disassembly**   Reverse the foregoing procedure to disassemble the mount. The green safety lock of the expando pins must be held open to release the cam handle. A helicopter mechanic must do the expando pin adjustment. Loosen the set screw on the side of the cam handle with a $^1/_8$-inch Allen wrench. Tighten or loosen the inner (threaded) shaft with a $^1/_8$-inch Allen wrench until desired tension is applied. Tighten the side set screw. The inner threaded shaft is a reverse thread; turning clockwise will loosen the adjustment. It often is necessary to insert the forward expando pins while they are in the locked position to clear the lower hanging chin bubbles. Therefore it is necessary first to loosen the expando pins (described earlier) and then tighten them again after insertion.

### Tyler Major Mount

Maximum camera weight for the Tyler model 806 major mount is 120 pounds.

### Installation of the Tyler Major Mount

Remove the PI pins or screws from the doors and remove the doors. Replace the PI pins or screws. Remove all seat and back cushions or other obstacles from the seat and floor.

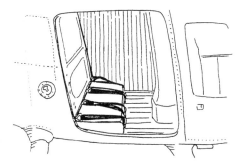

**Figure 58**   Preparation for installation of a Tyler major mount.

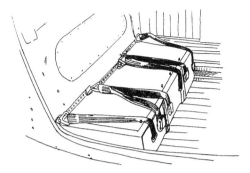

**Figure 59**  Preparation for installation, continued.

Lift the seat base into the helicopter around the center support column, placing the foot risers on bottom of seat base into the foot wells. The seat base should fit snugly against the support column and rear foot well area.

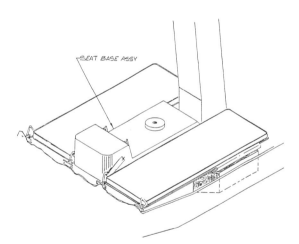

**Figure 60**  Installation of seat base.

Place the helicopter seat belt through the two D rings on the seat base. Buckle the seat belts together leaving them loose. A belly strap is already attached to one side of the seat base. Make sure that the bottom antennas are out of the way. Wrap the belly strap around the bottom of the helicopter and connect it to the D-ring strap attached under the seat cushion on the other side of the seat base. The belly strap should be pulled snug around the bottom of the helicopter.

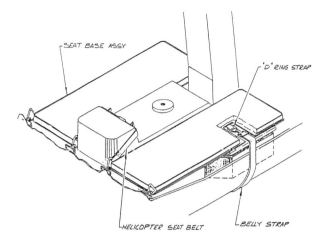

**Figure 61**    Installation of belts and straps.

Install the Lord mount unit. Line up the Lord mount unit with retaining bolt at the approximate center of the slot with the rubber Lord mount boot to the camera operator's right. The slot should line up with the nose and tail of the helicopter. Tighten the retaining bolt with the Allen wrench found on the Velcro patch on top of the seat base.

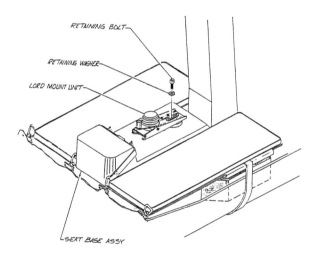

**Figure 62**    Installation of Lord mount.

Slip the tie-down bar through the right hand camera mount restraint strap then through the existing helicopter seat belt D ring. Continue by sliding the tie-down bar through camera operator's seat belt safety strap and then through the second existing helicopter seat belt D ring and the center camera mount restraint strap. Continue sliding the tie-down bar through the third and fourth existing helicopter seat belt D rings then through the left hand camera mount restraint strap. Secure with a bolt and nut through end of the tie-down bar.

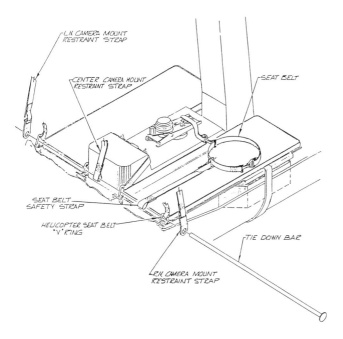

**Figure 63**    Installation of tie-down bar.

Install the major mount arm by lowering the mast post into the Lord mount assembly. Engage the vertical mount locks (red knobs at the top of the mast post). Rotate the mast post until it engages into a detent in the Lord mount.

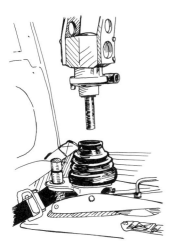

**Figure 64**    Installation of camera mount balance arm.

Attach the restraint strap bracket to the mast post with a PI pin. Attach the camera mount restraint straps to the restraint strap bracket in their appropriate positions. Adjust the restraint strap so there is sufficient slack to allow the camera mount to move on the yaw (pan) axis.

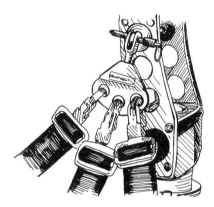

**Figure 65**    Attachment of restraining bracket.

Connect the hand grip assembly and rotate the red knob (marked "Arm Release") clockwise until securely engaged.

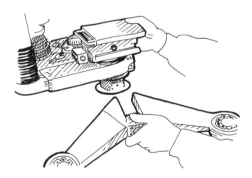

**Figure 66**    Installation of hand grip assembly.

Install the battery box by placing the box-support shaft onto the corresponding channel at the rear of the balance arm and raising the battery box until it automatically engages and locks.

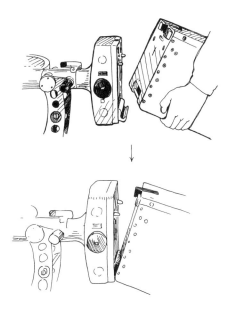

**Figure 67**    Installation of battery box.

Install the camera by sliding the dovetail of the quick release onto the camera support assembly. While depressing camera release lever, slide in the camera until the lock portion of the lever has cleared the edge of the camera support assembly. Let go of the lever while continuing to slide the camera in until the lock portion of the lever snaps into the camera support assembly. The camera release lever will be flush with the quick release plate.

**Figure 68**    Installation of camera.

Connect wiring from camera to camera mount assembly.

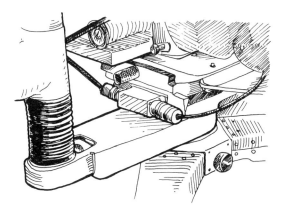

**Figure 69**   Wire connection.

Use the hinge pin to install the backrest assembly by connecting the hinge on the backrest to the hinge on forward right-hand side of the seat base. The headrest can be installed on the right side only.

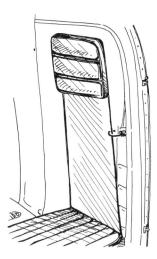

**Figure 70**   Installation of backrest.

Hook the two bungee cords into the holes in the backrest. Pull the bungee cords over the pilot's backrest and down to hook them into the pilot's seat belt D rings, one on each side.

**Figure 71**  Bungee cords hooked to pilot's backrest.

Install the Lexan windscreen to the existing door hinges. Secure with PI pins or the bolts and nuts that normally hold the door in place. Install on the right or left side, depending on the direction in which the camera mount is installed. This completes the camera mount installation for right-side filming. Reinstall the left rear door of the helicopter.

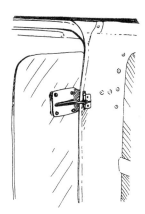

**Figure 72**  Installation of Lexan windscreen.

**Figure 73**   Camera operator's position during takeoff and landing when filming from the right side.

To film from the left side, follow these steps:

1. Remove left rear door.
2. Remove the camera, control handle, and battery box, in that order.
3. Pivot the camera mount balance arm to the left side by loosening the retaining bolt on the Lord mount unit, then retighten the retaining bolt.
4. Replace the battery box, control handle, and camera, in that order.
5. Remove the windscreen from the right side and install on the left side.
6. Install the right rear helicopter door.

During takeoff and landing, the camera operator sits facing forward and uses the left passenger seat belt and the camera mount seat belt.

## Mounts

A camera can be mounted on aircraft, cars, motorcycles, jet skis, boats, parasails, and elsewhere. You've got your work cut out for you. I list a few things that are a must when mounting a camera. Remember, you are under no pressure, none whatsoever, but remember a camera and lens usually cost $50,000 to $500,000. No oops allowed. If you want to be able to say, "I'll be back," do it right. Here are a few hints.

### Tricks of the Trade

1. If you are mounting a camera on a car, find out whether the car is strip painted (temporary latex paint applied over the original paint).

2. Determine whether the body can hold the weight of the mount and camera and the pressure applied by the motorcycle straps.
3. Put pads under everything that touches the vehicle.

**UVA F.A.C.T.**
Use a can of Dust-Off to blow away chalk lines.

There are many ways to rig a vehicle. First, if you can get equipment from Modern, American (8468 Kewen Ave, Sun Valley, CA 91352, Tel. (818) 768-8922), Matthews, or Norm's Studio Equipment (in North Hollywood, CA), rent it or buy it. It will pay for itself over and over again. Not only in money for rentals but also for the impression it leaves with DPs, directors, and producers. You look like a professional, and we all know what looks can do.

I use a combination of Modern and Speed-Rail® equipment. Seno Moussally (also known as Yoda), the owner of Modern, takes my designs, builds the rig exactly to my specifications, and usually enhances the design after he sees where I am going with it. All the other manufacturers mentioned have excellent equipment; I simply have developed a personal relationship with Seno. Eddie Phillips at Matthews is fantastic. He sold me my grip equipment. Norm, Jr., at Norm's is a grip turned business executive. He really knows the ins and outs. Lance at American has always built a better mouse trap. With reliable vendors, cellular telephones, and overnight delivery services, there is no reason not to get the right piece of equipment immediately.

**UVA F.A.C.T.**
Put gaffer tape over the hard wheels of electric scissors lifts to prevent tire tracks on a painted surface.

At Modern, Seno has a huge showroom of widgets, gidgets, gadgets, tubes, sleeves, plates, and rigs already built. He really has "been there and rigged that." I had 4 hours to rig a side-mounted camera on a Mercedes. I drove the car to Modern, and Seno welded and fit what I needed on the spot. I drove back to the set, had a nice cup of coffee, and got shots I needed. What I am trying to say is that I only act like a genius. I use the Albert Einsteins of the film industry to further my projects. I can't do it all, but I know who can, and I just gave you their names. Learn from the masters.

Here is a trick I use when I mount clamps on motorcycle frames. I apply 2-inch-wide paper tape to the area where I will apply the starter clamp. Then I put gaffers tape over the paper tape. The paper tape is easier to peel off the painted frame than is gaffers tape. After you have wrapped the gaffers tape 2 to 3 times around the frame, cut out a piece of rubber mat and wrap it only once around the frame. Then attach the metal clamp. This system should hold the clamp in place without scraping or marring the tube of the motorcycle frame. Whenever you mount a camera on a motorcycle, try to get three or four starter points on each mount. This gives it stability, and when you are asked to adjust the rig angle of the camera, your work will be expedited. Trust me on this; no mount is rigged in stone. Film is moving art. Changes are often made. Be prepared for those changes. At first it may seem like it takes a little longer to get started, but I promise you it will pay off for you. It's called planning ahead. They say advice is worth what it cost you; you paid for the advice in this book, use it.

This book is about my making you into one of the best, safest, and fastest mount riggers in the west, east, and even Ohio. (Inside joke to Deb Schneider, Ohio Buckeye, absolutely the top gun of her craft.)

### UVA F.A.C.T.
Hammer a nail tip before driving it into a piece of lumber. It helps prevent the wood from splitting.

A car, truck, boat, or whatever vehicle you are using may have to have a camera mounted on it. This is where expertise and imagination come together. You may be called to mount a camera on a bicycle, airplane, train, or even a jet ski. (Believe me, a jet ski can be fitted with a camera.) There are several types of mounts, but there

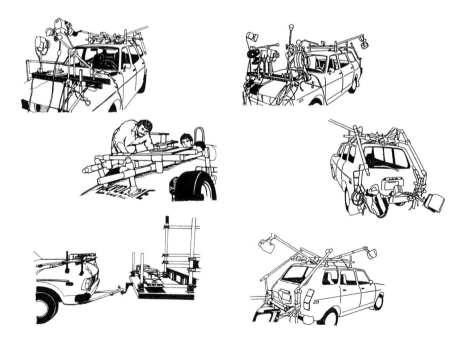

**Figure 74a**    Improvised rigs.

are no specific mounts for specific applications. This is where you step in as a grip. You will have to use the basic mounts available and design your own. It seems tough at first, but if you are someone who likes to build things you will enjoy this.

I provide illustrations of the mounts I have made with any materials at hand. Use the list of materials for a basic idea of what you will need to design and rig your own mounts. You can use wood, metal, plastic, or anything else that works safely. Observe one of my golden rules: There are ten ways to do the same job, and usually they all work.

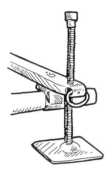

**Figure 74b**    Adjustable hood mount leg.

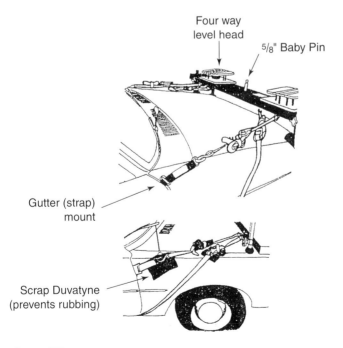

Four way
level head

⁵/₈" Baby Pin

Gutter (strap)
mount

Scrap Duvatyne
(prevents rubbing)

**Figure 74c**    Hood mount.

**Figure 74d**    Detail of Figure 74c.

---

**UVA F.A.C.T.**

The red, orange, or yellow plastic covers used on rebar (steel rods) at construction sights can be used as safety tips on any protruding objects, such as C-stand arms.

---

**UVA F.A.C.T.**

Safety all objects such as lights and clamps so that they will swing away from the set if they fall. This might prevent them from hitting the talent.

---

I prefer Speed-Rail® tubing and fittings. They can be assembled quickly; they are strong; and your rig looks like it was designed by a professional. You can add or subtract tubing by loosening two set screws. The standard-size tubing I have found to be used most is 1¹/₄ inches (1.680 inches OD, the outside diameter of the pipe [3.2 mm; 4.27 mm OD]), although larger tubing can be used. A trick of the trade for mounting a camera on a car or any vehicle is to check whether the vehicle has been strip painted. Strip painting is temporary paint that peels off after you are finished with the vehicle.

---

**UVA F.A.C.T.**

Poor man's light process: Cut a piece of 4-foot by 8-foot foamcore to 4 feet by 4 feet. Put it on a gobo arm to resemble a windmill. Cut holes through the foamcore. Shine a light through the holes as the arm spins. Gives a projector effect.

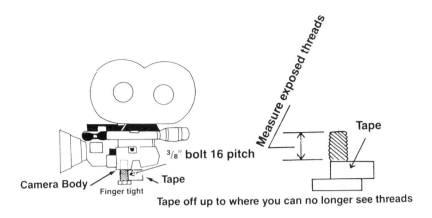

**Figure 75**  Tape method.

Strip painting sometimes is needed to match or change the color of a car for a certain type of scene. Then it is changed back to the original color for a matching scene, days or even weeks later. Our job as a grip is to ensure that the camera is mounted securely and safely without ruining the paint or damaging the car.

Installing a camera on a mount you have safely and securely rigged on a vehicle usually is accomplished with one bolt—a $^3/_8$-inch × 16 pitch bolt. This bolt cannot be too tight, or you will bend or pull the thread out of the $100,000 camera. If the bolt is too loose, the camera may move, ruining the shot, and possibly your career. Screw the bolt into the base of camera until it bottoms, mark the remaining threads with a marking pen or tape, back out the bolt, and measure the amount of threaded portion of the bolt that went into the camera body.

A trick of the trade is that usually about a $^1/_4$ inch to $^1/_2$ inch of thread can be inserted into the camera base. If you cannot mark the threaded portion of the bolt that is sticking out, mark the head of the bolt and count how many completed 360-degree counterclockwise revolutions or fractions thereof it takes to back out the bolt. Record this information to use later when you are mounting the camera for your shot.

---

**UVA F.A.C.T.**
Poor man's vehicle process: Put a lever under the frame of the car and pump it up and down while filming. It gives the effect of movement.

---

Never insert the bolt too deeply, but don't use too few of the threads either. My suggestion is to know how deep the bolt can and will go into the camera body,

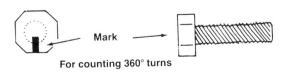

**Figure 76**  Marker method.

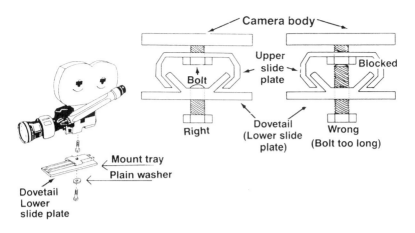

**Figure 77** Dovetail method.

measure the thickness of the plate or mounting surface, and add this and a flat washer's thickness to the length of the bolt. I use a washer (usually flat) because when tightening the bolt to the base, the bolt grinds (galls) its way into the metal and produces a locking action. These mounts usually are expensive and usually are rented from a rental house. You don't want to ruin an expensive mount when an inexpensive washer can take the beating instead. It shows you are a professional.

If too much bolt enters the base of the camera, the camera will jam or short circuit. You must work with someone who has experience before you start mounting cameras. A dovetail plate is a slide plate for the base of a camera. It allows quick mounting and dismounting of a camera. Insert a bolt through the mount plate base to the dovetail (slide plate) to ensure that the thread of the bolt does not exceed the height of the wings or lip of the dovetail plate. If the threads are too high, the camera will not slide on the plate. This should tell you something is wrong. You should not have any problems if you use this plate. If there is no dovetail (slide plate) to use, you must mount the camera body directly with a bolt as described earlier.

### Mounting Materials
6-inch extension pin
Hood mount
C stand head and arm
Speed-rail® tubing and fittings
Motorcycle strap
Hood mount and leveling heads
Two camera shot
Scrap rap to prevent rubbing
Leveling head
Back of insert car
Zip light (turn these on with red gel to achieve a breaking effect)
Tweenie 650 lamp
Double gobo head arm
Gobo head menace arm

Adjustable gobo head with pin
Grip clip with pin
Gutter mount (strap)
Scrap Duvatyne to prevent rubbing

**Mounting and Rigging Kit**

Ball level (Matthews, Modern, Norm's, or American)
Low level tilt plate (Matthews, Modern, Norm's, or American)
Hood mount (Matthews, Modern, Norm's, or American)
Side mount (Matthews, Modern, Norm's, or American)
Gutter mount clips (Matthews, Modern, Norms, or American)
Motorcycle straps
Common hardware, such as C-47, $^3/_8$-inch × 16 pitch hex head bolts of
    assorted lengths, and $^3/_8$-inch × 16 pitch nuts
Bailing wire (stove pipe)
Tape: gaffer and paper 1- × 2-inch black
Washers to fit a $^3/_8$-inch bolt, large area
Common flat and lock washers various sizes, $^3/_8$-inch most common
S hooks in various sizes
Rigid electric conduit $^3/_4$-inch OD down to $^1/_4$-inch OD
Self-taping lag bolts, $^1/_4$- to $^3/_8$-inch
Duvatyne cloth, black
Super grips suction cups for glass
$^1/_4$-inch hex head bolts, nuts, washers in various lengths
Various bolts, nuts, and washers
Tube brackets
Aluminum plate: flat, 90-degree angle, and channel aluminum

NOTE: Names in parentheses are suppliers.

## Power Grip or Super Grip

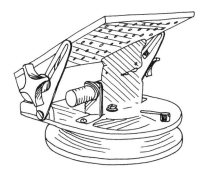

**Figure 78**   Tilt plate on super grip.

**UVA F.A.C.T.**
Use rubber-coated lead in a swimming pool. Rent from Fisher dollies or a crane company.

## Camera Clamp

Fastened with a screwdriver for greater holding power, a 16 mm clamp is especially designed for a lightweight film or TV camera; it is not a "make do" solution borrowed from carpenters. A 35 mm camera clamp is a heavy duty camera clamp that assures the safest protection for expensive and valuable equipment. Construction is steel core, cadmium plated, and electro painted.

**UVA F.A.C.T.**
Get the feel of each dolly. Turn the knob a few times to become familiar with the hydraulics of each dolly and the lifting beam (arm up and arm down).

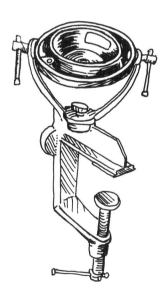

**Figure 79**   Camera clamp.

**UVA F.A.C.T.**
Tennis balls make excellent safety tips on stands or any protruding object on which they will fit after being punctured.

## Specifications

|  | 16 mm | 35 mm |
|---|---|---|
| Depth | 0.10 m | 0.21 m |
| Span | 0.24 m | 0.25 m |
| Weight | 3.9 kg | 8.0 kg |
| Ball cups | All sizes to fit any type head | |

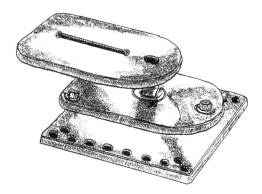

**Figure 80**   Ball level head.

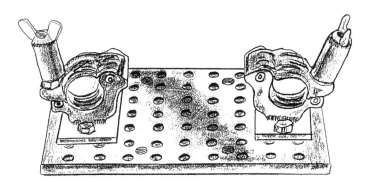

**Figure 81**   Rail drilled flat plate with double grid clamp.

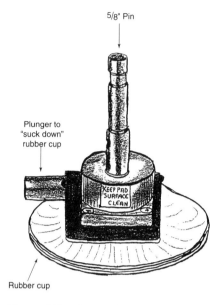

**Figure 82**    Super grip with pin. A plunger is used to "suck down" a rubber cup.

**Figure 83**    Junior grid clamp.

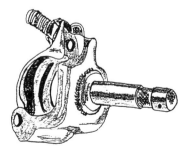

**Figure 84**    Baby grid clamp.

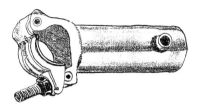

**Figure 85**    Grid clamp with female receiver.

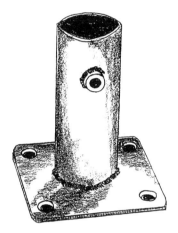

**Figure 86**    Rail flange plate.

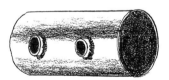

**Figure 87**    Four-inch rail sleeve.

**UVA F.A.C.T.**
Always carry earplugs in your personal bag.

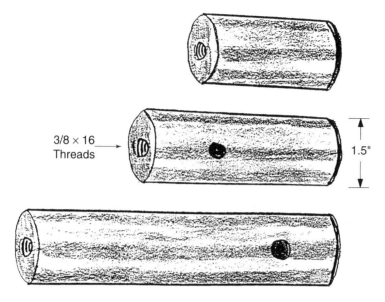

3/8 × 16
Threads

1.5"

**Figure 88**   Starter pins for rail.

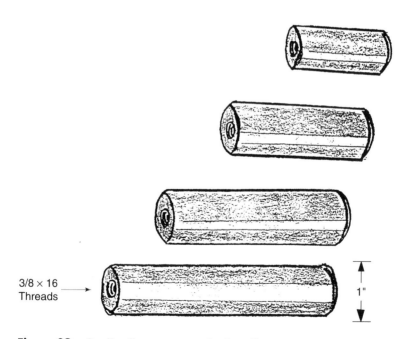

3/8 × 16
Threads

1"

**Figure 89**   Smaller-diameter starter pins for rail.

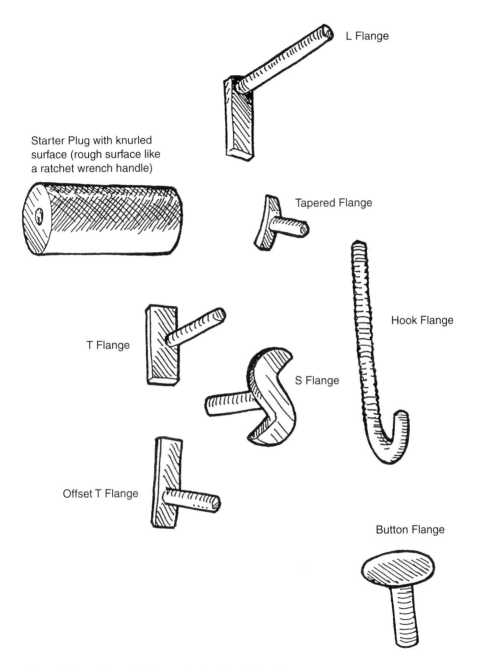

**Figure 90a** Threaded flange adapters for starter plugs.

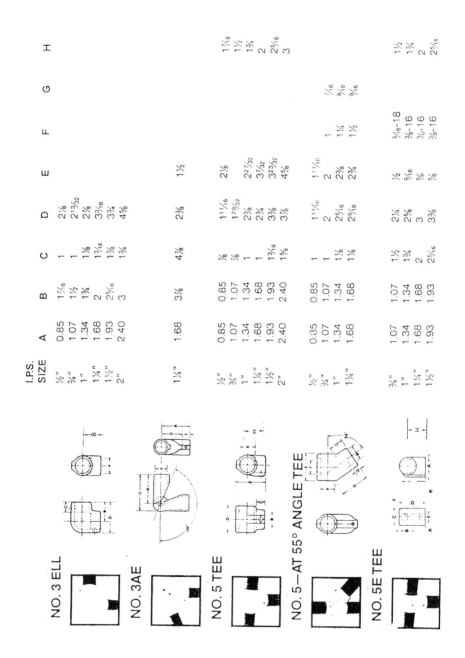

NO. 3 ELL

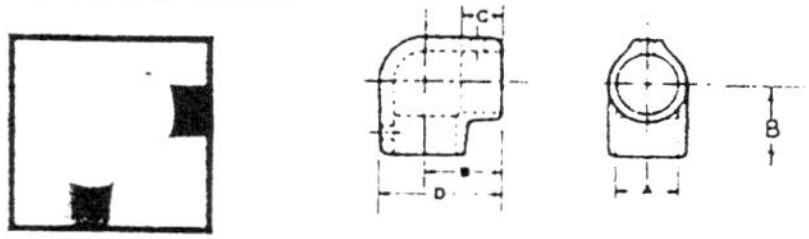

| I.P.S. SIZE | A | B | C | D | E | F | G | H |
|---|---|---|---|---|---|---|---|---|
| ½" | 0.85 | 1 7/16 | 1 | 2⅛ | | | | |
| ¾" | 1.07 | 1½ | 1 | 2 13/32 | | | | |
| 1" | 1.34 | 1¾ | 1⅛ | 2⅞ | | | | |
| 1¼" | 1.68 | 2 | 1 3/16 | 3 3/16 | | | | |
| 1½" | 1.93 | 2 5/16 | 1⅜ | 3¾ | | | | |
| 2" | 2.40 | 3 | 1¾ | 4⅝ | | | | |

NO. 3AE

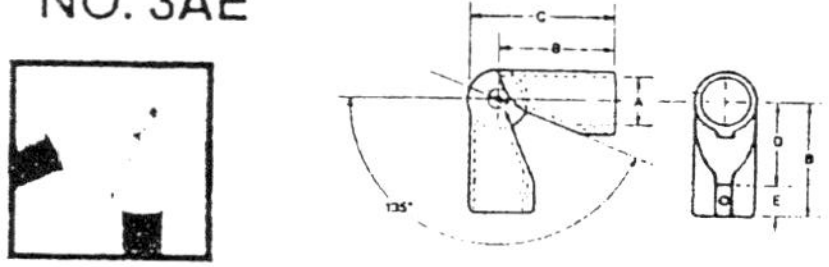

| I.P.S. SIZE | A | B | C | D | E | F | G | H |
|---|---|---|---|---|---|---|---|---|
| 1¼" | 1.68 | 3⅞ | 4⅞ | 2⅜ | 1½ | | | |

NO. 5 TEE

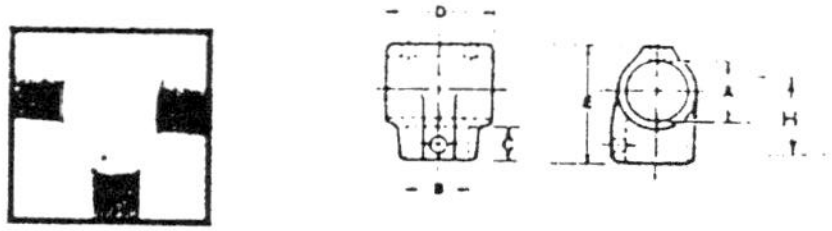

| I.P.S. SIZE | A | B | C | D | E | F | G | H |
|---|---|---|---|---|---|---|---|---|
| ½" | 0.85 | 0.85 | ⅞ | 1 11/16 | 2⅛ | | | 1 7/16 |
| ¾" | 1.07 | 1.07 | ⅞ | 1 29/32 | | | | 1½ |
| 1" | 1.34 | 1.34 | 1 | 2⅜ | 2 27/32 | | | 1¾ |
| 1¼" | 1.68 | 1.68 | 1 | 2¾ | 3 7/32 | | | 2 |
| 1½" | 1.93 | 1.93 | 1 3/16 | 3⅜ | 3 23/32 | | | 2 5/16 |
| 2" | 2.40 | 2.40 | 1⅝ | 3⅞ | 4⅝ | | | 3 |

NO. 5—AT 55° ANGLE TEE

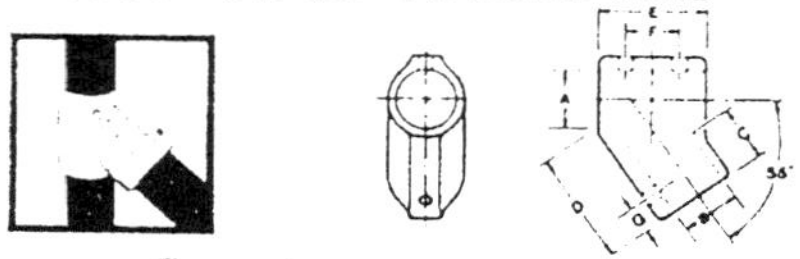

| I.P.S. SIZE | A | B | C | D | E | F | G | H |
|---|---|---|---|---|---|---|---|---|
| ½" | 0.85 | 0.85 | 1 | 1 11/16 | 1 11/16 | | | |
| ¾" | 1.07 | 1.07 | 1 | 2 | 2 | 1 | 7/16 | |
| 1" | 1.34 | 1.34 | 1⅛ | 2 5/16 | 2⅜ | 1¼ | 9/16 | |
| 1¼" | 1.68 | 1.68 | 1⅛ | 2 9/16 | 2¾ | 1½ | 9/16 | |

NO. 5E TEE

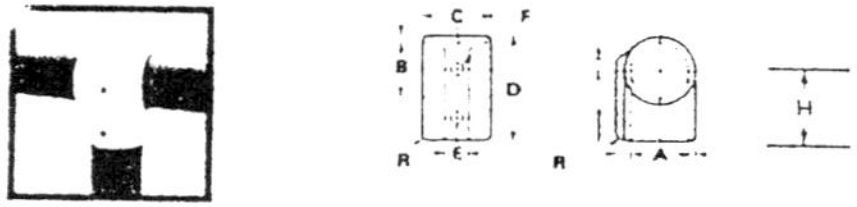

| I.P.S. SIZE | A | B | C | D | E | F | G | H |
|---|---|---|---|---|---|---|---|---|
| ¾" | 1.07 | 1.07 | 1½ | 2¼ | ½ | 5/16-18 | | 1½ |
| 1" | 1.34 | 1.34 | 1¾ | 2⅝ | 9/16 | ⅜-16 | | 1¾ |
| 1¼" | 1.68 | 1.68 | 2 | 3 | ⅝ | ⅜-16 | | 2 |
| 1½" | 1.93 | 1.93 | 2 5/16 | 3⅜ | ⅝ | ⅜-16 | | 2 5/16 |

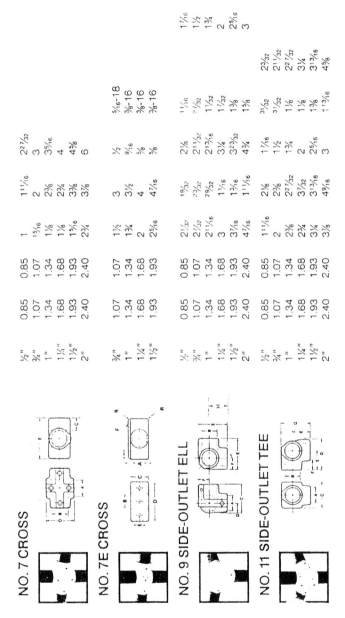

## NO. 7 CROSS

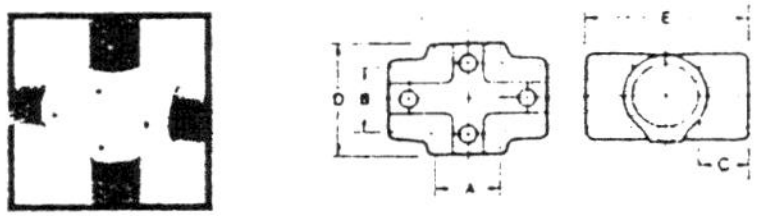


| | | | | | |
|---|---|---|---|---|---|
| 1/2" | 0.85 | 0.85 | 1 | 1 11/16 | 2 27/32 |
| 3/4" | 1.07 | 1.07 | 15/16 | 2 | 3 |
| 1" | 1.34 | 1.34 | 1 1/8 | 2 3/8 | 3 9/16 |
| 1 1/4" | 1.68 | 1.68 | 1 1/8 | 2 3/4 | 4 |
| 1 1/2" | 1.93 | 1.93 | 1 5/16 | 3 3/8 | 4 5/8 |
| 2" | 2.40 | 2.40 | 2 3/4 | 3 7/8 | 6 |

## NO. 7E CROSS

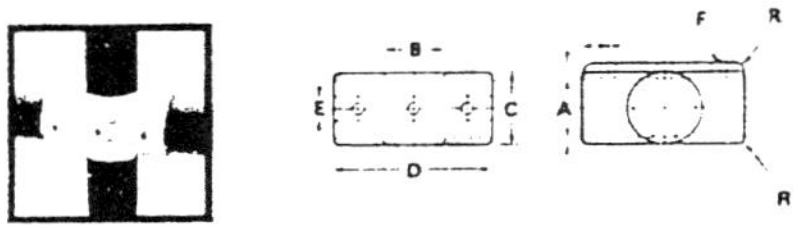


| | | | | | | |
|---|---|---|---|---|---|---|
| 3/4" | 1.07 | 1.07 | 1 1/2 | 3 | 1/2 | 5/16-18 |
| 1" | 1.34 | 1.34 | 1 3/4 | 3 1/2 | 9/16 | 3/8-16 |
| 1 1/4" | 1.68 | 1.68 | 2 | 4 | 5/8 | 3/8-16 |
| 1 1/2" | 1.93 | 1.93 | 2 5/16 | 4 7/16 | 5/8 | 3/8-16 |

## NO. 9 SIDE-OUTLET ELL

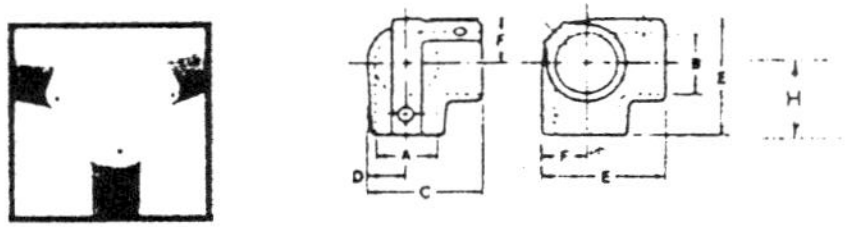


| | | | | | | | | |
|---|---|---|---|---|---|---|---|---|
| 1/2" | 0.85 | 0.85 | 2 1/32 | 19/32 | 2 1/8 | 11/16 | | 1 7/16 |
| 3/4" | 1.07 | 1.07 | 2 7/32 | 23/32 | 2 11/32 | 27/32 | | 1 1/2 |
| 1" | 1.34 | 1.34 | 2 11/16 | 29/32 | 2 13/16 | 1 1/32 | | 1 3/4 |
| 1 1/4" | 1.68 | 1.68 | 3 | 1 1/16 | 3 1/4 | 1 7/32 | | 2 |
| 1 1/2" | 1.93 | 1.93 | 3 7/16 | 1 3/16 | 3 23/32 | 1 3/8 | | 2 5/16 |
| 2" | 2.40 | 2.40 | 4 7/16 | 1 11/16 | 4 3/4 | 1 5/8 | | 3 |

## NO. 11 SIDE-OUTLET TEE

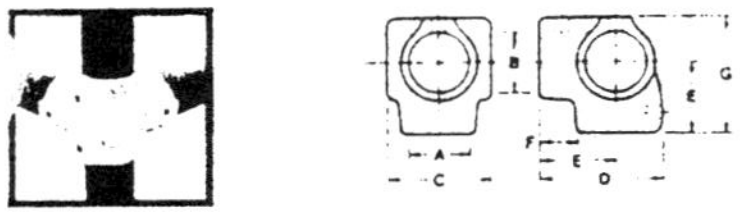


| | | | | | | | |
|---|---|---|---|---|---|---|---|
| 1/2" | 0.85 | 0.85 | 1 11/16 | 2 1/8 | 1 7/16 | 31/32 | 2 3/32 |
| 3/4" | 1.07 | 1.07 | 2 | 2 3/8 | 1 1/2 | 31/32 | 2 11/32 |
| 1" | 1.34 | 1.34 | 2 3/8 | 2 27/32 | 1 3/4 | 1 1/8 | 2 27/32 |
| 1 1/4" | 1.68 | 1.68 | 2 3/4 | 3 7/32 | 2 | 1 1/8 | 3 1/4 |
| 1 1/2" | 1.93 | 1.93 | 3 1/4 | 3 13/16 | 2 5/16 | 1 3/8 | 3 13/16 |
| 2" | 2.40 | 2.40 | 3 3/8 | 4 9/16 | 3 | 1 13/16 | 4 5/8 |

FOR NEAREST STOCKING DISTRIBUTOR CALL 1-800-772-8800

**Figure 90b** Speed-Rail® slip-on in-line fittings.

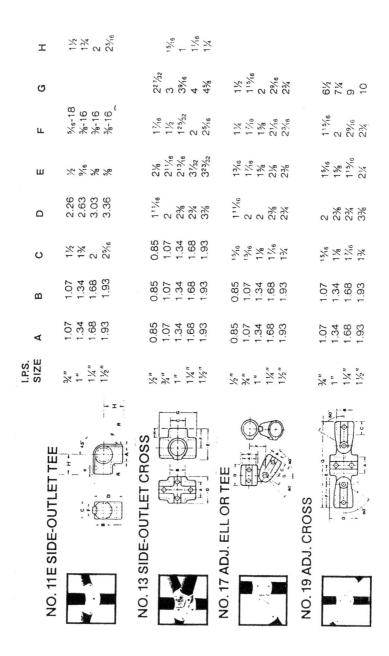

## NO. 11E SIDE-OUTLET TEE

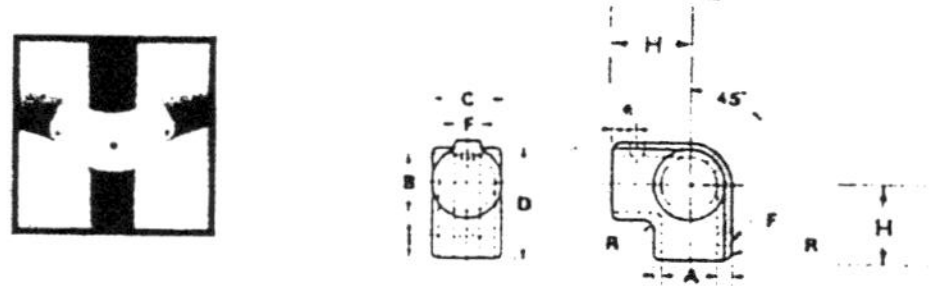

| I.P.S. SIZE | A | B | C | D | E | F | G | H |
|---|---|---|---|---|---|---|---|---|
| ¾" | 1.07 | 1.07 | 1½ | 2.26 | ½ | 5⁄16-18 | | 1½ |
| 1" | 1.34 | 1.34 | 1¾ | 2.63 | 9⁄16 | ⅜-16 | | 1¾ |
| 1¼" | 1.68 | 1.68 | 2 | 3.03 | ⅝ | ⅜-16 | | 2 |
| 1½" | 1.93 | 1.93 | 25⁄16 | 3.36 | ⅝ | ⅜-16 | | 25⁄16 |

## NO. 13 SIDE-OUTLET CROSS

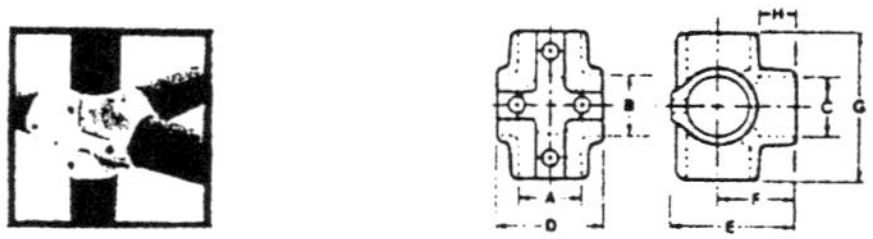

| | | | | | | | | |
|---|---|---|---|---|---|---|---|---|
| ½" | 0.85 | 0.85 | 0.85 | 111⁄16 | 2⅛ | 17⁄16 | 227⁄32 | |
| ¾" | 1.07 | 1.07 | 1.07 | 2 | 211⁄16 | 1½ | 3 | 15⁄16 |
| 1" | 1.34 | 1.34 | 1.34 | 2⅜ | 213⁄16 | 125⁄32 | 39⁄16 | 1 |
| 1¼" | 1.68 | 1.68 | 1.68 | 2¾ | 37⁄32 | 2 | 4 | 11⁄16 |
| 1½" | 1.93 | 1.93 | 1.93 | 3⅜ | 323⁄32 | 25⁄16 | 4⅝ | 1¼ |

## NO. 17 ADJ. ELL OR TEE

| | | | | | | | | |
|---|---|---|---|---|---|---|---|---|
| ½" | 0.85 | 0.85 | 15⁄16 | 111⁄16 | 13⁄16 | 1¼ | 1½ | |
| ¾" | 1.07 | 1.07 | 15⁄16 | 2 | 17⁄16 | 17⁄16 | 115⁄16 | |
| 1" | 1.34 | 1.34 | 1⅛ | 2 | 1⅝ | 1⅝ | 2 | |
| 1¼" | 1.68 | 1.68 | 17⁄16 | 2⅜ | 2⅛ | 21⁄16 | 29⁄16 | |
| 1½" | 1.93 | 1.93 | 1¾ | 2¾ | 2⅜ | 23⁄16 | 2¾ | |

## NO. 19 ADJ. CROSS

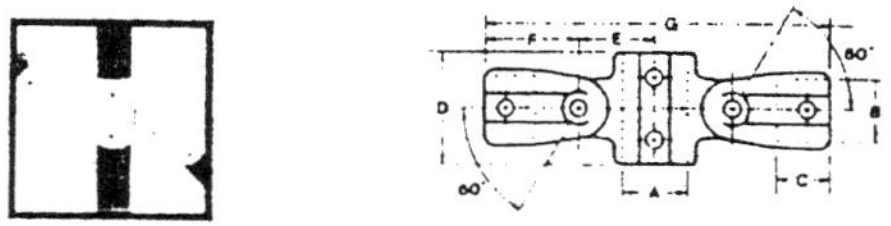

| | | | | | | | | |
|---|---|---|---|---|---|---|---|---|
| ¾" | 1.07 | 1.07 | 15⁄16 | 2 | 15⁄16 | 115⁄16 | 6½ | |
| 1" | 1.34 | 1.34 | 1⅛ | 2⅜ | 1⅝ | 2 | 7¼ | |
| 1¼" | 1.68 | 1.68 | 17⁄16 | 2¾ | 115⁄16 | 29⁄16 | 9 | |
| 1½" | 1.93 | 1.93 | 1¾ | 3⅜ | 2¼ | 2¾ | 10 | |

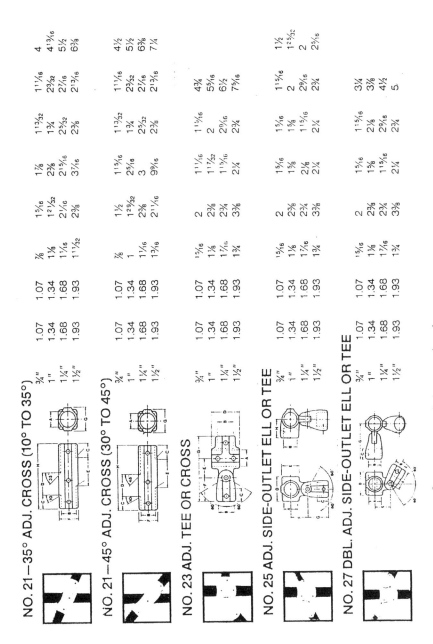

**Figure 90c**   Speed-Rail® slip-on in-line fittings, continued.

## NO. 10 CROSS

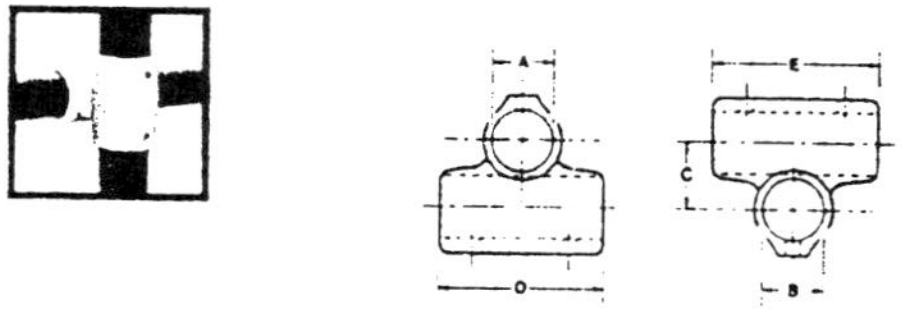

| I.P.S. SIZE | A | B | C | D | E | F | G |
|---|---|---|---|---|---|---|---|
| | *Straight Sizes* | | | | | | |
| ¾" | 1.07 | 1.07 | 1³⁄₁₆ | 2½ | 2½ | | |
| 1" | 1.34 | 1.34 | 1⁷⁄₁₆ | 3½ | 3½ | | |
| 1¼" | 1.68 | 1.68 | 1¹³⁄₁₆ | 3½ | 3½ | | |
| 1½" | 1.93 | 1.93 | 2 | 3½ | 3½ | | |
| 2" | 2.40 | 2.40 | 2½ | 4 | 4 | | |
| | *Reducing Sizes* | | | | | | |
| 1"x¾" | 1.34 | 1.07 | 1⁵⁄₁₆ | 2½ | 3 | | |
| 1¼"x1" | 1.68 | 1.34 | 1⅝ | 3½ | 3½ | | |
| 1½"x1¼" | 1.93 | 1.68 | 1²⁹⁄₃₂ | 3½ | 3½ | | |
| 2"x1½" | 2.40 | 1.93 | 2⁹⁄₃₂ | 3½ | 4 | | |

## NO. 12 SHORT BARREL CROSS

| I.P.S. SIZE | A | B | C | D | E | F | G |
|---|---|---|---|---|---|---|---|
| ¾" | 1.07 | 1½ | 1³⁄₁₆ | 1¹³⁄₃₂ | ²³⁄₃₂ | (¾" size has one setscrew in each barrel) | |
| 1" | 1.34 | 1⅞ | 1⁷⁄₁₆ | 1²⁵⁄₃₂ | ²⁹⁄₃₂ | | |
| 1¼" | 1.68 | 2¼ | 1¹³⁄₁₆ | 2⁵⁄₃₂ | 1¹⁄₁₆ | | |
| 1½" | 1.93 | 2½ | 2¹⁄₃₂ | 2⁷⁄₁₆ | 1¼ | | |

## NO. 15 OFFSET TEE

| I.P.S. SIZE | A | B | C | D | E | F | G |
|---|---|---|---|---|---|---|---|
| 1¼" | 1.68 | 2¼ | 1¹³⁄₁₆ | 5⅛ | | | |

## NO. 20 OUTSIDE CORNER

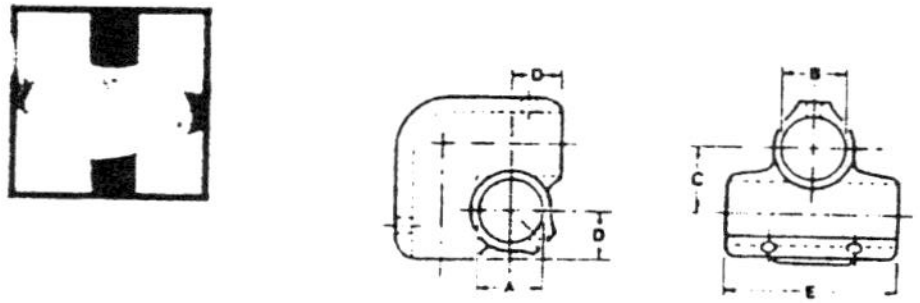

| I.P.S. SIZE | A | B | C | D | E | F | G |
|---|---|---|---|---|---|---|---|
| | *Straight Sizes* | | | | | | |
| ¾" | 1.07 | 1.07 | 1⁵⁄₁₆ | ¾ | 2½ | | |
| 1" | 1.34 | 1.34 | 1⁷⁄₁₆ | 1 | 3½ | | |
| 1¼" | 1.68 | 1.68 | 1¹³⁄₁₆ | 1³⁄₁₆ | 3½ | | |
| 1½" | 1.93 | 1.93 | 2 | 1⁵⁄₁₆ | 3½ | | |
| 2" | 2.40 | 2.40 | 2½ | 1⁹⁄₁₆ | 4 | | |
| | *Reducing Sizes* | | | | | | |
| 1"x¾" | 1.34 | 1.07 | 1⁵⁄₁₆ | ⅞ | 3 | | |
| 1¼"x1" | 1.68 | 1.34 | 1³⁷⁄₆₄ | 1³⁄₁₆ | 3½ | | |
| 1½"x1¼" | 1.93 | 1.68 | 1⅞ | 1⁵⁄₁₆ | 3½ | | |
| 2"x1½" | 2.40 | 1.93 | 2²⁹⁄₃₂ | 1⁹⁄₁₆ | 4 | | |

## NO. 30 ADJ. CROSS

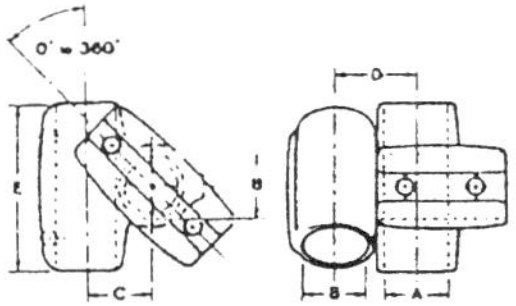

| | | | | | |
|---|---|---|---|---|---|
| ¾" | 1.07 | 1.07 | 1³⁄₁₆ | 1⅜ | 2½ |
| 1" | 1.34 | 1.34 | 1⁷⁄₁₆ | 1²¹⁄₃₂ | 3½ |
| 1¼" | 1.68 | 1.68 | 1¹³⁄₁₆ | 2 | 3½ |
| 1½" | 1.93 | 1.93 | 2 | 2¼ | 3½ |
| 2" | 2.40 | 2.40 | 2½ | 2¹³⁄₁₆ | 4 |
| | *Reducing Sizes* | | | | |
| 1"x¾" | 1.34 | 1.07 | 1⁹⁄₃₂ | 1⁷⁄₁₆ | 3 |
| 1¼"x1" | 1.68 | 1.34 | 1³⁷⁄₆₄ | 1⁵³⁄₆₄ | 3½ |
| 1½"x1¼" | 1.93 | 1.68 | 1⅞ | 2⅛ | 3½ |
| 2"x1½" | 2.40 | 1.93 | 2¹⁵⁄₆₄ | 2³¹⁄₆₄ | 4 |

## NO. 30-A MODIFIED CROSS

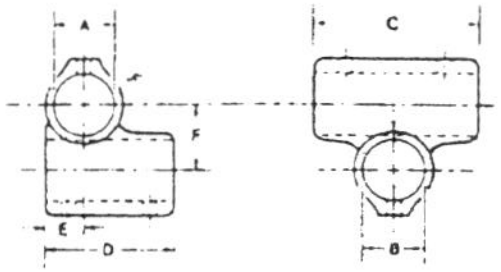

| | | | | | | |
|---|---|---|---|---|---|---|
| | *Straight Sizes* | | | | | |
| ¾" | 1.07 | 1.07 | 2½ | 2¼ | ¹¹⁄₁₆ | 1³⁄₁₆ |
| 1" | 1.34 | 1.34 | 3½ | 2¾ | ²¹⁄₃₂ | 1¹⁄₁₆ |
| 1¼" | 1.68 | 1.68 | 3½ | 2¾ | 1 | 1¹³⁄₁₆ |
| 1½" | 1.93 | 1.93 | 3½ | 3⅛ | 1⅛ | 2¹⁄₃₂ |
| 2" | 2.40 | 2.40 | 4 | 3⁵⁄₁₆ | 1⁷⁄₁₆ | 2½ |
| | *Reducing Sizes* | | | | | |
| 1"x¾" | 1.34 | 1.07 | 3 | 2¼ | ²⁷⁄₆₄ | 1⁵⁄₁₆ |
| 1¼"x1" | 1.68 | 1.34 | 3½ | 2¾ | 1 | 1⅝ |
| 1½"x1¼" | 1.93 | 1.68 | 3½ | 2¾ | 1⅛ | 1⅞ |
| 2"x1½" | 2.40 | 1.93 | 4 | 3⅛ | 1⅜ | 2¼ |

FOR NEAREST STOCKING DISTRIBUTOR CALL 1-800-772-8800

**Figure 90d** Nu-Rail® slip-on offset fittings.

NO. 30-B SWIVEL

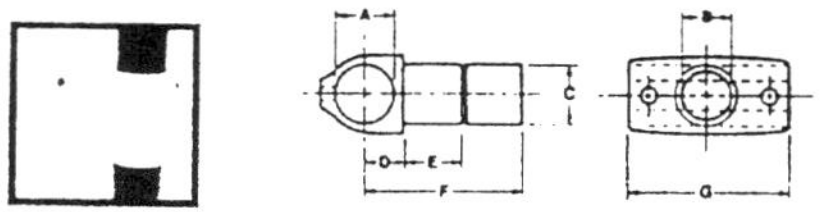

NO. 30-C ADJ. SWIVEL

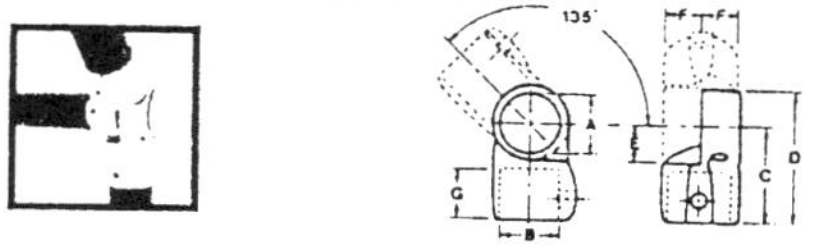

| I.P.S. SIZE | A | B | C | D | E | F | G | H |
|---|---|---|---|---|---|---|---|---|
| **NO. 30-B SWIVEL** | | | | | | | | |
| ¾" | 1.07 | 0.82 | 1.05 | 11/16 | 1⅛ | 2⅞ | 2½ | |
| 1" | 1.34 | 0.96 | 1.32 | 27/32 | 1⅜ | 3 17/32 | 3½ | |
| 1¼" | 1.68 | 1.38 | 1.66 | 1 | 1⅜ | 3 11/16 | 3½ | |
| 1½" | 1.93 | 1.61 | 1.90 | 1⅛ | 1 9/16 | 4 3/16 | 3½ | |
| 2" | 2.40 | 2.07 | 2.38 | 1⅜ | 1 11/16 | 4⅝ | 4 | |
| **NO. 30-C ADJ. SWIVEL** | | | | | | | | |
| ¾" | 1.07 | 1.07 | 1⅞ | 2 9/16 | ⅞ | 11/16 | 1 | |
| 1" | 1.34 | 1.34 | 2 5/16 | 3 5/16 | 1 1/16 | 27/32 | 1¼ | |
| 1¼" | 1.68 | 1.68 | 2 25/32 | 3⅞ | 1 9/32 | 1 1/16 | 1 7/16 | |
| 1½" | 1.93 | 1.93 | 3⅛ | 4⅜ | 1½ | 1 7/32 | 1⅝ | |
| 2" | 2.40 | 2.40 | 3½ | 4 31/32 | 1 17/32 | 1⅜ | 1¾ | |

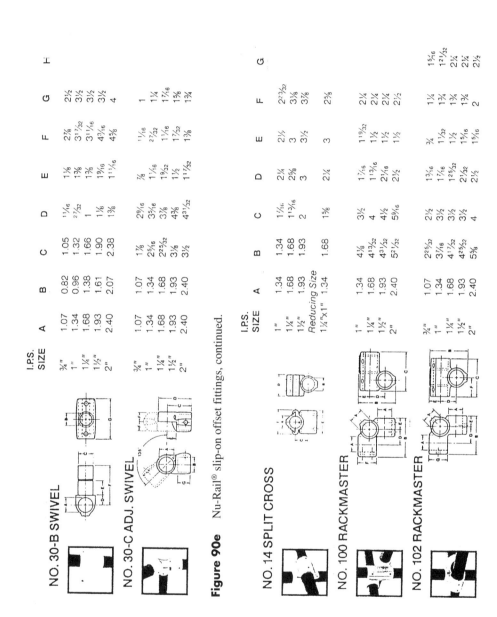

**Figure 90e** Nu-Rail® slip-on offset fittings, continued.

NO. 14 SPLIT CROSS

NO. 100 RACKMASTER

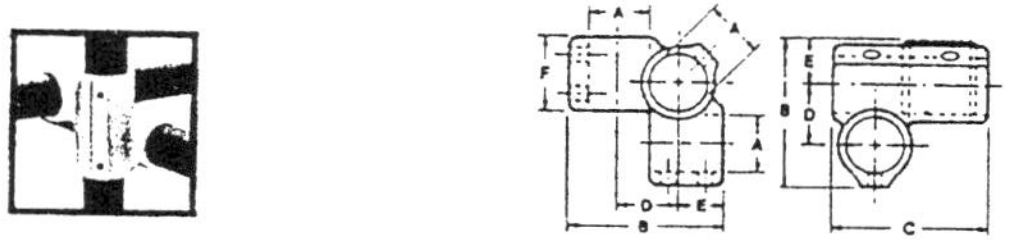

NO. 102 RACKMASTER

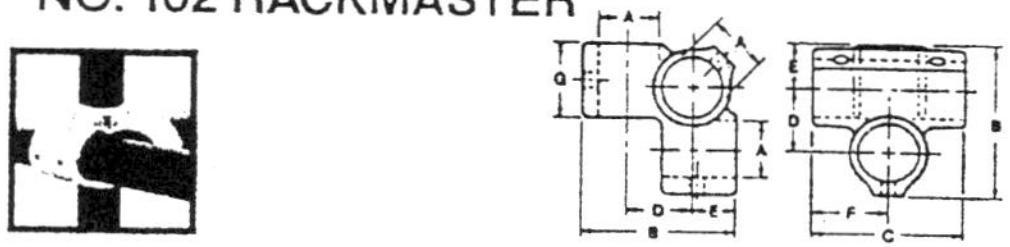

| I.P.S. SIZE | A | B | C | D | E | F | G |
|---|---|---|---|---|---|---|---|
| **NO. 14 SPLIT CROSS** | | | | | | | |
| 1" | 1.34 | 1.34 | 1 1/16 | 2¼ | 2½ | 2 23/32 | |
| 1¼" | 1.68 | 1.68 | 1 13/16 | 2⅝ | 3 | 3⅛ | |
| 1½" | 1.93 | 1.93 | 2 | 3 | 3½ | 3⅞ | |
| *Reducing Size* | | | | | | | |
| 1¼"x1" | 1.34 | 1.68 | 1⅝ | 2¼ | 3 | 2⅝ | |
| **NO. 100 RACKMASTER** | | | | | | | |
| 1" | 1.34 | 4⅛ | 3½ | 1 7/16 | 1 19/32 | 2¼ | |
| 1¼" | 1.68 | 4 13/32 | 4 | 1 13/16 | 1½ | 2¼ | |
| 1½" | 1.93 | 4 31/32 | 4½ | 2 1/16 | 1½ | 2¼ | |
| 2" | 2.40 | 5 21/32 | 5 9/16 | 2½ | 1½ | 2½ | |
| **NO. 102 RACKMASTER** | | | | | | | |
| ¾" | 1.07 | 2 25/32 | 2½ | 1 3/16 | ¾ | 1¼ | 1 5/16 |
| 1" | 1.34 | 3 7/16 | 3½ | 1 7/16 | 1 1/32 | 1¾ | 1 21/32 |
| 1¼" | 1.68 | 4 17/32 | 3½ | 1 25/32 | 1½ | 1¾ | 2¼ |
| 1½" | 1.93 | 4 25/32 | 3½ | 2 1/32 | 1 5/16 | 1¾ | 2¼ |
| 2" | 2.40 | 5⅝ | 4 | 2½ | 1 5/16 | 2 | 2½ |

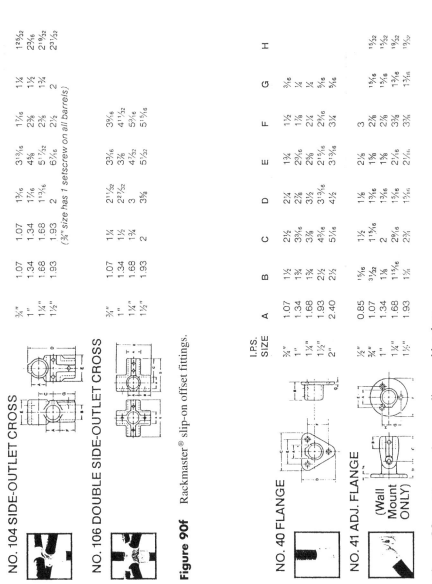

NO. 104 SIDE-OUTLET CROSS

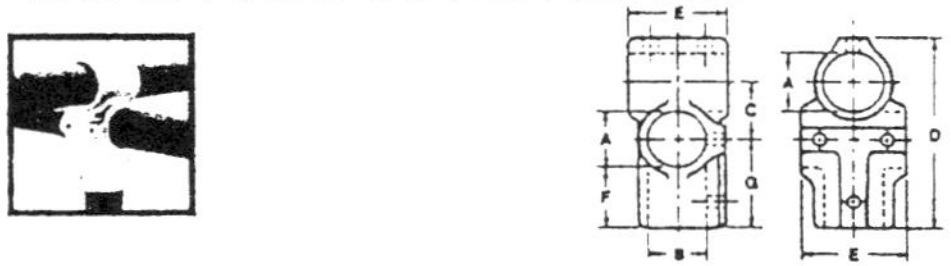

| | | | | | | | | |
|---|---|---|---|---|---|---|---|---|
| ¾" | 1.07 | 1.07 | 1³⁄₁₆ | 3¹³⁄₁₆ | 1⁷⁄₁₆ | 1¼ | 1²⁵⁄₃₂ |
| 1" | 1.34 | 1.34 | 1⁷⁄₁₆ | 4⅝ | 2⅜ | 1½ | 2³⁄₁₆ |
| 1¼" | 1.68 | 1.68 | 1¹³⁄₁₆ | 5¹⁷⁄₃₂ | 2⅜ | 1¾ | 2¹⁹⁄₃₂ |
| 1½" | 1.93 | 1.93 | 2 | 6⁷⁄₁₆ | 2½ | 2 | 2³¹⁄₃₂ |

*(¾" size has 1 setscrew on all barrels)*

NO. 106 DOUBLE SIDE-OUTLET CROSS

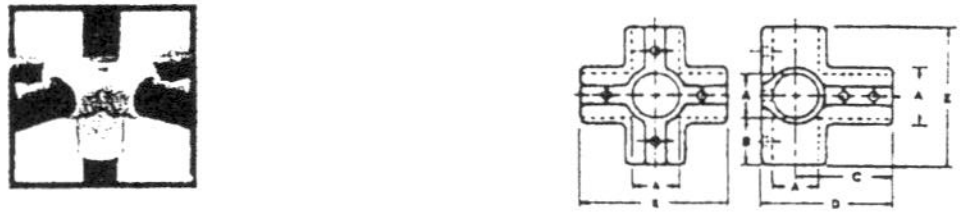

| | | | | | |
|---|---|---|---|---|---|
| ¾" | 1.07 | 1¼ | 2¹¹⁄₃₂ | 3³⁄₁₆ | 3⁹⁄₁₆ |
| 1" | 1.34 | 1½ | 2²⁷⁄₃₂ | 3⅞ | 4¹¹⁄₃₂ |
| 1¼" | 1.68 | 1¾ | 3 | 4⁷⁄₃₂ | 5³⁄₁₆ |
| 1½" | 1.93 | 2 | 3⅝ | 5¹⁄₃₂ | 5¹⁵⁄₁₆ |

**Figure 90f** Rackmaster® slip-on offset fittings.

NO. 40 FLANGE

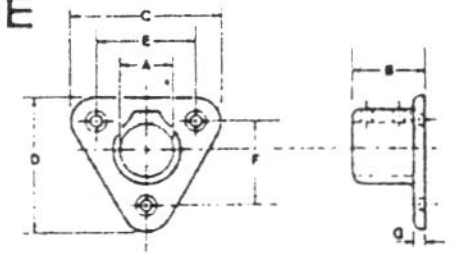

| I.P.S. SIZE | A | B | C | D | E | F | G | H |
|---|---|---|---|---|---|---|---|---|
| ¾" | 1.07 | 1½ | 2½ | 2¼ | 1¾ | 1½ | ³⁄₁₆ | |
| 1" | 1.34 | 1¾ | 3³⁄₁₆ | 2⅞ | 2³⁄₁₆ | 1⅞ | ¼ | |
| 1¼" | 1.68 | 1¾ | 3⅞ | 3½ | 2⅝ | 2¼ | ¼ | |
| 1½" | 1.93 | 2½ | 4³⁄₁₆ | 3¹³⁄₁₆ | 2¹⁵⁄₁₆ | 2⁹⁄₁₆ | ⁵⁄₁₆ | |
| 2" | 2.40 | 2½ | 5¹⁄₁₆ | 4½ | 3¹³⁄₁₆ | 3¼ | ⁵⁄₁₆ | |

NO. 41 ADJ. FLANGE

(Wall Mount ONLY)

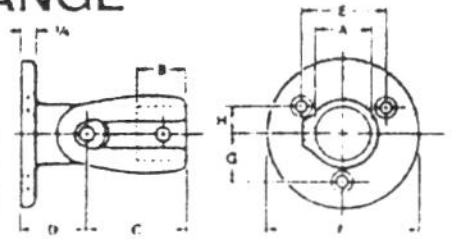

| I.P.S. SIZE | A | B | C | D | E | F | G | H |
|---|---|---|---|---|---|---|---|---|
| ½" | 0.85 | ¹⁵⁄₁₆ | 1½ | 1⅛ | 2⅛ | 3 | | |
| ¾" | 1.07 | ³¹⁄₃₂ | 1¹⁵⁄₁₆ | 1³⁄₁₆ | 1⅝ | 2⅞ | ¹⁵⁄₁₆ | ¹⁵⁄₃₂ |
| 1" | 1.34 | 1⅛ | 2 | 1³⁄₁₆ | 1⅝ | 2⅞ | ¹⁵⁄₁₆ | ¹⁵⁄₃₂ |
| 1¼" | 1.68 | 1¹⁵⁄₁₆ | 2⁹⁄₁₆ | 1⁵⁄₁₆ | 2¹⁄₁₆ | 3⅜ | 1³⁄₁₆ | ¹⁹⁄₃₂ |
| 1½" | 1.93 | 1⅝ | 2¾ | 1⁵⁄₁₆ | 2¹⁄₁₆ | 3⅜ | 1³⁄₁₆ | ¹⁹⁄₃₂ |

**Figure 90g** Flanges, plugs, couplings, and brackets.

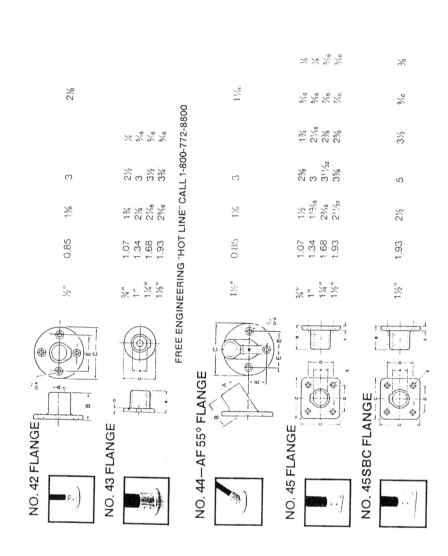

## NO. 42 FLANGE

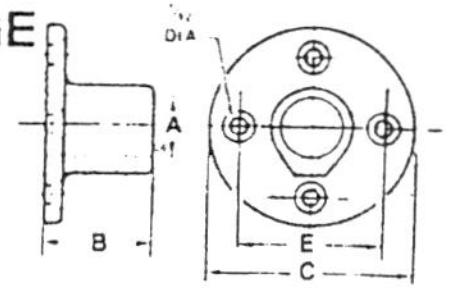

| | | | | | | |
|---|---|---|---|---|---|---|
| ½" | 0.85 | 1⅝ | 3 | | 2⅛ | |

## NO. 43 FLANGE

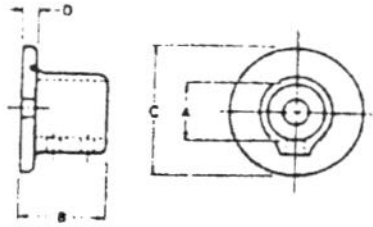

| | | | | | | |
|---|---|---|---|---|---|---|
| ¾" | 1.07 | 1¾ | 2½ | ¼ | | |
| 1" | 1.34 | 2⅛ | 3 | 5⁄16 | | |
| 1¼" | 1.68 | 2 7⁄16 | 3½ | 5⁄16 | | |
| 1½" | 1.93 | 2 9⁄16 | 3¾ | 5⁄16 | | |

FREE ENGINEERING "HOT LINE" CALL 1-800-772-8800

## NO. 44—AF 55° FLANGE

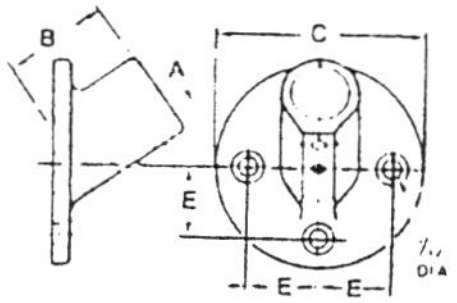

| | | | | | | |
|---|---|---|---|---|---|---|
| 1½" | 0.85 | 1⅝ | 3 | | 1 1⁄16 | |

## NO. 45 FLANGE

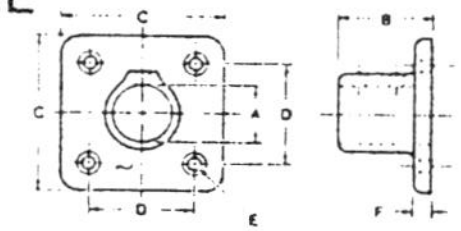

| | | | | | | |
|---|---|---|---|---|---|---|
| ¾" | 1.07 | 1½ | 2⅝ | 1¾ | 5⁄16 | ¼ |
| 1" | 1.34 | 1 13⁄16 | 3 | 2 1⁄16 | 5⁄16 | ¼ |
| 1¼" | 1.68 | 2 3⁄16 | 3 11⁄32 | 2⅜ | 7⁄16 | 5⁄16 |
| 1½" | 1.93 | 2 11⁄32 | 3⅝ | 2⅝ | 7⁄16 | 5⁄16 |

## NO. 45SBC FLANGE

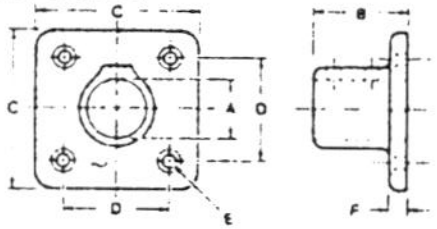

| | | | | | | |
|---|---|---|---|---|---|---|
| 1½" | 1.93 | 2½ | 5 | 3½ | 9⁄16 | ⅜ |

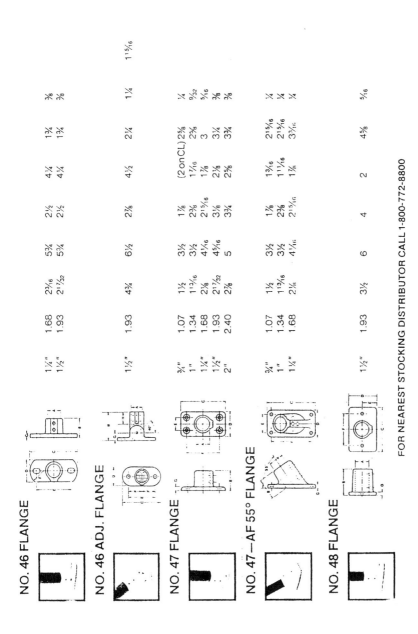

**Figure 90h**   Flanges, plugs, couplings, and brackets, continued.

FOR NEAREST STOCKING DISTRIBUTOR CALL 1-800-772-8800

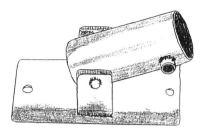

**Figure 91**   Rocker plate.

**Figure 92**   Adjustable-angle receiver.

**Figure 93**   Over-under sleeve.

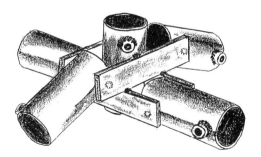

**Figure 94**   Pipe tower leg.

**UVA F.A.C.T.**
Don't stack large or small nets together; if they fall over, the pin might punch a hole through them.

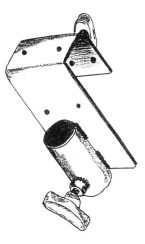

**Figure 95**  Door hanger.

**UVA F.A.C.T.**
Tape gels to the face of the frame on Xenons, not to the glass. This slows burnout of the gel.

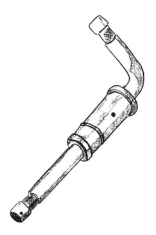

**Figure 96**  Baby to junior to baby adapter. Works in door hanger.

**UVA F.A.C.T.**
Tape the feet of metal stands. Do not tape factory plastic feet.

**Figure 97**   Spade adapter pin.

**Figure 98**   Baby four-pin adapter.

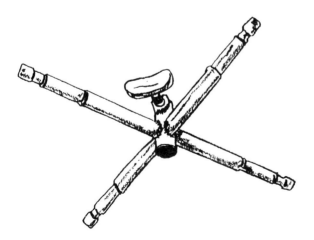

**Figure 99**   Baby star four-pin adapter.

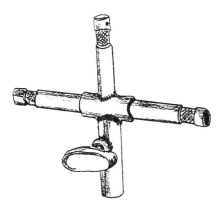

**Figure 100**   Baby three-pin adapter.

**UVA F.A.C.T.**
Use your hand first for shadow before setting a flag; it will save time.

**Figure 101**   Junior to baby adapter.

**Figure 102**   Baby pin to pin adapter.

**Figure 103**    *Top*, Junior to baby adapter. *Bottom*, baby to junior adapter.

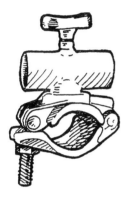

**Figure 104**    Junior 90-degree Cheeseborough clamp.

**UVA F.A.C.T.**
The angle of a flag should match the angle of light.

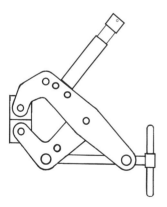

**Figure 105**    Kant twist clamp with baby pin.

1-1/8" Receiver

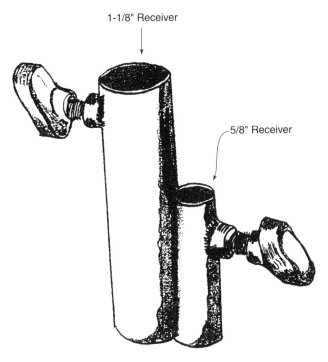

5/8" Receiver

**Figure 106**   Five-eighths-inch baby receiver with junior 1¹/₈-inch receiver.

## Dolly

### Minislider Dolly

The Minislider dolly requires no assembly. It is a skate-wheel dolly that glides securely within black anodized aluminum channel beams. Wheel tension can be adjusted to control slider flow. A locking brake allows rigid camera positioning. Beam end clamps have 1¹/₄-inch Speed-Rail® flanges mounted to facilitate rigging (the Speed-Rail®, elbows, and tees are not included). The package includes one set of 4-foot (1.2 m) beams; optional 8-foot (2.4) beams also are available). A longer channel beam can be used. The minislider dolly comes with a Mitchell plate on 4-inch (10 cm) riser stands. The Mitchell plate can be secured to the dolly base for lower mounting of a fluid head or secured to the underside of the dolly base for use with a remote or Weaver Steadman head.

**UVA F.A.C.T.**
Don't move, talk, or make eye contact with actors during filming.

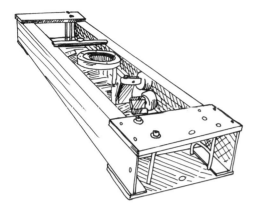

**Figure 107** Minislider dolly.

### SR71 Dolly

**Features**

Ultrasmooth linear bearing movement
Quick and easy setup with no assembly required
Carrying case
Four models: 2-foot, 3-foot, 5-foot, 6-foot
Use with any camera movement from 0 to 6 inches
Use with any Mitchell detail head

**Mounting Suggestions**

Two apple boxes as a sliding high hat
Any camera dolly to make adjustments

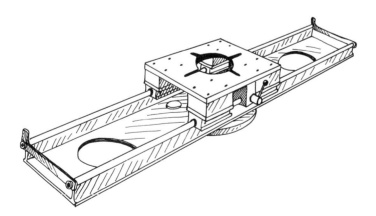

**Figure 108** SR71 dolly.

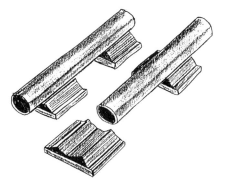

**Figure 109**   Speed-Rail® rubber flange.

Any camera dolly to make camera moves without a track
A tripod to make camera moves
Speed-Rail® pipe for a sliding car mount
A process trailer to make moves without a dolly track
A car to make moves on the interior of a car
An undersling on a crane arm to make the crane arm more versatile
A Condor to make camera moves wherever the Condor takes you
A camera car to add a new dimension to camera car moves

It is easy to be creative with the SR-71. The manufacturer is available for questions and comments. For the listed mounting suggestions as well as many others, the manufacturer strongly suggests employing a qualified grip. The manufacturer can be reached at telephone (323) 769-0650 or fax (323) 461-2338. I have used this piece of equipment on many car shoots. The camera operators are very pleased with the shots they get. Don't limit your shot to car shoots.

**Figure 110**   Portable track wheels.

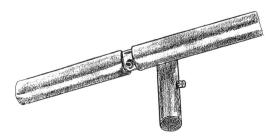

**Figure 111**    Track joiner.

**UVA F.A.C.T.**
A good safety practice when letting a camera operator off a riding crane is to step on the arm, have another grip take the place of the camera operator, lock the brakes, put an arm on the chains, and reduce the lead or mercury for counterbalance.

**Figure 112**    Grip clip with pin for light.

**Figure 113**    Adjustable gobo head with pin.

**Figure 114**   Double header gobo head. Used for rigging on cars, stage, locations.

**Figure 115**   Dulling-spray holder strap.

**Figure 116**   Tool ditty bag.

## Specialized Rigging

### Rig on Jet Ski

Water housing for camera
Homemade, center to center, steel drilled plates cut to form with holes 1-inch
  apart
Channel drilled plates
Flat drilled plates
Ridged conduit (flattened and bent to working angle)
Drilled angle plates
Common hardware

### UVA F.A.C.T.

The proper angle of an extension ladder is 4 to 1 (i.e., for every four feet the
length of the ladder is extended, its base should be moved 1 foot away from
the wall).

### Rig on Parasail Aircraft

Rigid conduit
Drilled plates
Common hardware
Lightweight 35 mm camera
Wide lens for vibration

**Figure 117**   Rig on jet ski.

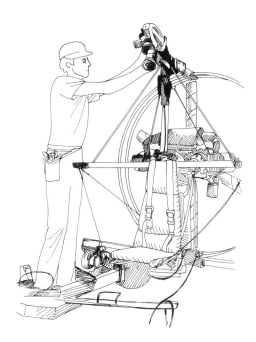

**Figure 118**    Rig on parasail aircraft.

## Platform Rig of Plywood and 2-by-4-inch and 2-by-6-inch Wooden Planks

C clamps
Motorcycle strap
Sand bags
Common hardware

**Figure 119**    Platform rig of plywood and 2-by-4-inch and 2-by-6-inch wooden planks.

**Figure 120** Rig on DC3 Aircraft. Each fitting was drilled and a bolt and self-locking nut were installed through the fitting and tube before this rig left the ground.

### Rig on DC3 Aircraft

Speed-Rail® tubes and flanges.

You must use aircraft hardware on the airplane. All bolts must be torqued to proper poundage.

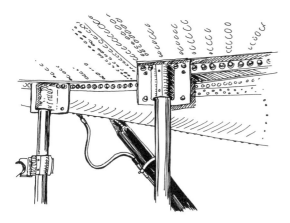

**Figure 121** Rig on DC3 aircraft flange.

### Rig on the Front of High Speed Train

Speed-Rail® tubing and fittings
Drilled plates
Motorcycle straps
C stand head and arms

**Figure 122a**    Rig on the front of high speed train.

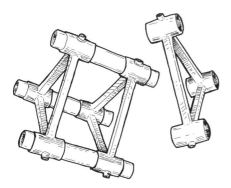

**Figure 122b**    Portable truss system for rigging.

**UVA F.A.C.T.**
Always move the crane arm after releasing the brake to ensure the brake is fully off.

### Special Effects Rig

Several cameras mounted on Speed-Rail® for motion picture effect

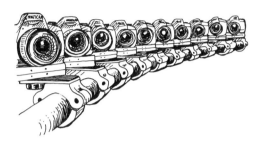

**Figure 123**   Several cameras mounted on rail for motion.

**UVA F.A.C.T.**
Know all your exits on stage.

**UVA F.A.C.T.**
Put a steel double in front of a large HMI light before you shut it down on an extremely cold day. This helps the Fresnel cool more slowly. It may prevent a crack. (Contributed by Gaffer Mike Laws.)

### *Hardware*

The following hardware can be carried in a parachute bag:

| Screws | Bolts | Nails | Miscellaneous |
|---|---|---|---|
| Drywall | Combo round | Common | Cotter pin |
| Exterior | Phillips pan head | Finish | Turnbuckle |
| Slotted pan head | Threaded eye | Sinker | Turnbuckle with hook end |
| Combo pan head | | Roofing | and eye end |
| Hex head | | Masonry | Screw hook |
| Turned eye | | | |
| Phillips pan head | | | |
| Phillips oval head | | | |
| Slotted hex head | | | |

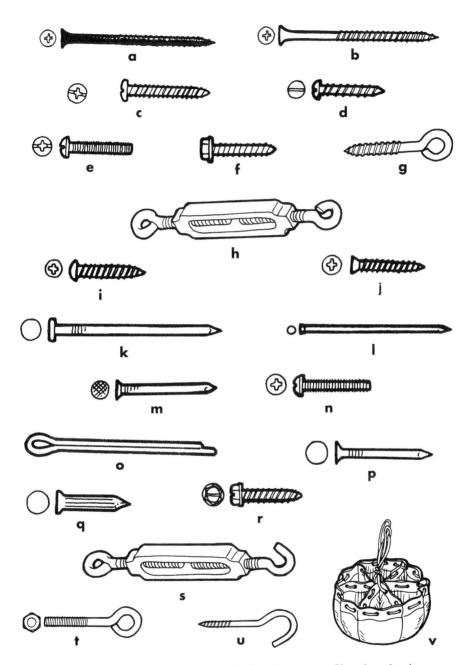

**Figure 124**    Hardware. *a*, Drywall screw. *b*, Exterior screw. *c*, Slotted pan head screw. *d*, Combo pan head screw. *e*, Combo round head screw. *f*, Hex head screw. *g*, Turnbuckle. *h*, Turned eye screw. *i*, Phillips pan head screw. *j*, Phillips oval head screw. *k*, Common nail. *l*, Finish nail. *m*, Sinker nail. *n*, Phillips pan head bolt. *o*, Cotter pin. *p*, Roofing nail. *q*, Masonry nail. *r*, Slotted hex head screw. *s*, Turnbuckle with eye end and hook end. *t*, Threaded eye bolt. *u*, Screw hook. *v*, Parachute bag.

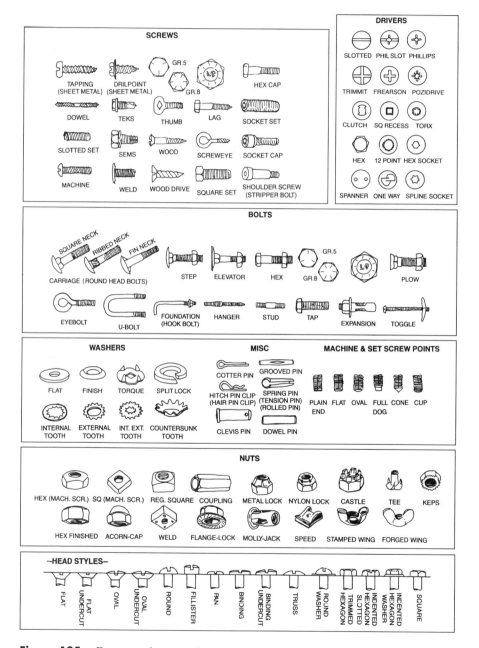

**Figure 125**    Fastener reference guide.

128

## High Hat

### J. L. Fisher Leveling High Hat

**Features**

Standard four-way leveling head same as used on models 10 and 9 dollies
Mitchell mount
Mounting hole pattern matches standard hole plates $^3/_8$-inch × 1-inch
(1 × 2.5 mm) layout

---

**UVA F.A.C.T.**
Know the placement of fire extinguishers.

---

### Dexter High Hats

**The Camera Model**   The three legs are adjustable every 10 degrees in lock-ing 3-inch (7.6 mm) rosettes that allow loads of more than 200 pounds (90 kg). The bottom legs adjust continuously for final leveling. This model works with all gear heads. The bottom legs adjust to allow one-handed adjustment.

**The Rigger Model**   This is an update of the original Dexter Hi-Hat. Four clamps are attached to an aluminum plate with an extension for bolting or clamping to the rest of the world. The legs for this model also have rosettes that allow infinite adjustment for height and level. The clamps attach to $1^1/_4$- and $1^1/_2$-inch (3.2 × 3.8 mm) Speed-Rail® pipe and 2-inch (5.9 mm) camera car tube. Almost no clamps made in the United States adjust for all these sizes. Both styles are provided with Mitchell and 150 mm tops and 150 mm camera bases for rigging. Both styles adjust

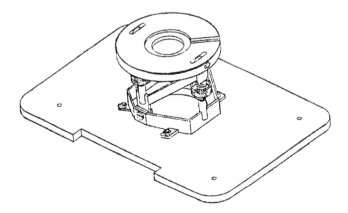

**Figure 126**   J. L. Fisher leveling high hat.

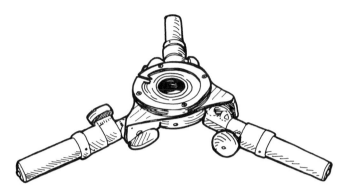

**Figure 127**   Dexter Hi-Hat.

from 5 to 21 inches (12.8 to 53.3 mm). The 150 mm top and camera rigging base are available separately.

The advantages of the Dexter Hi-Hat over the Hi-Hat on a board are as follows:

1. Ease of leveling
2. Three-point contact with the ground at a distance
3. Ease of adjusting height
4. Rigidity for long lenses
5. Something new to talk about
6. No wedges, no sand bags, no hassles
7. Support for the heaviest of cameras

A few safety factors in camera mounting are important for use of Hi-Hats and tripods. Ball leveling tripod tops should be used only with light- to medium-weight cameras. It is possible to set up tripod legs in an unstable position and still level the tripod head. With a flat Mitchell base tripod, it is less possible. A Mitchell base tripod head or Hi-Hat places the head and camera closer to the top of the legs, and together the camera and fluid head are less top heavy. The shorter the legs the worse this problem becomes. Risers should not be used on a Hi-Hat or tripod. Extend the legs or put something under the legs. Cameras at a 60-degree angle to their contact with the earth or floor are the most stable. If the legs are too flat, there is a tendency to slide on dirt. A spreader helps, but at a very shallow angle puts a tremendous strain on the triangle or earth.

In vehicles it is important to place the tripod tip or Hi-Hat in close contact with the frame or solid section of the vehicle. Any movement between the Hi-Hat or tripod and the vehicle will show up on film. Many vehicles have few "hard points."

If you are working in a pickup bed, 1-inch (2.54 cm) plywood is better than $^3/_4$-inch (1.9 mm) plywood. Tie the Hi-Hat or tripod down to the plywood for safety and stability. Pickup beds with stake holes allow a 2 × 4 to be clamped inside the bed to hold the plywood down against the bed. Always think about the comfort of the operator. If the operator is unstable, he or she cannot evaluate the stability of the shot, and operating becomes difficult. Too much padding makes the operator unstable.

If you are using pipe to rig a Hi-Hat, attach the Hi-Hat as closely as possible to solid points. Avoid the center of a long span of pipe unless the pipe is braced near the Hi-Hat. Legs can be made from Speed-Rail® if the regular legs don't fit. Consider using one leg and Speed-Rail® for the other if it works.

For welding rigs, always consider including fittings that should be added before welding. They don't always have to be used. I don't recommend the Speed-Rail® split cross for rigging. It easily slides apart in one direction.

**Dexter 150 mm Rigging Ball**   The rigging ball allows locked-off cameras to be attached closer and lower to the pipes supporting the Hi-Hat. A regular tripod head adds unnecessary weight and height. The rigging ball is intended for attaching the camera directly to the Hi-Hat without a regular head for rigged and locked-off shots. It is not intended to be attached to a flat-bottomed tripod head. It would raise the camera too high. If you use 150 mm ball top tripods, rent or buy the factory 150 mm base for your tripod head.

**Hood Rigs**   The Hi-Hat allows easy adjustment on two pipes that span the hood. Many hoods allow a blade to slide between the hood and the fender. A piece of stiff steel or aluminum with relief in the middle attaches to a thicker piece with holes for Speed-Rail® floor flanges. Consider adjustment for different curved hoods. Build or order pipe-to-light adapters. Secure the rig to the wheel wells or the screws that hold the fender to the engine compartment wall. If ever in doubt, use a back-up tie-down system.

**Door Rig**   Door rigs have to be welded up. Consider the curve of most car doors. The rig often can be strapped to the door and the door slammed on the straps. Any "tray" rig should be adjustable so that the door jam and possibly the rearview mirror can be seen in camera. Always consider the size of the actor and driving position before locking everything off.

**Airplane or Van Door-off Rig**   Preventing motion between the camera and the vehicle is important. A horse made of Speed-Rail® cinched down to the seat rails of a plane work well. You will have to make some seat rail clamps out of aluminum angle and S hooks. Consider an intercom for the operator, pilot, and director. Consider air temperature at altitude and air sickness when looking through camera. Video assist through a Sony Watchman with a hood will help the director.

### Maintenance and Modifications of the Dexter Hi-Hat

**Leg spike position**   If you don't like the position of the spike, loosen the set screws in the leg casting and adjust the spike to a suitable position.

**Leg length**   If you want to shorten any or all legs, remove the lower leg section by loosening the set screws in the leg casting and saw off some length. The legs are hard-anodized and resist cutting with a hacksaw but are cut easier once the surface is broken.

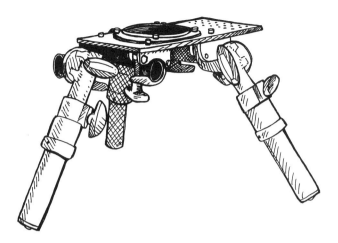

**Figure 128**   Dexter Hi-Hat System.

If the leg locking knob fails to lock the sliding leg, remove the knob, plug the threaded hole with cotton or rag and file the extended part of the casting off to make the knob handle stud go deeper. The knobs and casting are designed to be durable and easy to adjust.

> **UVA F.A.C.T.**
> No block zone: A yellow line on stage marks an area 4 feet from the stage walls. If the stage were to fill with thick, black smoke, you would not be able to see anything. Make your way to any wall and feel your way to an emergency exit.

## Other Materials

### The Mystery of Pipe, Tube, Conduit, etc., *by Ron Dexter*

Searching for pipe, tube, and conduit can be confusing and frustrating. You may not know the right language, and the salesperson may not know what she has or what it's called. Here is a rule to remember: The terms that you use should be tailored to the person to whom you are talking. A hardware store clerk will not know as much as an industrial pipe and tube salesperson. When your request is passed to a production person, then to a supplier, it can become garbled in transmission. Talk to the supplier yourself, if possible.

**Water Pipe**   Water pipe should be galvanized steel with threaded ends, maximum length 21 feet (6.3 m). Pipe is sold according to its *inside diameter* (ID). Many people don't understand *diameter* but only read what's printed on the rack or the pipe itself. For example, $1^1/_4$-inch pipe has an OD (outside diameter) of $1^5/_8$ inch and $1^1/_2$-inch pipe has an OD of $1^7/_8$ ($1^1/_2$-inch pipe often is called 2-inch pipe). Pipe comes in a standard ID size (not always its actual ID). Tube always comes in OD size.

Water pipe is available in most areas, except sometimes in the tropics. Pipe is heavy, but when it's all that's available, it is fine. On flat surfaces water pipe makes good dolly track with or without ties. The threads must be cut off to join the water pipe. Bring your internal couplers and a rat-tail file. A pipe cutter is used to cut it square to remove the threads but leaves ridges that must be carefully filed flat. It is difficult to accurately cut pipe with a hand hacksaw. It can be screwed to ties with much effort. Steel is more difficult to cut than is aluminum. Use oversize tapping drills. Water pipe also can be used for rigging with Speed-Rail®. If you are asked what "schedule" pipe you want, schedule 40 is the most common. Don't confuse people if they don't ask. Many salespersons have not heard of schedule.

**Gas Pipe**   Gas pipe is made of steel. It usually is rough and sometimes is tar-coated. It is less expensive than water pipe. You had better see it before you buy it.

**Electrical Conduit**   Electrical metallic tubing (EMT) conduit (thin wall) is available almost everywhere except the tropics. It is inexpensive, galvanized, comes in 10-foot (3 meter) lengths, and is sold according to ID. A 10-inch (2.5 cm) piece of EMT thin wall has an ID of 1.040 inches (2.64 cm) and an OD of 1.160 inches (2.95 cm), a bit more than $1^1/_{16}$ inches). Confusing? It's very useful though. Progressive sizes telescope inside one another, and the tubing is fairly strong for its weight. It also can be bent smoothly with a conduit bender (the right size and type). One-half-inch and three-quarter-inch EMT is great for rigging. One and one-quarter and one and one-half inch EMT is good for short dolly track. The ends are square and smooth. Track couplers cut with a rat-tail file can be used for longer moves. Ten-foot-long tracks with pine ties make good location track that you can leave. It's easy to drill and tap. EMT thin wall is available from building suppliers, electrical suppliers, and hardware stores. This conduit does not fit any Speed-Rail® fittings well.

**Aluminum Electrical Conduit**   Aluminum electrical conduit is acceptable only for one-time rigging. It is soft and weak, has threads, and comes only in 10-foot lengths.

**Rigid Steel Electrical Conduit**   Rigid steel electrical conduit is a bit thinner than water pipe and a bit less expensive, but it comes only in 10-foot lengths. It has threads on the ends and is the same size as water pipe.

**PVC Plastic Pipe and PVC Electrical Conduit**   Polyvinyl chloride (PVC) plastic pipe and PVC electrical conduit are good for curved track. It can be used for straight track if screwed to plywood. Ties are not used. PVC pipe comes in pipe sizes like water pipe. You want schedule 40. One-inch, $1^1/_4$-inch, and $1^1/_2$-inch PVC pipes all make inexpensive dolly track for flat surfaces. Make sure that your dolly tracks work on the size that you choose. A 6-inch piece of pipe one size smaller than the rails can be cut lengthwise with a saw to make a good track coupler. The pipe is drilled with a regular drill bit and screwed in place with drywall screws and a drywall screw bit. Battery-operated drills are best. PVC in smaller sizes is available from most hardware, building, gardening tools, irrigation, and plumbing suppliers. For larger sizes you have to find dealers of plastic pipe. Couplers can be made out of wood dowel and can be spliced with tape in an emergency. PVC is clean, light, and flexible. Don't try very long lens moves on it unless it is screwed down and aligned.

**Tube**   *Tube* is exact language. Tube is always referred to by OD and wall thickness (wall). For example, 2-inch by 0.065-inch has an OD of 2 inches plus or minus 0.002 inch. The ID is 2 inches minus two times the wall thickness (0.065 inch) or 1.870 inches (4.74 cm). Most camera cars use 2-inch tubing.

For dolly track you must find an industrial pipe or metal supply house. These suppliers know all about pipe and tubing, and their catalogs will help you understand. They usually deal in large quantities, and your price will reflect the amount that you buy. The insides and outsides of the ends of the pipes or tubes should be slightly filed to remove the sharp edges. It is desirable to have aluminum pipe or tube anodized. It will be cleaner, be protected from corrosion, and have a harder surface. Clear, hard anodizing is best for track. For fancy camera work, black is impressive but becomes hot in the sun. Be very careful about anodizing Speed-Rail® fittings. Some methods corrode and weaken cast aluminum fittings.

For dolly track 1$^1$/$_2$-inch, 6061-T6, schedule 40 aluminum pipe is best. In the number, 6061 is the alloy and T-6 is the hardness. It can be welded. *Schedule* indicates the thickness of pipe (the higher the number the thicker is the wall of the pipe). Aluminum pipe comes in schedule 5, 10, 20, 40, 80, and 160. Schedule 40 is the most common and least expensive. You may be able to get a deal on any other alloy that is as strong, but avoid 6063-T3. It is for railings, is soft, and bends easily.

**Fence Post Pipe**   Fence post pipe comes in typical sizes, is light, and is useful for rigging. Some fence post fittings are useful for rigging, but you must remember they are made for building fences and not for flying people and equipment.

### Starter Plugs and Starter Connectors

I use the Modern Studio starter plugs on most of my rig shoots. The angled threaded connectors fit in holes, under plates, or clamped between metal places on cars. I suggest you get at least eight different starter connectors. The S type, the L type, and the offset tee are always used. The others are helpful for odd places. Each connector usually is nothing more than a $^3$/$_8$-inch × 16 pitch common hardware threaded rod. If you want to make them yourself, you had better be an expert welder. Remember, it's usually a $100,000 to $500,000 camera and lens riding on your rig. Your career is at stake. This isn't written to scare you, it is written to prepare you.

I want to hear through the grape vine (*uva* means "grape") that your rigs were great, solid, and nice-looking. Speed-Rail® and starter plugs seem to make this happen. Even my worst rig on a bad day looks good. All joking aside, Speed-Rail® is what most grips use.

**Tilt Plates**   Tilt plates are made by several manufacturers, and they all work pretty well. You have to decide which one will do the most jobs for you. I own three different types, and I can usually get the job done. A Super Grip with a tilt plate works well but not for all occasions. A drilled-base tilt plate also may not work for all occasions. I often use a combination of plates to achieve the desired effect or shot.

**Speed-Rail® by Hollaender**   Two words—fantastic, fantastic. I first discovered Speed-Rail® twenty years ago. I knew at that time that I had died and gone to grip heaven. This system is like a tinker toy or erector set for adults. I normally use a Speed-Rail® size designed as 1¹/₄ inches, which is 1.680 inches in actual size; 1.500 inches equates to 1¹/₂ inches.

This may be confusing for as many years as you use any railing. What seems to happen is you go on a location shoot and order a Speed-Rail® rig kit or a pipe organ. A pipe organ usually consists of four each of cut Speed-Rail® starting anywhere from 8 inches to 1 foot. The lengths increase by 1 foot, that is, 1 foot, 2 feet, 3 feet, and so on, up to about 6 feet. These loose pieces of pipe are put into an organized wooden box on rollers. When fully loaded, the box has the appearance of an old time pipe organ.

The rental house usually takes your order by telephone or fax. For example, you order 1¹/₄-inch pipe and fittings. What sometimes happens is that the person pulling the order may not know how Speed-Rail® is measured. The shop person may measure it and decide that 1¹/₄ inches is actually 1.680 inches or just over 1¹/₂ inches. Get the picture? Make sure you clarify the order, and make sure the salesperson understands you. Don't assume, give attention to detail. Remember the commercials that say, "Check with your physician before use." The same words of wisdom apply here. Don't think, "Well it might work." Know that it will work safely. Check with the experts first.

## Insert Camera Cars

An insert car is a fantastic tool. There are a few things you should know and think about.

1. Always move the arm after you have released the brake if the car has an arm or crane on it. This will let you know that the brake has not lodged or become stuck.
2. Allow air space for bumps while traveling. Don't rest the arm against its stops.
3. Always run the course in the midarm position first at half speed. This may save a life.
4. Level to the camber of the road once the route is chosen.
5. If filming in a tunnel, account for the curve of the walls to the ceiling.
6. Use as many personnel as needed to control the arm.
7. Tie and ensure the safety of all loose equipment.
8. Check for wires on the course.

These are only a few of the many things you should watch for. Be safe.

### Insert Car Facts

The Shotmaker® Elite insert car has an automatic leveling system. Turn on the leveling system when you line up the shot on the desired roadway. Turn off the system while driving down the road. You don't want the system to autolevel during the middle of a take because it can throw off the camera operator's desired final position.

The Elite also has an electric braking system with a light to indicate whether the brakes are off or on. *Always* move the arm up and down and side to side after you have released the brake. This gives you a check to see whether the brakes are off. If they are off, the system is mobile. *Never* go strictly by the lights. Lights burn out. After you set the brake, also try to move the arm. No movement ensures the brakes are on.

I always ask for a half-speed rehearsal the first time through a shot. I usually get them. It is not because I am the rich and powerful Oz. It's because I have been blessed to work with professionals who understand safety. There are times when everything happens fast. You are losing light because the sun is setting. The talent is heading fast into double time. Whatever the reason, don't be stupid. Make the right decision; make a safe decision. I sometimes have to remind myself when these situations arise, "I was looking for a job when I found this one." Is it worth making a stupid mistake by rushing? Think about it.

### Shotmaker® Camera Cars

The Shotmaker® Elite is one of the newest tools in the film industry. It has already won several awards, including The Academy of Motion Pictures Arts and Sciences Engineering Award. It is an excellent addition to the tool inventory of key grips. It's a camera car, a crane, a generator, and much more. The Shotmaker® is the most versatile and hardworking moviemaking vehicle.

**Figure 129**    Shotmaker® Elite.

**UVA F.A.C.T.**
To measure how much time is left before the direct sun ball sinks behind a mountain or building, extend your hand and arm toward the sun with your fingers parallel to the horizon. Place your lower fingers at the top of the mountain. The thickness of each finger between the top of the mountain and the bottom of the sun represents 10 to 15 minutes. Wear your shades.

### Shotmaker® Elite

### Features

Crane reaches a lens height of 23 feet (6.9 meters) (higher with risers).

Arm rotates through 360 degrees without cable wrap-up.

Center post hydraulically adjusts to compensate for camber in the road.

Front camera platform has an arc of 6 feet (1.8 meters) with a lens height of 5 feet 6 inches (1.65 meters) to 11 feet 6 inches (3.45 meters) with a standard mount.

System runs on a 500 A DC generator. Camera car carries an on-board 500 A DC generator and a 200 A DC battery pack used for lighting or to drive the Shotmaker® Elite up to 20 miles per hour for silent running shots. The key grip can drive the vehicle forward or backward from the rear platform.

Inverter provides silent AC power: 120 V AC, 70 A, 60.00001 Hz.

Arm extends to a lens height of 23 feet (6.9 meters), has a 600-pound (270 kilograms) lifting capacity, and can continuously rotate past 360 degrees with no cable wrap-up.

Front platform rises from ground level to a lens height of 13 feet, 6 inches (4 meters), even while vehicle is in motion.

Vibration-absorbing air suspension system corrects 15 times per second. This provides continuous self-leveling, even over difficult terrain, and almost eliminates camera chatter.

Tow dolly sets up fast and tracks precisely and safely. Can tow up to three vehicles or motorcycles in a variety of configurations by means of three axles, six wheels, and four-wheel drive.

Rear wheels crab in both directions for running shots and enable the vehicle to turn its own length.

Process trailer expands from 8 feet (2.4 meters) to 13 feet, 6 inches (4 meters) wide, with an 11-foot, 6-inch (3.5-meter)-wide by 26-foot (7.8-meter)-long working surface. The trailer has an 8,000-pound capacity and full air suspension.

Rear license plate flips down for immediate access to compressed air and electrical power outlets. Illuminated for night use.

**Figure 130a**   Shotmaker® Premier.

### Shotmaker® Premier

### Features

Crane arm reaches a lens height of 21 feet (6.3 meters) (higher with risers).
Hydraulically adjusted center post compensates for road camber.
Camera car carries an onboard 200 A DC generator and a 200 A DC battery
   pack.
Three axles for maximum safety and load-carrying capacity.

### Shotmaker® Classic

The Classic is a state-of-the-art insert car with three-axle construction for a
longer, wider stance.

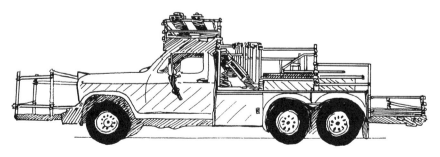

**Figure 130b**   Shotmaker® Classic.

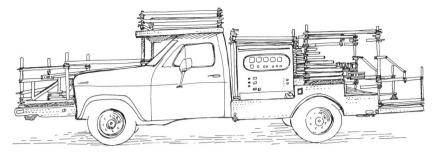

**Figure 130c**   Shotmaker® Standard.

## Features
Rear air suspension is self-correcting.
Front camera platform can be repositioned high or low on either side of
the vehicle.
Available with 28-foot-long (8.4 meters) process trailer that expands
to a shooting width of 11 feet, 6 inches (3.5 meters), 9 feet, 6 inches
(2.9 meters) between wheel wells.
Camera car carries an onboard 200 A AC generator.

### Shotmaker® Standard

#### Features
The Standard insert car rides on spring plus air-assist suspension for smooth
running shots.
Vehicle carries an onboard 200 A AC generator.
Picture vehicles can be towed from five hook-on points around the camera car.

## Underwater Camera Rigs
### *HydroFlex®*
#### Underwater Camera Housings
The HydroFlex® underwater camera housings are as follows:

43-5 remote AquaCam
35-3 remote AquaCam
Deep water housing
35-3 shallow water housing
HydroFlex® 35-3 surf housing
Panavision 65 deep water housing
Mini Vistacam
VistaVision™ Butterfly deep water housing
Eyemo
16SR 3 shallow water

**Figure 131a**   43-5 Remote AquaCam.

**Figure 131b**   35-3 Remote AquaCam.

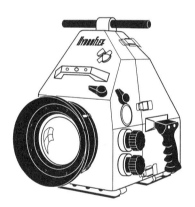

The Hydroflex 35-3 Deep Water Housing.

## SPECIFICATIONS

**CAMERA:** Arri 35-3
**OPERATING DEPTH:** 150 ft.
**WEIGHT IN AIR:** 85 lbs. loaded
**WEIGHT IN SALTWATER:** 3 lbs. loaded
**LENSES:** Zeiss PL T1.3 &
2.1 Series &
Panavision

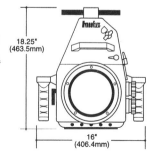
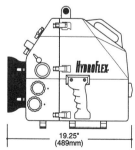

18.25"
(463.5mm)

16"
(406.4mm)

19.25"
(489mm)

**Figure 132**   Deep water housing.

The Hydroflex Shallow Water Housing.

## SPECIFICATIONS

**CAMERA:** Arri 35-3
**OPERATING DEPTH:** 12 ft.
**WEIGHT IN AIR:** 52 lbs. loaded
**WEIGHT IN SALTWATER:** 2 lbs. w/lead pack
**LENSES:** Zeiss PL T1.3 &
2.1 Series &
Panavision

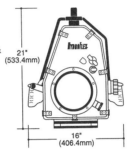

21"
(533.4mm)

16"
(406.4mm)

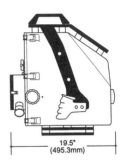

19.5"
(495.3mm)

**Figure 133**  35-3 Shallow water housing.

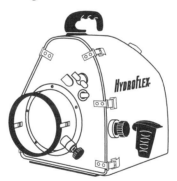

The Hydroflex 35-3 Surf Housing.

## SPECIFICATIONS

**CAMERA:** Arri 35-3
**OPERATING DEPTH:** 2 ft., Surface Only
**LENSES:** Zeiss PL T1.3 &
2.1 Series &
Panavision

16"
(406.4mm)

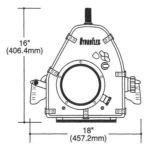

18"
(457.2mm)

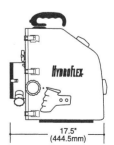

17.5"
(444.5mm)

**Figure 134**  HydroFlex® 35-3 surf housing.

**141**

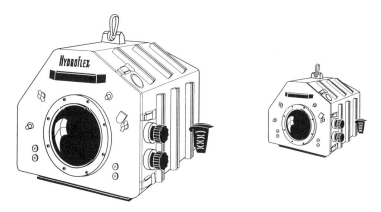

**Figure 135**    Panavision 65 deep water housing.

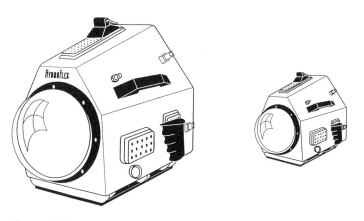

**Figure 136**    Mini Vistacam.

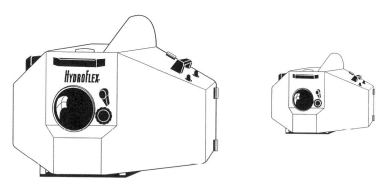

**Figure 137**    VistaVision™ Butterfly deep water housing.

The HydroFlex® 35 mm Eyemo underwater housing is designed for through-the-lens or video viewing, 100-foot film loads, and use of on-board batteries. It is depth rated to 40 feet (12 meters). The housing is built of PVC and Plexiglas. Other features include video to the surface, remote run, exterior focus and iris controls and mounting surfaces on top, bottom, and both sides. The Eyemo camera uses Nikon lenses and has preselected crystal-controlled film speeds of 6 to 50 feet per second.

The HydroFlex® 16SR 3 is designed around the Arriflex 16SR 3 camera with video assist, 400-foot magazines, and an on-board camera battery. Designed primarily for above-water filming in wet environments, the 16SR 3 shallow water housing has an optional lead pack to allow the housing to go underwater to a depth of 20 feet. Features include video-out, remote run, exterior focus and iris controls, and top and bottom mounting surfaces.

**Underwater Camera Accessories**

The following are underwater camera accessories:

Underwater speakers
Focus charts
Underwater tripods
Tilt and mounting plates
Sekonic marine meters
Spectra Pro housings
Minolta 1-degree spot housing
Minolta color temperature housings
Underwater monitors

Much lighter and smaller than a spinning glass spray deflector, the HydroFlex® spray deflector keeps water spots from ruining shots. This accessory is ideal when shooting in the rain or on the water where spray can be a problem. The system uses

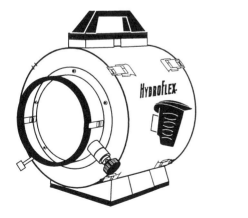

**Figure 138**   Eyemo underwater camera housing.

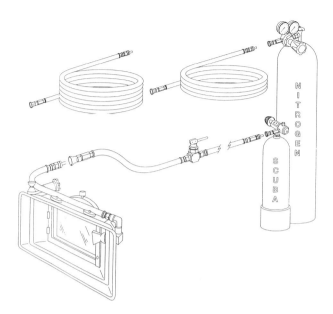

**Figure 139**  HydroFlex® air-powered spray deflector.

standard scuba nitrogen tanks for the air supply and is controlled by an in-line on-off valve. Also available are modified lightweight matte boxes that incorporate the air-blower system for use in wet situations.

Digital and Hi-8 underwater video is used primarily for location scouting and behind the scenes coverage. HydroFlex® offers Digital and Hi-8 housings that allow one to feed video out to the surface through an underwater video cable.

**Exposure Meter Housings**

HydroFlex® has designed waterproof housing for the Minolta 1-degree spot meter, the Minolta Auto IV incident meter, and the Spectra Pro IV meter. These housings allow use of exposure meters with equal ease in wet or dry conditions. Crafted from aluminum and Plexiglas, the incident meter housings are depth-rated to 40 feet and the spot meter

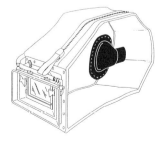

**Figure 140**  HydroFlex® splashbags.

**Figure 141**    HydroFlex® housings for Minolta and Spectra Pro meters.

to 150 feet (45 meters). These meter housings also provide ideal protection on land against damage from sand and rain. HydroFlex® has produced the most form-fitting design possible. Meters fit in the housings without any special modification or setup. Quick-release latches allow for easy installation or removal.

### Underwater Lighting Systems

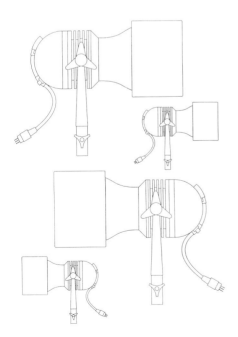

**Figure 142**    HydroFlex® 4000W SE HMI.

**145**

HydroPar 2500W lighting system includes barn
doors, snoots, GFI's, and ballast.

## SPECIFICATIONS

| | |
|---|---|
| **BULB:** | 2500W SE |
| **VOLTAGE:** | 120 VAC |
| **COLOR TEMP:** | 5600° K |
| **OPERATING DEPTH:** | 120 feet |
| **WEIGHT IN AIR:** | 30 pounds |
| **WEIGHT IN WATER:** | 3.5 pounds |

**DIFFUSION LENSES:**

| BEAM | BEAM ANGLE | CANDLE POWER |
|---|---|---|
| VNSP | 7 x 10 | 3,600,000 |
| NSP | 8 x 11 | 2,600,000 |
| MFL | 10 x 22 | 1,200,000 |
| WFL | 19 x 54 | 340,000 |
| JWFL | 36 x 62 | 180,000 |

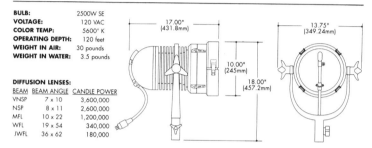

**Figure 143**  HydroPar® 2500W HMI.

HydroPar 1200W lighting
system includes barn doors,
snoots, GFI's, and ballast.

## SPECIFICATIONS

| | |
|---|---|
| **BULB:** | 1200SE/1200PAR 64 |
| **VOLTAGE:** | 120 VAC |
| **COLOR TEMP:** | 5600° K |
| **OPERATING DEPTH:** | 120 feet |
| **WEIGHT IN AIR:** | 29 pounds |
| **WEIGHT IN WATER:** | 2 pounds |

**DIFFUSION LENSES:**

| BEAM | BEAM ANGLE | CANDLE POWER |
|---|---|---|
| VNSP | 7 x 10 | 1,800,000 |
| NSP | 8 x 11 | 1,300,000 |
| MFL | 10 x 22 | 600,000 |
| WFL | 19 x 54 | 170,000 |
| UWFL | 36 x 62 | 90,000 |

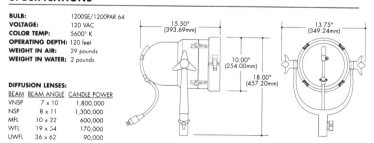

**Figure 144**  HydroPar® 1200W HMI.

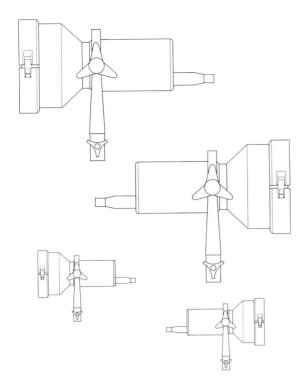

**Figure 145**   SeaPar 1200W HMI.

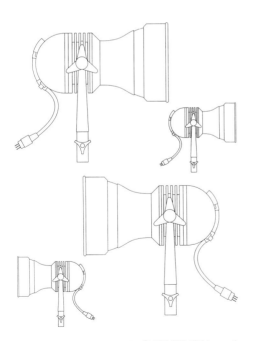

**Figure 146**   HydroFlex® 5000W SE incandescent.

The HydroPar 2000W offers a safe, more powerful incandescent light.

## SPECIFICATIONS

**BULB:** CYX
**VOLTAGE:** 120 VAC/VDC
**COLOR TEMP:** 3200° K
**OPERATING DEPTH:** 120 feet
**WEIGHT IN AIR:** 24 pounds
**WEIGHT IN WATER:** 3.5 pounds

**DIFFUSION LENSES:**

| BEAM | BEAM ANGLE | CANDLE POWER |
|------|-----------|--------------|
| VNSP | 7 x 10 | 1,000,000 |
| NSP | 8 x 11 | 740,000 |
| MFL | 10 x 22 | 340,000 |
| WFL | 19 x 54 | 95,000 |
| UWFL | 36 x 62 | 50,000 |

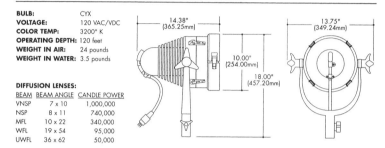

**Figure 147**  HydroPar® 2000W incandescent.

The HydroPar 1000W incandescent is a simple lightweight multipurpose light source suitable for key or fill light from a fixed position or hand-held to follow the action.

## SPECIFICATIONS

**BULB:** PAR 64
**VOLTAGE:** 120 VAC/VDC
**COLOR TEMP:** 3200°/5200°K
**OPERATING DEPTH:** 120 feet
**WEIGHT IN AIR:** 14 pounds
**WEIGHT IN WATER:** 4 oz.

**BULB OPTIONS:**

| ANSI | BEAM | BEAM ANGLE | CANDLE PWR | COLOR TEMP |
|------|------|-----------|------------|-----------|
| FFN | VNSP | 12 x 6 | 400,000 | 3200°K |
| FFP | NSP | 14 x 7 | 330,000 | 3200°K |
| FFR | MFL | 26 x 12 | 125,000 | 3200°K |
| FFS | WFL | 40 x 24 | 40,000 | 3200°K |
| FGM | NSP | 24 x 12 | 200,000 | 5200°K |
| FGN | MFL | 27 x 11 | 70,000 | 5200°K |

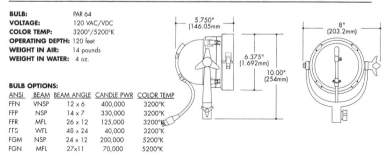

**Figure 148**  HydroPar® 1000W incandescent.

**148**

## SPECIFICATIONS

**BULB:** PAR 36
**VOLTAGE:** 120 VAC/VDC
**COLOR TEMP:** 3200°/5000°K
**OPERATING DEPTH:** 120 feet
**WEIGHT IN AIR:** 5.25 pounds
**WEIGHT IN WATER:** 1 pound

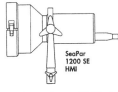

**BULB OPTIONS:**

| ANSI | BEAM | BEAM ANGLE | CANDLE PWR | COLOR TEMP |
|------|------|-----------|-----------|-----------|
| DWE | MFL | 40° x 30° | 24,000 | 3200°K |
| FBO | SP | 25° x 15° | 75,000 | 3400°K |
| FGK | NFL | 30° x 20° | 24,000 | 5000°K |
| FBE | SP | 25° x 15° | 35,000 | 5000°K |

The HydroPar 650W incandescent is a simple lightweight multipurpose light source suitable for key or fill light from a fixed position or hand-held to follow the action.

**Figure 149a**   HydroPar® 650W incandescent.

The HydroPar® and SeaPar® lighting systems are state-of-the-art underwater lights specifically designed for feature and commercial film production. Modular components, underwater mateable connectors and integrated ground fault sensors (GFCI's) which prevent electrical accidents, make these lighting systems very safe, flexible and easy to set up.

Each lamp is compact and lightweight, and can be tailored to any shooting situation. Barn doors and specially designed snoots are easily added by simply removing the lamphead retainer ring and inserting the accessory. Filter gels and scrims may also be added. All the lamps mate to a 5/8" spud to be compatible with standard grip and lighting equipment. With the exception of the HydroPar 2500 SE HMI, all lamps can be used above water for timed intervals, which allows them to work well on partially wet or rainy sets. All lights are depth rated to 120'.

All HydroPar and SeaPar lighting systems are fitted with our custom underwater mateable connectors which utilize an extended ground pin for *Mate First/Break Last* grounding of the lamp. HMI lamps are run on AC power only and incandescent lighting can be powered with AC or DC.

### HydroPar® 2500 SE HMI

The HydroPar 2500 SE HMI represents the latest generation of HydroPar underwater lighting. The main body of the lamp was designed with cooling fins to dissipate the heat generated by the lamp, and a Teflon® spacer isolates the ignitor electronics to keep them cool. The lamphead can rotate on axis in the yoke assembly and tailor the beam pattern to the subject. On the surface this lamp weighs 30 lbs., and it weighs only 3.5 lbs. in saltwater.

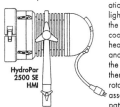

### HydroPar 1200 SE HMI

The HydroPar 1200 HMI has been refitted with a single-ended globe to allow the lamphead to rotate in its yoke assembly. Changing fresnels to adjust the light's beam pattern is fast and simple. On the surface this lamp weighs 26 lbs, and it only weighs 2.5 lbs. in saltwater, making it easy to handhold to follow the action.

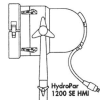

### SeaPar® 1200w HMI

The original *Wet or Dry HMI*, designed for the movie *The Abyss* in 1988, these lamps have been extensively used in the motion picture and commercial industries on countless projects worldwide. In 1991, the SeaPar 1200w HMI received a Technical Achievement Award from the Academy of Motion Picture Arts and Sciences for: *Safety and Portability On Wet or Dry Sets*. On the surface the SeaPar 1200w HMI weighs 27 lbs, and it weighs just 3.5 lbs. in saltwater.

### HydroPar 2000w Incandescent

Designed in response to the increasing demands of the industry, the HydroPar 2000w incandescent uses the 2000w single-ended CYX globe and offers a safe and more powerful tungsten lamp. Changing fresnels to adjust the beam pattern is quick and easy. The HydroPar 2000w weighs 24 lbs. in air and 3.5 lbs. in saltwater.

### HydroPar 1000w Incandescent

Designed primarily as a simple, lightweight multipurpose light source, the HydroPar 1000w achieves its high output by using interchangeable PAR 64 globes. Various beam widths and color temperatures are easily obtained by simply switching globes. The HydroPar 1000w weighs 14 lbs. in air and 4 oz. in saltwater.

### HydroPar 650w Incandescent

The HydroPar 650w is the most compact, ultra light member of our underwater lighting systems. Using Par 36 globes, Spot or Wide beam patterns are available in 3200° or 5000° Kelvin. On the surface this lamp weighs 5.25 lbs., and in saltwater it weighs 1 lb.

**Figure 149b**   HydroFlex® underwater and incandescent lighting overview.

**149**

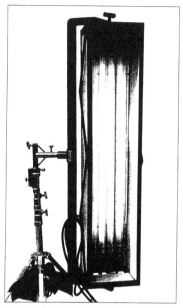

HydroFlow Four-Bank Underwater Soft Box with
4 ft. fluorescent lamps.

## SPECIFICATIONS

**Photometrics for 4 ft., Four-Bank Soft Box:**

| Feet | 4 | 6 | 8 | 10 | 12 |
|---|---|---|---|---|---|
| Meters | 1.2 | 1.8 | 2.4 | 3.0 | 3.6 |
| Footcandles | 170 | 80 | 45 | 35 | 25 |

*Values are approximate and based on Kino Flo KF55 and KF32 tubes. HydroFlow underwater fixtures will accept any standard 2 ft. or 4 ft. medium bi-pin fluorescent tube.*

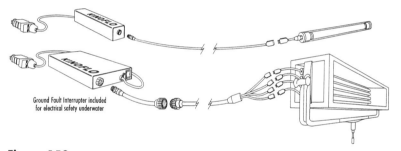

Ground Fault Interrupter included
for electrical safety underwater

**Figure 150**   HydroFlow™ fluorescent system.

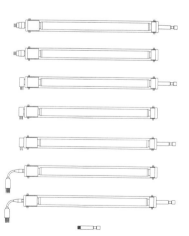

**Figure 151**   HydroFlow™ fluorescent system, continued.

**150**

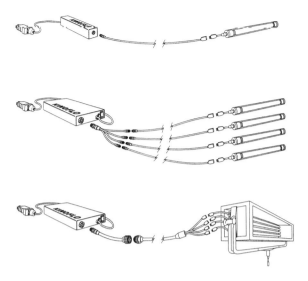

**Figure 152**   HydroFlow™ fluorescent system, continued.

### *Scubacam*

**Splash Housings for Betacam Cameras**

**SCU 1**   This model is for the 400/600 series Betacam cameras.

**SCU 2**   This model is for the 5/7 series Betacam cameras. Both of the SCU 1 and the SCU 2 units are supplied with an audio input and can have a video output. Adapter rings are supplied to securely locate the lens in the front port. These units can only be handheld.

**SCU 3**   This model is for Aaton 35 mm cameras with a Chrosziel follow focus. The widest lens that can be used is 18 mm. A clip-on 4 by 4 filter holder is supplied, and the housing can be handheld or mounted on a tripod. A 10-foot video cable is supplied as standard, and there is an external handle with a watertight film-run switch.

**SCU 5**   This model is for Arri SR2 and ST3 cameras. It has an external handle with two watertight film-run switches and interchangeable eyepieces for the two cameras. A full glove allows access to the lens, and there are ports to view camera and lens functions. This housing can be either handheld or mounted on a tripod. The housing comes with a clip-on filter holder, and a 10-foot video output cable.

**SCU 6**   This unit is for the Arri 35/3 camera. It is supplied with a 10-meter power and video loom, and the camera can be run at 130 feet per second. This housing has an external film-run switch and can be either handheld or mounted on a tripod. The camera is mounted on a Ronford quick-release system and has a double

4 by 4 filter holder. The widest lens that can be used is 12 mm, and there is an external follow focus.

**SCU 7**    This model is for the Aaton XTR and Prod cameras. It has an external handle with a watertight film-run switch and interchangeable eyepieces. There is a full glove to access the lens and there are viewing ports to see camera and lens functions. The unit can be either handheld or mounted on a tripod. It comes supplied with a clip-on filter holder and a 10-foot video cable.

### Rain Covers

Scubacam has rain covers for Arri and Aaton 16 mm cameras, Arri 35/3, Arri 435, Arri 535, Aaton 35, and Betacam cameras. All Scubacam splash housings are made from 2- to 2.5-millimeter thick natural latex and sealed with very high quality watertight zips. They are all equipped with an audible leak detector and can be easily modified to customer requirements. When the zips are fully closed, the splash housing can be submerged to a maximum depth of 3 meters.

## ShowRig Truss Systems
### Framework

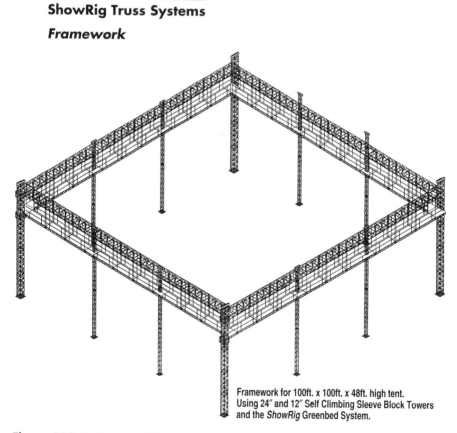

Framework for 100ft. x 100ft. x 48ft. high tent.
Using 24″ and 12″ Self Climbing Sleeve Block Towers
and the *ShowRig* Greenbed System.

**Figure 153a**    Framework for tent.

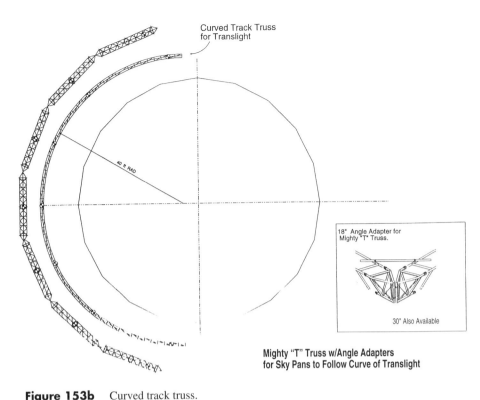

Curved Track Truss
for Translight

40 ft RAD

18" Angle Adapter for
Mighty "T" Truss.

30° Also Available

**Mighty "T" Truss w/Angle Adapters
for Sky Pans to Follow Curve of Translight**

**Figure 153b**    Curved track truss.

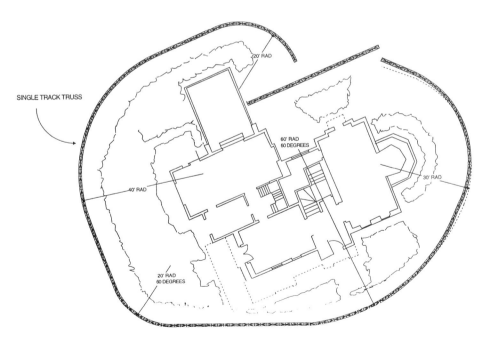

20' RAD

SINGLE TRACK TRUSS

60' RAD
60 DEGREES

30' RAD

40' RAD

20' RAD
60 DEGREES

**Figure 153c**    Track truss layout.

**153**

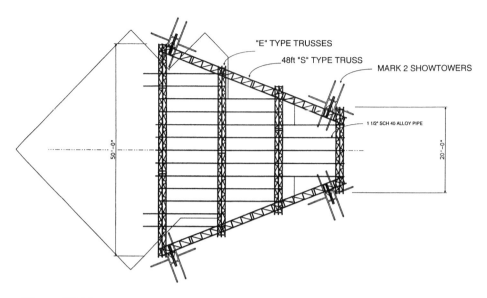

**Figure 153d**   E truss, S truss, and show towers.

## MARK 1 BGS SYSTEM
FOR BLUE/GREEN SCREENS AS TALL AS 28FT.
ALLOWING EASY RIGGING AND REPOSITIONING
OF SCREENS, BACKINGS AND TRANSLIGHTS ***

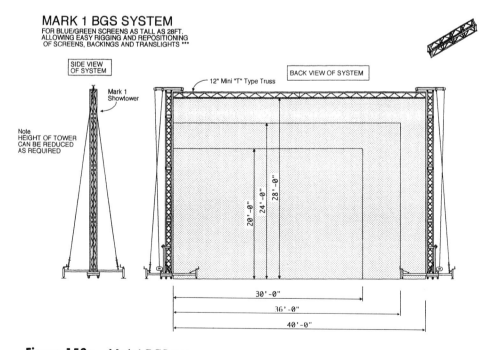

**Figure 153e**   Mark 1 BGS system.

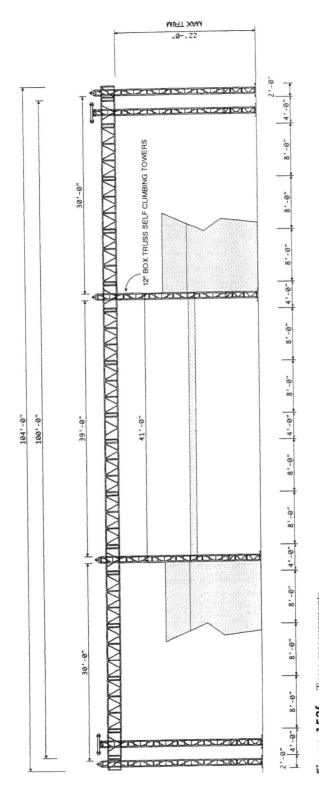

**Figure 153f** Truss measurements.

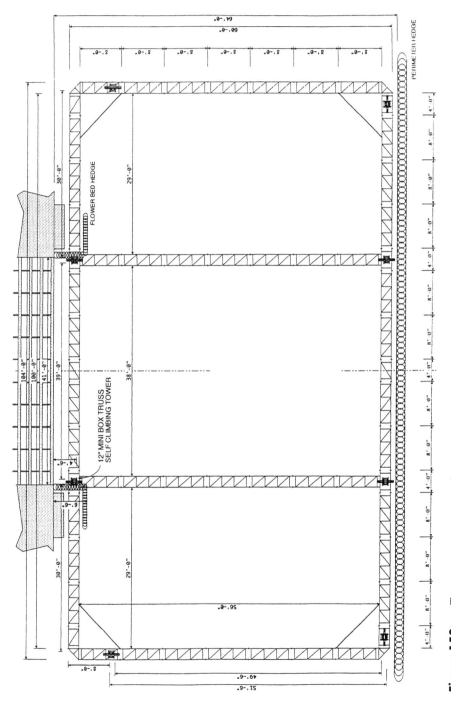

**Figure 153g** Truss measurements, continued.

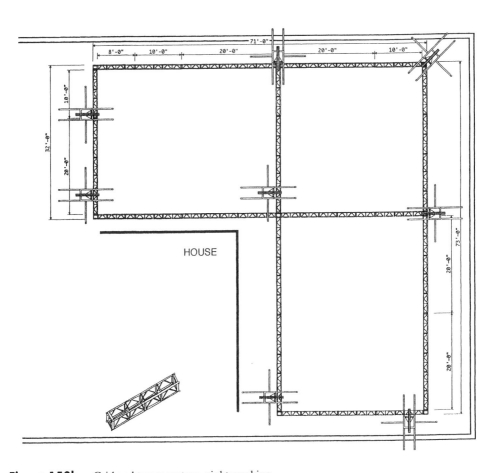

**Figure 153h**   Grid and tower system, night masking.

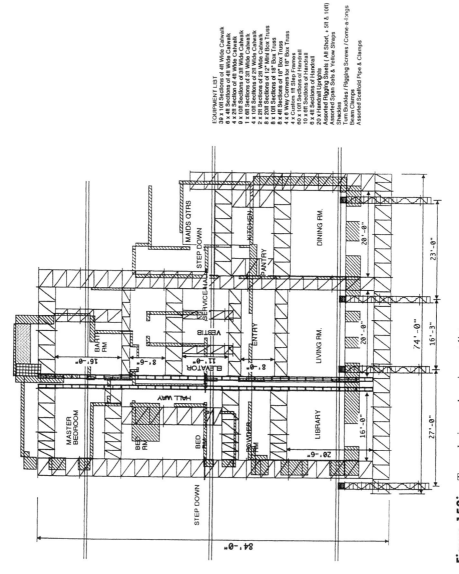

EQUIPMENT LIST
39 x 10ft Sections of 4ft Wide Catwalk
6 x 4ft Sections of 4ft Wide Catwalk
4 x 2ft Section of 4ft Wide Catwalk
9 x 10ft Sections of 3ft Wide Catwalk
1 x 6ft Sections of 3ft Wide Catwalk
4 x 10ft Sections of 2ft Wide Catwalk
2 x 2ft Sections of 2ft Wide Catwalk
8 x 20ft Sections of 12" Mini Box Truss
8 x 10ft Sections of 18" Box Truss
8 x 4ft Sections of 18" Box Truss
4 x 6 Way Corners for 18" Box Truss
4 x Custom 1ft Step Frames
60 x 10ft Sections of Handrail
10 x 4ft Sections of Handrail
6 x 4ft Sections of Handrail
20 x Handrail Uprights
Assorted Rigging Steels ( All Short, + 5ft & 10ft)
Assorted Span Sets & Yellow Straps
Shackles
Turn Buckles / Rigging Screws / Come-a-longs
Beam Clamps
Assorted Scaffold Pipe & Clamps

**Figure 153i** Truss design and equipment list.

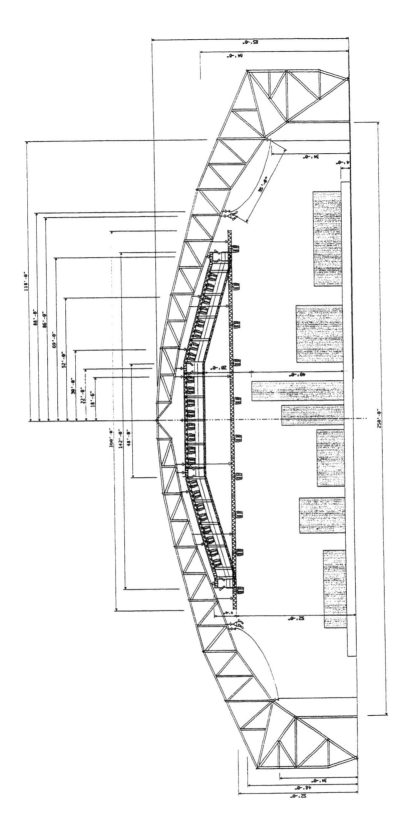

**Figure 153j** Side view of catwalk and truss layout.

159

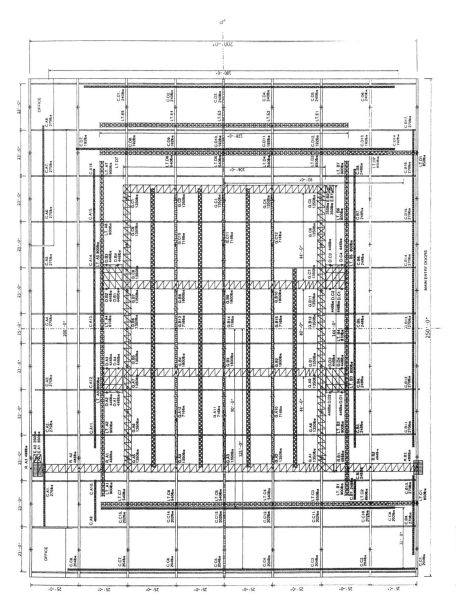

**Figure 153k** Catwalk system, rigging layout.

## Chain Motors and Controls

1 Ton CM Load Star
• Unit Weight w/ 60ft Chain 147lbs
• Shipping Weight 2 Motors w/ Case 421lbs

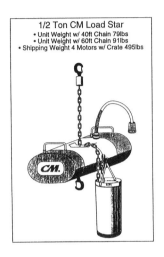

1/2 Ton CM Load Star
• Unit Weight w/ 40ft Chain 79lbs
• Unit Weight w/ 60ft Chain 91lbs
• Shipping Weight 4 Motors w/ Crate 495lbs

300 Lb. CM Pro Star
• Unit Weight w/ 40ft Chain 39lbs

**Figure 153l**   Chain motors.

This Power Distribution and control unit can control from 1 to 6 motors. Each motor circuit can be controlled separately. Because the PD is compact and light weight it can be mounted on the truss, easily hauled up into the perms or left on the floor taking up very little space.

The power connection is on the back panel. Power cable comes with each PD. For the power tie-in we can provide bare ends, sister lugs, or tweko connectors. Additionally on the back panel is a power output allowing for the use of "jumpers" to feed other PDs. Eliminating the need for multiple power tie-ins.

**Power Requirement:**
For use with 1/2 ton motors   30 amps 208v/3 phase
For use with 1 ton motors      60 amps 208v/3 phase

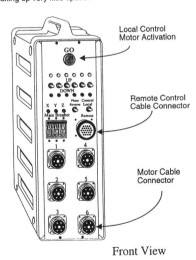

Local Control
Motor Activation

Remote Control
Cable Connector

Motor Cable
Connector

Front View

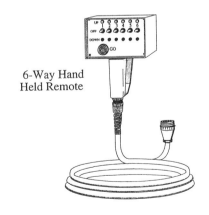

6-Way Hand
Held Remote

**Figure 153m**   Six-way motor control.

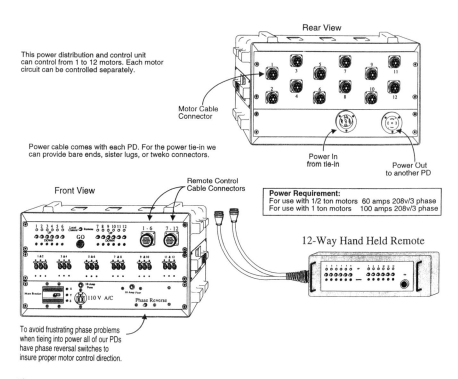

Rear View

This power distribution and control unit can control from 1 to 12 motors. Each motor circuit can be controlled separately.

Motor Cable Connector

Power cable comes with each PD. For the power tie-in we can provide bare ends, sister lugs, or tweko connectors.

Power In from tie-in

Power Out to another PD

Front View

Remote Control Cable Connectors

**Power Requirement:**
For use with 1/2 ton motors  60 amps 208v/3 phase
For use with 1 ton motors   100 amps 208v/3 phase

12-Way Hand Held Remote

To avoid frustrating phase problems when tieing into power all of our PDs have phase reversal switches to insure proper motor control direction.

**Figure 153n**   Twelve-way motor control.

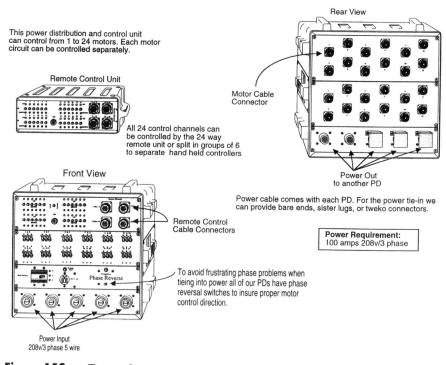

Rear View

This power distribution and control unit can control from 1 to 24 motors. Each motor circuit can be controlled separately.

Remote Control Unit

Motor Cable Connector

All 24 control channels can be controlled by the 24 way remote unit or split in groups of 6 to separate hand held controllers

Power Out to another PD

Front View

Power cable comes with each PD. For the power tie-in we can provide bare ends, sister lugs, or tweko connectors.

Remote Control Cable Connectors

**Power Requirement:**
100 amps 208v/3 phase

To avoid frustrating phase problems when tieing into power all of our PDs have phase reversal switches to insure proper motor control direction.

Power Input
208v/3 phase 5 wire

**Figure 153o**   Twenty-four-way motor control.

## Speed Grid Systems

THE "X &Y" LADDER BEAM GRID

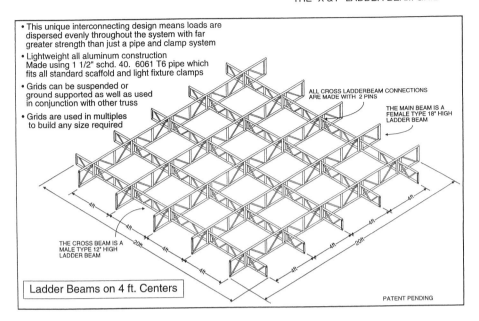

- This unique interconnecting design means loads are dispersed evenly throughout the system with far greater strength than just a pipe and clamp system
- Lightweight all aluminum construction Made using 1 1/2" schd. 40. 6061 T6 pipe which fits all standard scaffold and light fixture clamps
- Grids can be suspended or ground supported as well as used in conjunction with other truss
- Grids are used in multiples to build any size required

ALL CROSS LADDERBEAM CONNECTIONS ARE MADE WITH 2 PINS

THE MAIN BEAM IS A FEMALE TYPE 18" HIGH LADDER BEAM

THE CROSS BEAM IS A MALE TYPE 12" HIGH LADDER BEAM

4ft 4ft 4ft 20ft 20ft 4ft 4ft 4ft

Ladder Beams on 4 ft. Centers

PATENT PENDING

**Figure 153p**    Ladder beams on 4-foot centers.

THE "X &Y" LADDER BEAM GRID

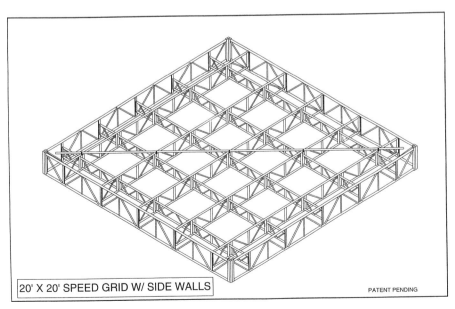

20' X 20' SPEED GRID W/ SIDE WALLS

PATENT PENDING

**Figure 153q**    Twenty-foot by twenty-foot speed grid with side walls.

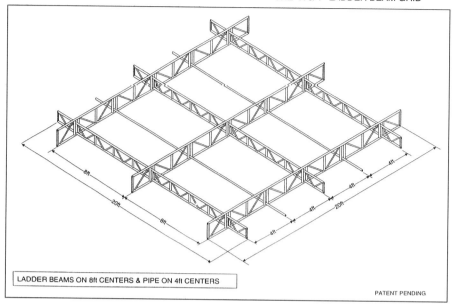

**Figure 153r**    Ladder beams on 8-foot centers and pipe on 4-foot centers.

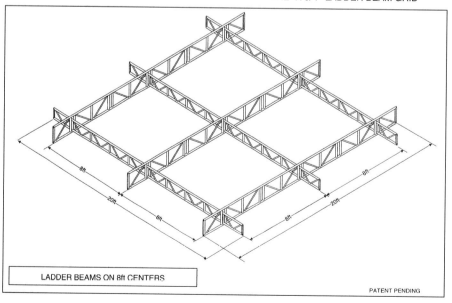

**Figure 153s**    Ladder beams on 8-foot centers.

THE "X &Y" LADDER BEAM GRID

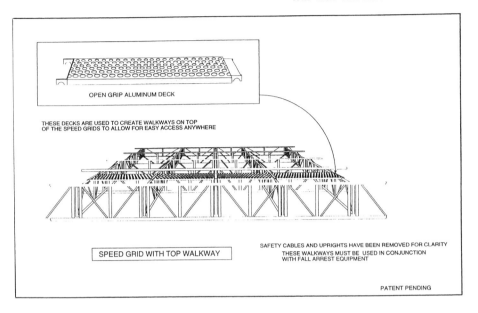

OPEN GRIP ALUMINUM DECK

THESE DECKS ARE USED TO CREATE WALKWAYS ON TOP
OF THE SPEED GRIDS TO ALLOW FOR EASY ACCESS ANYWHERE

SPEED GRID WITH TOP WALKWAY

SAFETY CABLES AND UPRIGHTS HAVE BEEN REMOVED FOR CLARITY
THESE WALKWAYS MUST BE USED IN CONJUNCTION
WITH FALL ARREST EQUIPMENT

PATENT PENDING

**Figure 153t**   Speed grid with top walkway.

THE "X &Y" LADDER BEAM GRID

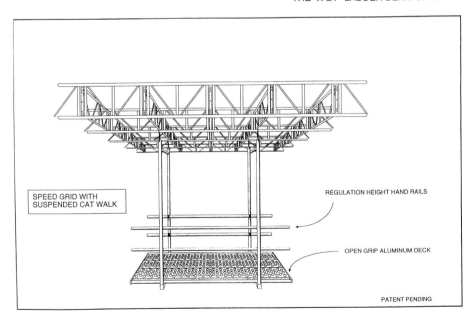

SPEED GRID WITH
SUSPENDED CAT WALK

REGULATION HEIGHT HAND RAILS

OPEN GRIP ALUMINUM DECK

PATENT PENDING

**Figure 153u**   Speed grid with suspended cat walk.

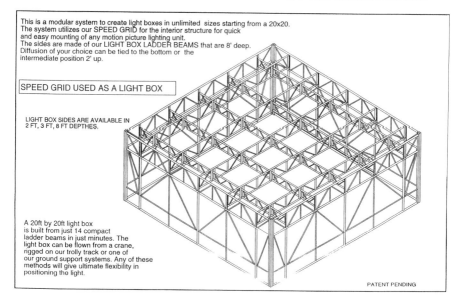

This is a modular system to create light boxes in unlimited sizes starting from a 20x20. The system utilizes our SPEED GRID for the interior structure for quick and easy mounting of any motion picture lighting unit. The sides are made of our LIGHT BOX LADDER BEAMS that are 8' deep. Diffusion of your choice can be tied to the bottom or the intermediate position 2' up.

SPEED GRID USED AS A LIGHT BOX

LIGHT BOX SIDES ARE AVAILABLE IN 2 FT, 3 FT, 8 FT DEPTHES.

A 20ft by 20ft light box is built from just 14 compact ladder beams in just minutes. The light box can be flown from a crane, rigged on our trolly track or one of our ground support systems. Any of these methods will give ultimate flexibility in positioning the light.

PATENT PENDING

**Figure 153v**   Speed grid used as a light box.

## *Trusses*

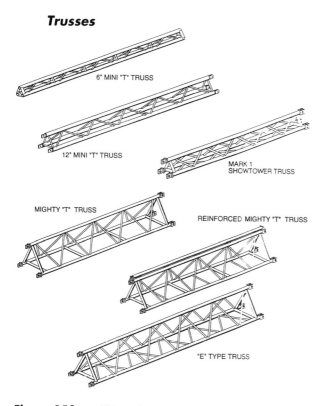

6" MINI "T" TRUSS

12" MINI "T" TRUSS

MARK 1 SHOWTOWER TRUSS

MIGHTY "T" TRUSS

REINFORCED MIGHTY "T" TRUSS

"E" TYPE TRUSS

**Figure 153w**   Triangular trusses.

**166**

PATENT PENDING
Designed and Manufactured by
**SGPS,Inc.**

• Use it for framing translights, painted backings and green screens.

• Mini T is a low profile truss that has been designed as a lighter weight, stiffer alternative to steel water pipe and irrigation pipe.

Chords are made using
1 1/4" Speed Rail

•6" Mini-"T" weighs 62 lbs. per 20 ft. section
A 20 ft piece of 1 1/2" schedule 40 black water pipe weighs 54.5 lbs. Three times the rigidity for almost the same weight.

• Our framing corners are designed so the single pipe is on the inside for easy tensioning of soft goods in the frame.

• A 20 ft. section is easily carried by one person.

• Hang curtains and masking on less points.

**Unit Weight**
• 20ft 60lbs.

Available in 5′, 8′, 10′, 20′ sections

Securely bolts together using
Grade 8 Hardened Bolts

**Figure 153x**   Six-inch mini-T truss.

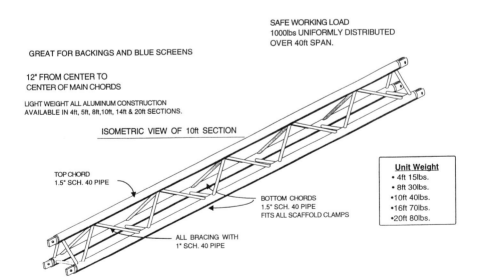

SAFE WORKING LOAD
1000lbs UNIFORMLY DISTRIBUTED
OVER 40ft SPAN.

GREAT FOR BACKINGS AND BLUE SCREENS

12" FROM CENTER TO
CENTER OF MAIN CHORDS

LIGHT WEIGHT ALL ALUMINUM CONSTRUCTION
AVAILABLE IN 4ft, 5ft, 8ft,10ft, 14ft & 20ft SECTIONS.

ISOMETRIC VIEW OF 10ft SECTION

TOP CHORD
1.5" SCH. 40 PIPE

BOTTOM CHORDS
1.5" SCH. 40 PIPE
FITS ALL SCAFFOLD CLAMPS

ALL BRACING WITH
1" SCH. 40 PIPE

**Unit Weight**
• 4ft 15lbs.
• 8ft 30lbs.
•10ft 40lbs.
•16ft 70lbs.
•20ft 80lbs.

**Figure 153y**   Twelve-inch mini-T truss.

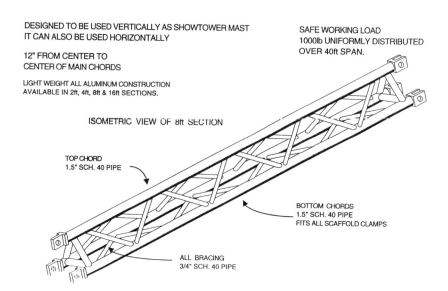

DESIGNED TO BE USED VERTICALLY AS SHOWTOWER MAST
IT CAN ALSO BE USED HORIZONTALLY

12" FROM CENTER TO
CENTER OF MAIN CHORDS

LIGHT WEIGHT ALL ALUMINUM CONSTRUCTION
AVAILABLE IN 2ft, 4ft, 8ft & 16ft SECTIONS.

SAFE WORKING LOAD
1000lb UNIFORMLY DISTRIBUTED
OVER 40ft SPAN.

ISOMETRIC VIEW OF 8ft SECTION

TOP CHORD
1.5" SCH. 40 PIPE

BOTTOM CHORDS
1.5" SCH. 40 PIPE
FITS ALL SCAFFOLD CLAMPS

ALL BRACING
3/4" SCH. 40 PIPE

**Figure 153z**   Mark 1 show tower mast truss.

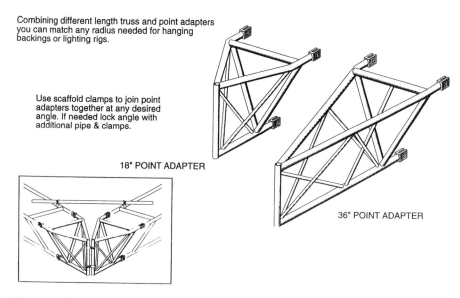

Combining different length truss and point adapters
you can match any radius needed for hanging
backings or lighting rigs.

Use scaffold clamps to join point
adapters together at any desired
angle. If needed lock angle with
additional pipe & clamps.

18" POINT ADAPTER

36" POINT ADAPTER

**Figure 153aa**   Point adapters and angle adapters for Mighty T and E type truss.

SAFE WORKING LOAD
2,000 lb UNIFORMLY
DISTRIBUTED OVER 40ft SPAN

23 1/4" OD OF CORDS

LIGHT WEIGHT ALL ALUMINUM CONSTRUCTION
AVAILABLE IN 2ft, 4ft, 8ft, & 16ft SECTIONS
EVERY CONCEIVABLE ADAPTOR IN STOCK.
INTER-CONNECTS WITH OUR "E"-TYPE TRUSS

QUICK SAFE CONNECTION
BY HARDENED STEEL PINS

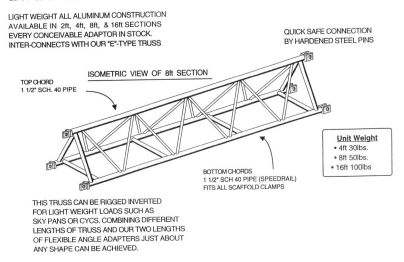

ISOMETRIC VIEW OF 8ft SECTION

TOP CHORD
1 1/2" SCH. 40 PIPE

BOTTOM CHORDS
1 1/2" SCH 40 PIPE (SPEEDRAIL)
FITS ALL SCAFFOLD CLAMPS

**Unit Weight**
• 4ft 30lbs.
• 8ft 50lbs.
• 16ft 100lbs

THIS TRUSS CAN BE RIGGED INVERTED
FOR LIGHT WEIGHT LOADS SUCH AS
SKY PANS OR CYCS. COMBINING DIFFERENT
LENGTHS OF TRUSS AND OUR TWO LENGTHS
OF FLEXIBLE ANGLE ADAPTERS JUST ABOUT
ANY SHAPE CAN BE ACHIEVED.

**Figure 153bb**  Mighty T truss.

DESIGNED FOR OUT-DOOR APPLICATIONS

LIGHT WEIGHT ALL ALUMINUM CONSTRUCTION
AVAILABLE IN 3'6", & 16ft SECTIONS
TWO & THREE WAY ADAPTORS IN STOCK.

SAFE WORKING LOAD
3,000 lb UNIFORMLY
DISTRIBUTED OVER 40ft SPAN

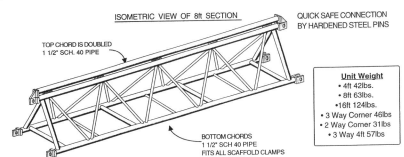

ISOMETRIC VIEW OF 8ft SECTION

QUICK SAFE CONNECTION
BY HARDENED STEEL PINS

TOP CHORD IS DOUBLED
1 1/2" SCH. 40 PIPE

BOTTOM CHORDS
1 1/2" SCH 40 PIPE
FITS ALL SCAFFOLD CLAMPS

**Unit Weight**
• 4ft 42lbs.
• 8ft 63lbs.
• 16ft 124lbs.
• 3 Way Corner 46lbs
• 2 Way Corner 31lbs
• 3 Way 4ft 57lbs

THIS UNIQUE DESIGN ALLOWS THIS
TRUSS TO HANDLE SOME WIND LOADING.
MAKING THIS TRUSS THE IDEAL CHOICE
FOR LARGE EXTERIOR DIFFUSION FRAMES.
EITHER GROUND SUPPORTED OR CRANE FLOWN.

**Figure 153cc**  Reinforced Mighty T.

**Also Known as MARK 2 SHOWTOWER MAST TRUSS**

23 1/4" OD OF CHORDS

LIGHT WEIGHT ALL ALUMINUM CONSTRUCTION
AVAILABLE IN 5ft, 10ft, & 20ft SECTIONS
EVERY CONCEIVABLE ADAPTOR IN STOCK.
INTER-CONNECTS WITH OUR MIGHTY "T" TRUSS

ISOMETRIC VIEW OF 10ft SECTION

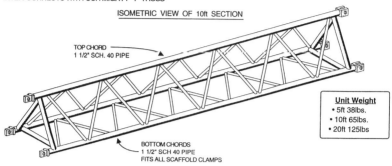

TOP CHORD
1 1/2" SCH. 40 PIPE

**Unit Weight**
- 5ft 38lbs.
- 10ft 65lbs.
- 20ft 125lbs

BOTTOM CHORDS
1 1/2" SCH 40 PIPE
FITS ALL SCAFFOLD CLAMPS

QUICK SAFE CONNECTION
BY HARDENED STEEL PINS

**Figure 153dd**   E-type truss.

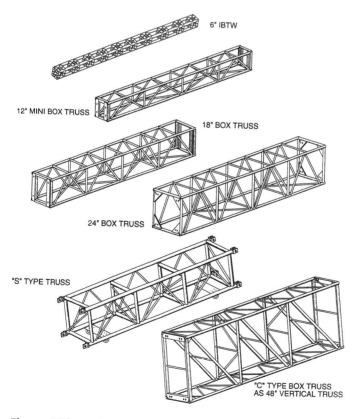

6" IBTW

12" MINI BOX TRUSS

18" BOX TRUSS

24" BOX TRUSS

"S" TYPE TRUSS

"C" TYPE BOX TRUSS
AS 48" VERTICAL TRUSS

**Figure 153ee**   Box trusses.

**170**

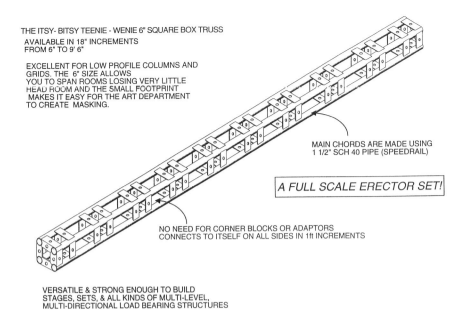

THE ITSY- BITSY TEENIE - WENIE 6" SQUARE BOX TRUSS
AVAILABLE IN 18" INCREMENTS
FROM 6" TO 9' 6"

EXCELLENT FOR LOW PROFILE COLUMNS AND
GRIDS. THE 6" SIZE ALLOWS
YOU TO SPAN ROOMS LOSING VERY LITTLE
HEAD ROOM AND THE SMALL FOOTPRINT
MAKES IT EASY FOR THE ART DEPARTMENT
TO CREATE MASKING.

MAIN CHORDS ARE MADE USING
1 1/2" SCH 40 PIPE (SPEEDRAIL)

A FULL SCALE ERECTOR SET!

NO NEED FOR CORNER BLOCKS OR ADAPTORS
CONNECTS TO ITSELF ON ALL SIDES IN 1ft INCREMENTS

VERSATILE & STRONG ENOUGH TO BUILD
STAGES, SETS, & ALL KINDS OF MULTI-LEVEL,
MULTI-DIRECTIONAL LOAD BEARING STRUCTURES

**Figure 153ff**    IBTW 6-inch box truss.

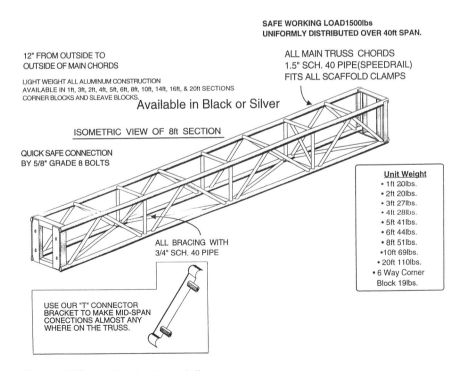

SAFE WORKING LOAD1500lbs
UNIFORMLY DISTRIBUTED OVER 40ft SPAN.

12" FROM OUTSIDE TO
OUTSIDE OF MAIN CHORDS

ALL MAIN TRUSS CHORDS
1.5" SCH. 40 PIPE(SPEEDRAIL)
FITS ALL SCAFFOLD CLAMPS

LIGHT WEIGHT ALL ALUMINUM CONSTRUCTION
AVAILABLE IN 1ft, 3ft, 2ft, 4ft, 5ft, 6ft, 8ft, 10ft, 14ft, 16ft, & 20ft SECTIONS
CORNER BLOCKS AND SLEAVE BLOCKS.

Available in Black or Silver

ISOMETRIC VIEW OF 8ft SECTION

QUICK SAFE CONNECTION
BY 5/8" GRADE 8 BOLTS

| Unit Weight |
| --- |
| • 1ft 20lbs. |
| • 2ft 20lbs. |
| • 3ft 27lbs. |
| • 4ft 28lbs. |
| • 5ft 41lbs. |
| • 6ft 44lbs. |
| • 8ft 51lbs. |
| •10ft 69lbs. |
| • 20ft 110lbs. |
| • 6 Way Corner Block 19lbs. |

ALL BRACING WITH
3/4" SCH. 40 PIPE

USE OUR "T" CONNECTOR
BRACKET TO MAKE MID-SPAN
CONECTIONS ALMOST ANY
WHERE ON THE TRUSS.

**Figure 153gg**    Twelve-inch minibox truss.

**171**

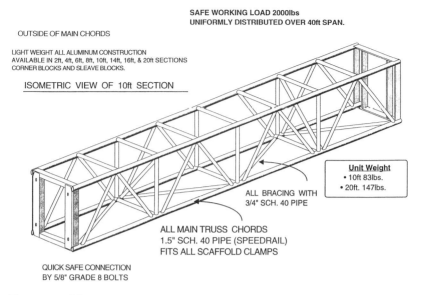

SAFE WORKING LOAD 2000lbs
UNIFORMLY DISTRIBUTED OVER 40ft SPAN.

OUTSIDE OF MAIN CHORDS

LIGHT WEIGHT ALL ALUMINUM CONSTRUCTION
AVAILABLE IN 2ft, 4ft, 6ft, 8ft, 10ft, 14ft, 16ft, & 20ft SECTIONS
CORNER BLOCKS AND SLEAVE BLOCKS.

ISOMETRIC VIEW OF 10ft SECTION

**Unit Weight**
• 10ft 83lbs.
• 20ft. 147lbs.

ALL BRACING WITH
3/4" SCH. 40 PIPE

ALL MAIN TRUSS CHORDS
1.5" SCH. 40 PIPE (SPEEDRAIL)
FITS ALL SCAFFOLD CLAMPS

QUICK SAFE CONNECTION
BY 5/8" GRADE 8 BOLTS

**Figure 153hh**   Eighteen-inch box truss.

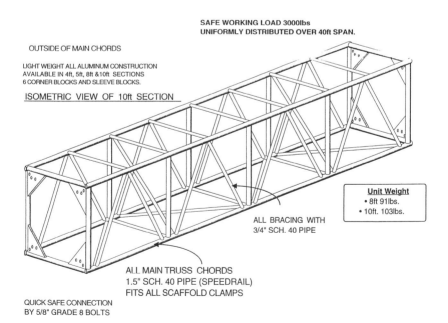

SAFE WORKING LOAD 3000lbs
UNIFORMLY DISTRIBUTED OVER 40ft SPAN.

OUTSIDE OF MAIN CHORDS

LIGHT WEIGHT ALL ALUMINUM CONSTRUCTION
AVAILABLE IN 4ft, 5ft, 8ft &10ft SECTIONS
6 CORNER BLOCKS AND SLEEVE BLOCKS.

ISOMETRIC VIEW OF 10ft SECTION

**Unit Weight**
• 8ft 91lbs.
• 10ft. 103lbs.

ALL BRACING WITH
3/4" SCH. 40 PIPE

ALL MAIN TRUSS CHORDS
1.5" SCH. 40 PIPE (SPEEDRAIL)
FITS ALL SCAFFOLD CLAMPS

QUICK SAFE CONNECTION
BY 5/8" GRADE 8 BOLTS

**Figure 153ii**   Twenty-four-inch box truss.

SAFE WORKING LOAD **4,000 lb** UNIFORMLY
DISTRIBUTED OVER **40ft SPAN**

26" HIGH BY 22 1/2" WIDE

LIGHT WEIGHT ALL ALUMINUM CONSTRUCTION,
YET BUILT FOR VERY HEAVY LOADS
1 TON & 1/2 TON MOTORS CAN BE MOUNTED INTERNALLY.
AVAILABLE IN 4ft, & 8ft SECTIONS
STANDARD ANGLE ADAPTORS AND CORNER BLOCKS IN STOCK.

QUICK SAFE CONNECTION
BY HARDENED STEEL PINS

ISOMETRIC VIEW OF 8ft SECTION

TOP CHORD
1 1/2" SCH. 40 PIPE

**Unit Weight**
• 4ft 50lbs.
• 8ft 100lbs.

FOR ADDED STRENGTH THE
BOTTOM CHORD IS 1 1/2" SCH 80 PIPE
FITS ALL SCAFFOLD CLAMPS

COMES COMPLETE WITH WHEELS

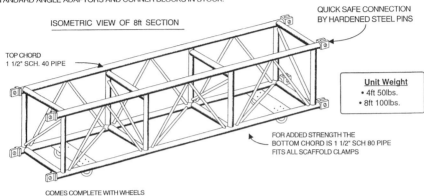

**Figure 153jj**   S-type truss.

WHEN USED IN A VERTICAL ORIENTATION
THIS TRUSS IS CAPABLE OF SPANNING **80 ft**,
WITH A SAFE WORKING LOAD OF **2000lbs**
UNIFORMLY DISTRIBUTED.

48in HIGH BY 18in WIDE
LIGHT WEIGHT, HIGH STRENGTH
ALUMINUM CONSTRUCTION

AVAILABLE IN 20ft, 10ft, 4ft, & 2ft SECTIONS

ISOMETRIC VIEW OF 10ft SECTION

**Unit Weight**
• 4ft 80lbs.
• 10ft 127lbs.

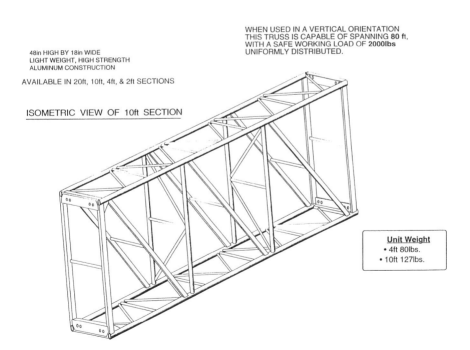

**Figure 153kk**   C-type truss, vertical.

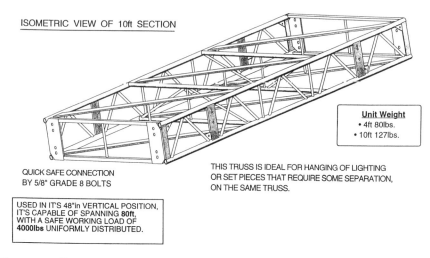

18in BY 48in LIGHT WEIGHT HIGH STRENGTH ALUMINUM CONSTRUCTION

AVAILABLE IN 20ft, 10ft, 4ft, & 2ft SECTIONS

WHEN USED IN A HORIZONTAL ORIENTATION THIS TRUSS IS CAPABLE OF SPANNING **40 ft,** WITH A SAFE WORKING LOAD OF **2000lbs** UNIFORMLY DISTRIBUTED.

ISOMETRIC VIEW OF 10ft SECTION

**Unit Weight**
- 4ft 80lbs.
- 10ft 127lbs.

QUICK SAFE CONNECTION
BY 5/8" GRADE 8 BOLTS

THIS TRUSS IS IDEAL FOR HANGING OF LIGHTING OR SET PIECES THAT REQUIRE SOME SEPARATION, ON THE SAME TRUSS.

USED IN IT'S 48"in VERTICAL POSITION, IT'S CAPABLE OF SPANNING **80ft,** WITH A SAFE WORKING LOAD OF **4000lbs** UNIFORMLY DISTRIBUTED.

**Figure 153ll**   C-type truss, horizontal.

## Ground Support Systems

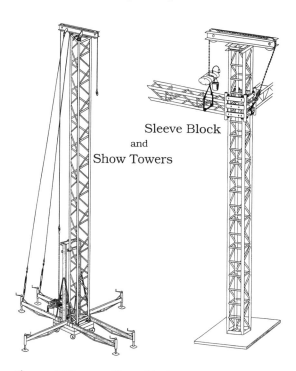

Sleeve Block
and
Show Towers

**Figure 153mm**   Sleeve block and show towers.

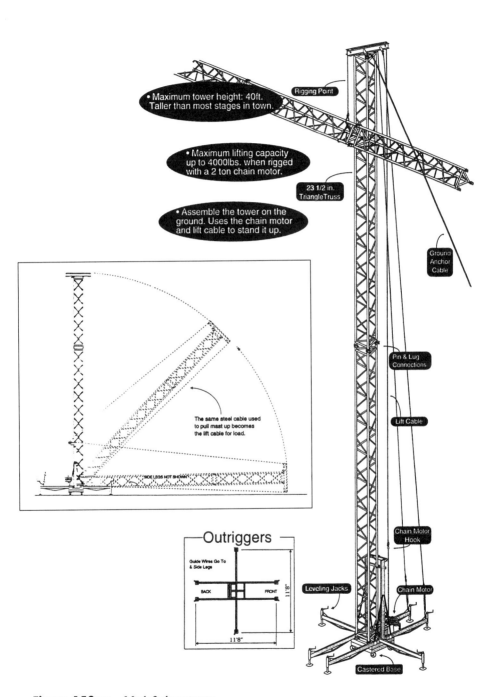

Maximum tower height: 40ft. Taller than most stages in town.

Maximum lifting capacity up to 4000lbs. when rigged with a 2 ton chain motor.

Assemble the tower on the ground. Uses the chain motor and lift cable to stand it up.

Rigging Point

23 1/2 in. TriangleTruss

Ground Anchor Cable

Pin & Lug Connections

Lift Cable

The same steel cable used to pull mast up becomes the lift cable for load.

SIDE LEGS NOT SHOWN

Chain Motor Hook

Outriggers

Guide Wires Go To & Side Legs

BACK      FRONT

11'8"

Leveling Jacks

Chain Motor

Castered Base

**Figure 153nn**   Mark 2 show tower.

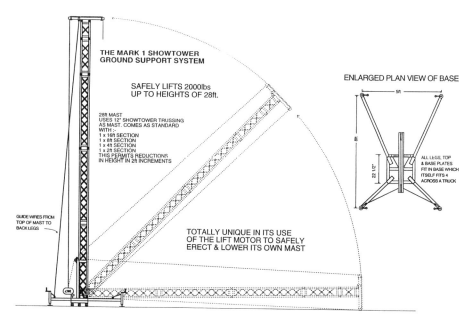

THE MARK 1 SHOWTOWER
GROUND SUPPORT SYSTEM

SAFELY LIFTS 2000lbs
UP TO HEIGHTS OF 28ft.

28ft MAST
USES 12" SHOWTOWER TRUSSING
AS MAST. COMES AS STANDARD
WITH :-
1 x 16ft SECTION
1 x 8ft SECTION
1 x 4ft SECTION
1 x 2ft SECTION
THIS PERMITS REDUCTIONS
IN HEIGHT IN 2ft INCREMENTS

GUIDE WIRES FROM
TOP OF MAST TO
BACK LEGS

TOTALLY UNIQUE IN ITS USE
OF THE LIFT MOTOR TO SAFELY
ERECT & LOWER ITS OWN MAST

ENLARGED PLAN VIEW OF BASE

5ft

8ft

22 1/2"

ALL LEGS, TOP
& BASE PLATES
FIT IN BASE WHICH
ITSELF FITS 4
ACROSS A TRUCK

**Figure 153oo**   Mark 1 show tower.

SMALLEST FOOT PRINT OF ANY TOWER. EASY TO MASK.

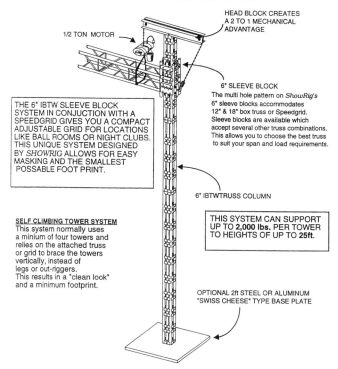

HEAD BLOCK CREATES
A 2 TO 1 MECHANICAL
ADVANTAGE

1/2 TON MOTOR

6" SLEEVE BLOCK
The multi hole pattern on *ShowRig's*
6" sleeve blocks accommodates
12" & 18" box truss or Speedgrid.
Sleeve blocks are available which
accept several other truss combinations.
This allows you to choose the best truss
to suit your span and load requirements.

THE 6" IBTW SLEEVE BLOCK
SYSTEM IN CONJUCTION WITH A
SPEEDGRID GIVES YOU A COMPACT
ADJUSTABLE GRID FOR LOCATIONS
LIKE BALL ROOMS OR NIGHT CLUBS.
THIS UNIQUE SYSTEM DESIGNED
BY *SHOWRIG* ALLOWS FOR EASY
MASKING AND THE SMALLEST
POSSABLE FOOT PRINT.

6" IBTWTRUSS COLUMN

SELF CLIMBING TOWER SYSTEM
This system normally uses
a minium of four towers and
relies on the attached truss
or grid to brace the towers
vertically, instead of
legs or out-riggers.
This results in a "clean look"
and a minimum footprint.

THIS SYSTEM CAN SUPPORT
UP TO **2,000 lbs.** PER TOWER
TO HEIGHTS OF UP TO **25ft.**

OPTIONAL 2ft STEEL OR ALUMINUM
"SWISS CHEESE" TYPE BASE PLATE

**Figure 153pp**   Six-inch IBTW self-climbing tower system.

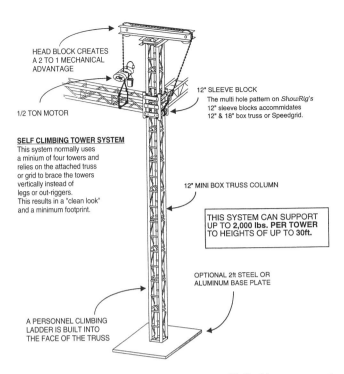

**Figure 153qq**   Twelve-inch box truss self-climbing tower system.

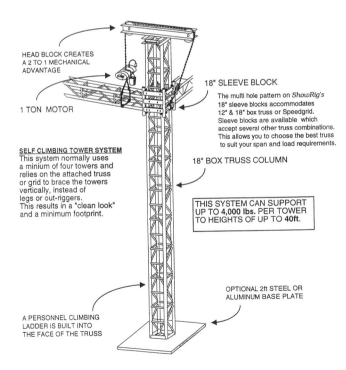

**Figure 153rr**   Eighteen-inch box truss self-climbing tower system.

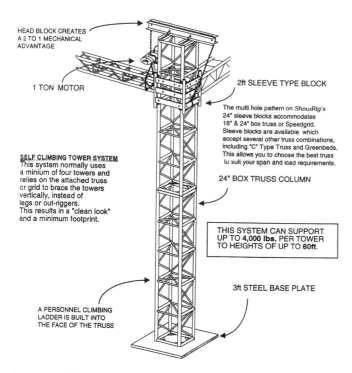

HEAD BLOCK CREATES
A 2 TO 1 MECHANICAL
ADVANTAGE

1 TON MOTOR

2ft SLEEVE TYPE BLOCK

The multi hole pattern on *ShowRig's*
24" sleeve blocks accommodates
18" & 24" box truss or Speedgrid.
Sleeve blocks are available which
accept several other truss combinations,
including "C" Type Truss and Greenbeds.
This allows you to choose the best truss
to suit your span and load requirements.

SELF CLIMBING TOWER SYSTEM
This system normally uses
a minium of four towers and
relies on the attached truss
or grid to brace the towers
vertically, instead of
legs or out-riggers.
This results in a "clean look"
and a minimum footprint.

24" BOX TRUSS COLUMN

THIS SYSTEM CAN SUPPORT
UP TO **4,000 lbs.** PER TOWER
TO HEIGHTS OF UP TO **60ft.**

3ft STEEL BASE PLATE

A PERSONNEL CLIMBING
LADDER IS BUILT INTO
THE FACE OF THE TRUSS

**Figure 153ss**   Twenty-four-inch box truss self-climbing tower system.

## *Hangers*

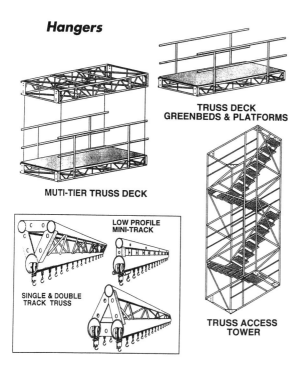

TRUSS DECK
GREENBEDS & PLATFORMS

MUTI-TIER TRUSS DECK

LOW PROFILE
MINI-TRACK

SINGLE & DOUBLE
TRACK TRUSS

TRUSS ACCESS
TOWER

**Figure 153tt**   Hanger and deck overview.

**178**

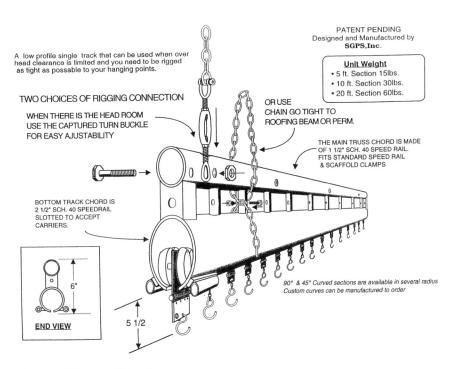

A low profile single track that can be used when over head clearance is limited and you need to be rigged as tight as possable to your hanging points.

TWO CHOICES OF RIGGING CONNECTION

WHEN THERE IS THE HEAD ROOM USE THE CAPTURED TURN BUCKLE FOR EASY AJUSTABILITY

OR USE CHAIN GO TIGHT TO ROOFING BEAM OR PERM.

PATENT PENDING
Designed and Manufactured by
SGPS,Inc.

**Unit Weight**
• 5 ft. Section 15lbs.
• 10 ft. Section 30lbs.
• 20 ft. Section 60lbs.

THE MAIN TRUSS CHORD IS MADE OF 1 1/2" SCH. 40 SPEED RAIL. FITS STANDARD SPEED RAIL & SCAFFOLD CLAMPS

BOTTOM TRACK CHORD IS 2 1/2" SCH. 40 SPEEDRAIL SLOTTED TO ACCEPT CARRIERS.

90° & 45° Curved sections are available in several radius
Custom curves can be manufactured to order

6"

END VIEW

5 1/2

**Figure 153uu**  Minitrack.

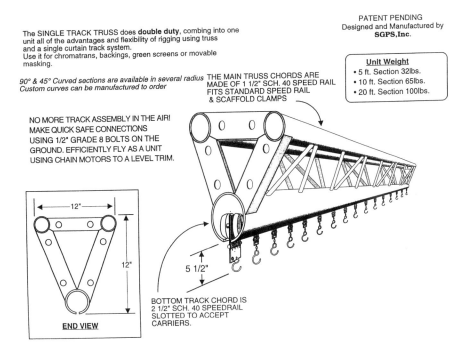

The SINGLE TRACK TRUSS does **double duty**, combing into one unit all of the advantages and flexibility of rigging using truss and a single curtain track system.
Use it for chromatrans, backings, green screens or movable masking.

90° & 45° Curved sections are available in several radius
Custom curves can be manufactured to order

THE MAIN TRUSS CHORDS ARE MADE OF 1 1/2" SCH. 40 SPEED RAIL FITS STANDARD SPEED RAIL & SCAFFOLD CLAMPS

PATENT PENDING
Designed and Manufactured by
SGPS,Inc.

**Unit Weight**
• 5 ft. Section 32lbs.
• 10 ft. Section 65lbs.
• 20 ft. Section 100lbs.

NO MORE TRACK ASSEMBLY IN THE AIR! MAKE QUICK SAFE CONNECTIONS USING 1/2" GRADE 8 BOLTS ON THE GROUND. EFFICIENTLY FLY AS A UNIT USING CHAIN MOTORS TO A LEVEL TRIM.

12"

12"

5 1/2"

BOTTOM TRACK CHORD IS 2 1/2" SCH. 40 SPEEDRAIL SLOTTED TO ACCEPT CARRIERS.

END VIEW

**Figure 153vv**  Single-track truss.

179

The Double Truss Track does **double duty**, combing into one unit all of the advantages and flexibility of rigging using truss and the convenience of a double curtain track system. Use it for day and night chromatrans, backings, green screens or movable masking.

*90° Curved sections are available in several radius Custom curves can be manufactured to order*

NO MORE TRACK ASSEMBLY IN THE AIR! MAKE QUICK SAFE CONNECTIONS USING 1/2" GRADE 8 BOLTS ON THE GROUND. EFFICIENTLY FLY AS A UNIT USING CHAIN MOTORS TO A LEVEL TRIM.

PATENT PENDING

Designed and Manufactured by **SGPS,Inc.**

THE MAIN TRUSS CHORD IS MADE OF 1 1/2" SCH. 40 SPEED RAIL. FITS STANDARD SPEED RAIL & SCAFFOLD CLAMPS

**Unit Weight**
• 5 ft. Section 35lbs.
• 10 ft. Section 70lbs.
• 20 ft. Section 110lbs.

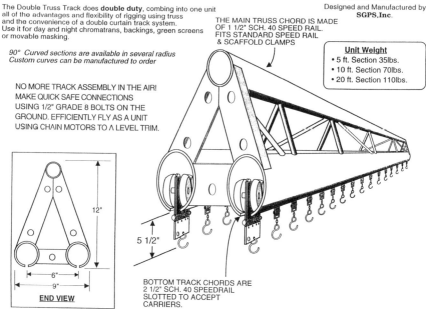

12"

5 1/2"

6"
9"
**END VIEW**

BOTTOM TRACK CHORDS ARE 2 1/2" SCH. 40 SPEEDRAIL SLOTTED TO ACCEPT CARRIERS.

**Figure 153ww**   Double-track truss.

## Decks

A safe and cost effective full featured greenbed system for places that "studio" beds don't work.This system can be rigged or ground supported in any warehouse or aircraft hanger.

THIS SYSTEM COMBINES THE STRUCTURAL STRENGTH OF AN ALUMINUM TRUSSING SYSTEM WITH A CONVENTIONAL GREENBED STYLE DECK SO YOU CAN SPAN THE DISTANCES BETWEEN THE BUILDINGS STRUCTURAL BEAMS.

LIGHT WEIGHT, HIGH STRENGTH ALUMINUM CONSTRUCTION ALLOWS FOR EASY ACCESS AND GREATER DECK CAPACITY WITHOUT EXCEEDING THE LOAD LIMITS OF THE BUILDING

**Unit Weight**
• 4' x 4' Deck 90lbs.
• 4' x 10' Deck 223lbs.

DECKS ARE AVAILABLE IN 2FT, 3FT & 4FT WIDE VERSIONS. VARIOUS LENGTHS ALONG WITH CORNER SECTIONS & "T" CONNECTIONS, ACCOMIDATES YOUR EXACT LAYOUT REQUIREMENTS

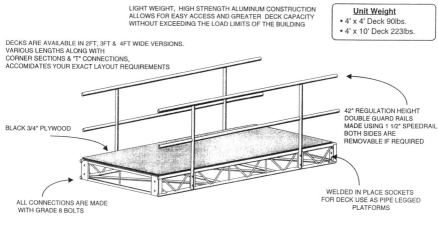

BLACK 3/4" PLYWOOD

42" REGULATION HEIGHT DOUBLE GUARD RAILS MADE USING 1 1/2" SPEEDRAIL BOTH SIDES ARE REMOVABLE IF REQUIRED

ALL CONNECTIONS ARE MADE WITH GRADE 8 BOLTS

WELDED IN PLACE SOCKETS FOR DECK USE AS PIPE LEGGED PLATFORMS

DECKS CAN BE CONNECTED SIDE BY SIDE TO CREATE WIDE WORKING PLATFORMS

**Figure 153xx**   Twelve-inch truss deck greenbed.

A safe and cost effective full featured heavy duty greenbed system for long spans or heavy loads in places that "studio" beds don't work. This system can be rigged or ground supported in any warehouse or aircraft hanger.

THIS SYSTEM COMBINES THE STRUCTURAL STRENGTH OF AN ALUMINUM TRUSSING SYSTEM WITH A CONVENTIONAL GREENBED STYLE DECK SO YOU CAN SPAN THE DISTANCES BETWEEN THE BUILDINGS STRUCTURAL BEAMS.

LIGHT WEIGHT, HIGH STRENGTH ALUMINUM CONSTRUCTION ALLOWS FOR EASY ACCESS AND GREATER DECK CAPACITY WITHOUT EXCEEDING THE LOAD LIMITS OF THE BUILDING

DECKS ARE AVAILABLE IN 2FT, 3FT & 4FT WIDE VERSIONS. VARIOUS LENGTHS ALONG WITH CORNER SECTIONS & "T" CONNECTIONS, ACCOMIDATES YOUR EXACT LAYOUT REQUIREMENTS

42" REGULATION HEIGHT DOUBLE GUARD RAILS MADE USING 1 1/2" SPEEDRAIL BOTH SIDES ARE REMOVABLE IF REQUIRED

BLACK 3/4" PLYWOOD TRIMMED BACK TO ALLOW ADDITIONAL RIGGING ATTACHMENTS

18"

ALL CONNECTIONS ARE MADE WITH GRADE 8 BOLTS

DECKS CAN BE CONNECTED SIDE BY SIDE TO CREATE WIDE WORKING PLATFORMS

**Figure 153yy**   Eighteen-inch heavy-duty truss deck.

Rig lights and cable on the overhead truss and service them from the suspended 4ft wide greenbed below . This system can be rigged or ground supported in any warehouse or aircraft hanger.

**Unit Weight**
• 4' x 10' Section 350lbs.

18" by 4'ft "C" TYPE BOX TRUSS, AVAILABLE IN 10' & 4' CORNER SECTIONS, CUSTOM LENGTHS ON REQUEST.

42" REGULATION HEIGHT DOUBLE GUARD RAILS ARE MADE USING 1 1/2" SPEEDRAIL BOTH SIDES ARE REMOVABLE IF REQUIRED

1/4" STEEL AIRCRAFT WIRE SUSPENSION SYSTEM FOR ADJUSTABLE CLEARANCE

DECKS CAN BE CONNECTED SIDE BY SIDE TO CREATE WIDE WORKING PLATFORMS

12" ALUMA "T" DECK
12" BY 4' ALUMA T DECK CAN BE USED WITH OR WITHOUT THE LIGHTING TRUSS ABOVE.

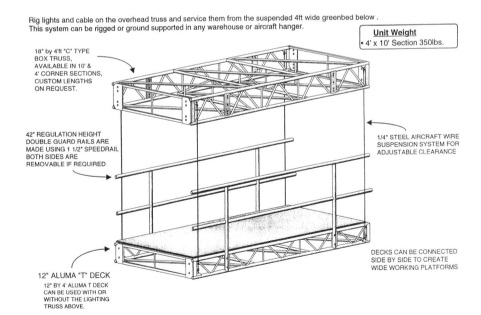

**Figure 153zz**   Multiple-tier truss deck catwalk system.

## Access Tower

A self contained light weight aluminum stair system to access installed catwalk, greenbed or grid systems.

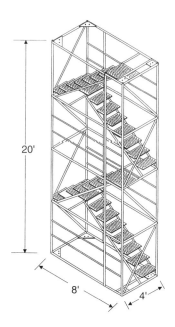

• Available in 10ft and 20ft bolt together sections.

• Ships pre-built, like a truss.

• Minimal footprint of only 4x8 - can be tucked away in a corner.

• Bolt together on the floor - lift up with one motor.

• Non-slip diamond plate landings and stair treads.

• Built in handrails.

20'

8'   4'

**Figure 153aaa**   Truss access tower.

## Trolleys and Track

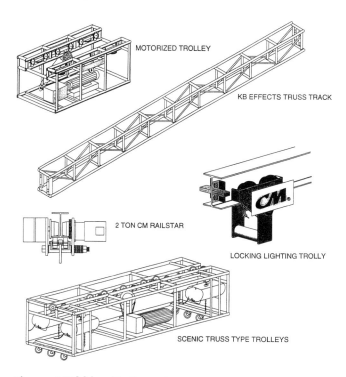

MOTORIZED TROLLEY

KB EFFECTS TRUSS TRACK

2 TON CM RAILSTAR

LOCKING LIGHTING TROLLY

SCENIC TRUSS TYPE TROLLEYS

**Figure 153bbb**   Trolley and track overview.

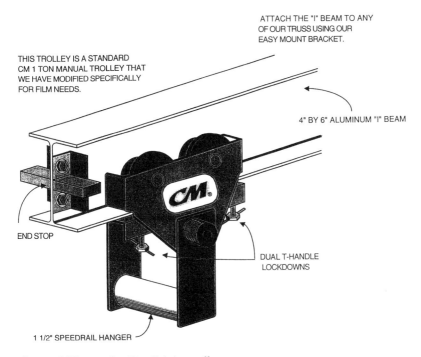

ATTACH THE "I" BEAM TO ANY
OF OUR TRUSS USING OUR
EASY MOUNT BRACKET.

THIS TROLLEY IS A STANDARD
CM 1 TON MANUAL TROLLEY THAT
WE HAVE MODIFIED SPECIFICALLY
FOR FILM NEEDS.

4" BY 6" ALUMINUM "I" BEAM

END STOP

DUAL T-HANDLE
LOCKDOWNS

1 1/2" SPEEDRAIL HANGER

**Figure 153ccc**   Locking lighting trolley.

Gives you remote repositioning capability, at a reasonable cost.
When sight Lines require that you rig from above, you are not locked in to one position or
a costly and time consuming re-rig.

END VIEW               12" MINI BOX TRUSS          SIDE VIEW

4" BY 6" ALUMINUM
"I" BEAM

←—TRAVEL—→

TRAVEL

**2 TON CM RAIL STAR**
FITTED WITH SHOWRIG'S
CUSTOM SPRING TENSIONED
ADJUSTABLE FRICTION WHEEL
ASSEMBLY FOR POSITIVE DRIVE
& POSITION HOLDING CAPABILITY

WE CAN PROVIDE A VERY SIMPLE 2 AXIS MOVEMENT  CAPABILITY
OR A MORE COMPLEX THREE AXIS SYSTEM

**Figure 153ddd**   Motorized repositioning trolley system.

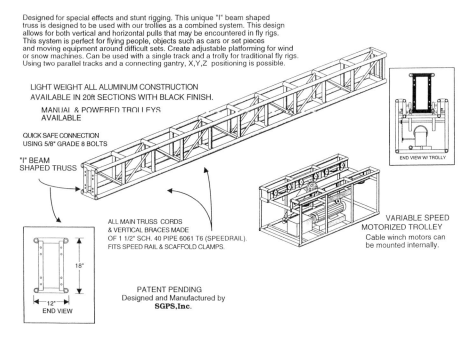

Designed for special effects and stunt rigging. This unique "I" beam shaped truss is designed to be used with our trollies as a combined system. This design allows for both vertical and horizontal pulls that may be encountered in fly rigs. This system is perfect for flying people, objects such as cars or set pieces and moving equipment around difficult sets. Create adjustable platforming for wind or snow machines. Can be used with a single track and a trolly for traditional fly rigs. Using two parallel tracks and a connecting gantry, X,Y,Z positioning is possible.

LIGHT WEIGHT ALL ALUMINUM CONSTRUCTION
AVAILABLE IN 20ft SECTIONS WITH BLACK FINISH.

MANUAL & POWERED TROLLEYS
AVAILABLE

QUICK SAFE CONNECTION
USING 5/8" GRADE 8 BOLTS

"I" BEAM
SHAPED TRUSS

ALL MAIN TRUSS CORDS
& VERTICAL BRACES MADE
OF 1 1/2" SCH. 40 PIPE 6061 T6 (SPEEDRAIL).
FITS SPEED RAIL & SCAFFOLD CLAMPS.

END VIEW W/ TROLLY

VARIABLE SPEED
MOTORIZED TROLLEY
Cable winch motors can
be mounted internally.

18"

12"
END VIEW

PATENT PENDING
Designed and Manufactured by
**SGPS,Inc.**

**Figure 153eee**   KB effects truss track.

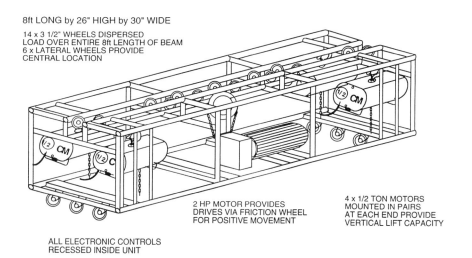

8ft LONG by 26" HIGH by 30" WIDE

14 x 3 1/2" WHEELS DISPERSED
LOAD OVER ENTIRE 8ft LENGTH OF BEAM
6 x LATERAL WHEELS PROVIDE
CENTRAL LOCATION

2 HP MOTOR PROVIDES
DRIVES VIA FRICTION WHEEL
FOR POSITIVE MOVEMENT

4 x 1/2 TON MOTORS
MOUNTED IN PAIRS
AT EACH END PROVIDE
VERTICAL LIFT CAPACITY

ALL ELECTRONIC CONTROLS
RECESSED INSIDE UNIT

**Figure 153fff**   Scenic truss type trolley.

## Cable, Slings, and Hardware

When picking cable for a project, I usually use aircraft-rated cable. It's strong and flexible. It does nicely for most jobs. Seven by nineteen (see later) usually seems to work best. Use the fixture with which you can accomplish the job safely. If you don't have a great deal of experience with cable, contact VER Sales in Burbank, California. They are as close to experts as anyone can be. I did a car spot in Japan with a hot young actor. My crew had to fly a 60-foot by 80-foot frame with silk on it. We used aircraft cable locks, span sets, and a 70-ton crane with a spreader beam on it to distribute the weight. I tell this story because years ago, when I first started keying, my budget was for rope, not cable. As my jobs grew I had to ask a lot of folks for a lot of advice. I went to VER Sales and explained that I really didn't have a lot of experience, told them what the shot entailed, and asked them to help me decide what equipment I needed. Don't try to be a know-it-all. There are plenty of folks who will help (see Contributing Companies).

What follows is a list of different types of hardware. This is only a glimpse of the equipment, cables, and attaching hardware that I have used over a period of thirty years. The facts and figures sometimes change. The charts are only a reference. Contact the manufacturers and vendors before you go into the unknown. I really can't emphasize that enough. This book contains a few examples to get you started. Devise what you think you may need, and map it out. Then call a local merchant or the manufacturer.

### *Miniature Cable*

Miniature cable line is perfect for special effects and mechanical design that require sharp bends and confined space situations.

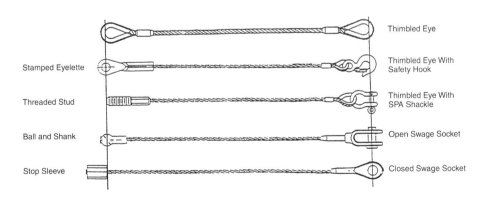

**Figure 154a**   Miniature cable.

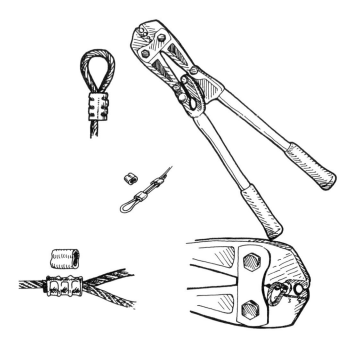

**Figure 154b** Press and sleeve.

**1 × 7** One center wire with six wires laid around the center. More flexible than 1 × 3. Used for push-pull applications and for conductive needs with low flexibility.

**7 × 7** Most standard cable construction. Six 1 × 7 outside strands cabled around a 1 × 7 center. Very flexible, good cycle life and breaking strength.

**1 × 19** Twelve wires laid around a 1 × 7 center. For more flexible needs than 1 × 7 in push-pull and conductive applications. Almost as high breaking strength as 1 × 7 with same diameter.

**7 × 19** Most flexible standard construction for cable. Six 1 × 19 strands around a 1 × 19 center. Lower breaking strength, more expensive than 7 × 7. High cycle life.

## *Wire Rope*

Wire rope consists of three basic components. These components vary in complexity and configuration to produce ropes for specific purposes or characteristics. The three basic components of a standard wire rope design are (1) wires that form the strand, (2) multiwire strands laid in a helix around a core, and (3) the core.

### Wires

Wire for rope is made in several materials and types. These include steel, iron, stainless steel, monel metal, and bronze. By far the most widely used material is high-carbon steel. This is available in a variety of grades, each of which has properties re-lated to the basic curve for steel rope wire. Wire rope manufacturers select the wire type that is most appropriate for requirements of the finished product.

**Steel**   The strength of steel wire is appropriate to the particular grade of the wire rope in which the wires are used. Grades of wire rope are referred to as traction steel (TS), improved plow steel (MPS), plow steel (PS), improved steel (IPS), and extra-improved plow steel (EIP). These names originated at the earliest stages of development of wire rope and have been retained as references to the strength of a particular size and grade of rope. The plow steel strength curve forms the basis for calculating the strength of all steel rope wires. The tensile strength (in pounds per square inch [psi]) of any grade of steel wire is not constant. It varies with diameter and is highest in the smallest wires.

The most common finish for steel wire is *bright* or uncoated. Steel wire also may be galvanized, that is, coated with zinc. *Drawn galvanized* wire has the same strength as bright wire, but wire *galvanized at finished size* usually is 10 percent lower in strength. In certain applications, *tinned* wire is used, but tin does not provide the sacrificial, that is, cathodic, protection for steel that zinc does. Different coatings are available for other applications.

**Iron**   Iron wire actually is drawn from low-carbon steel and has a fairly lim-ited use except in older elevator installations. When iron is used for other than elevator applications, it is most often galvanized.

**Stainless Steel**   Stainless steel ropes, listed in order of frequency of use, are made of American Iron and Steel Institute (AISI) types 302/304, 316, and 305. Contrary to general belief, hard-drawn stainless steel type 302/304 is magnetic. Type 316 is less magnetic, and type 305 has a permeability low enough to qualify as nonmagnetic.

**Monel Metal**   Monel metal is steel that contains 68 percent nickel. Monel metal wire usually is type 400 and conforms to federal specification QQ-N-281.

**Bronze**   Bronze wire usually is type A phosphor bronze (Composite Design and Analysis Code [CDA] 510), although other bronzes can be specified.

**Strands**
Strands are made up of two or more wires laid in one of many specific geo-metric arrangements or in a combination of steel wires and another material such as natural or synthetic fibers. A strand can be composed of any number of wires, and a rope can have any number of strands.

**Core**
The core is the foundation of a wire rope. It is made of materials that support the strands under normal bending and loading conditions. Core materials include

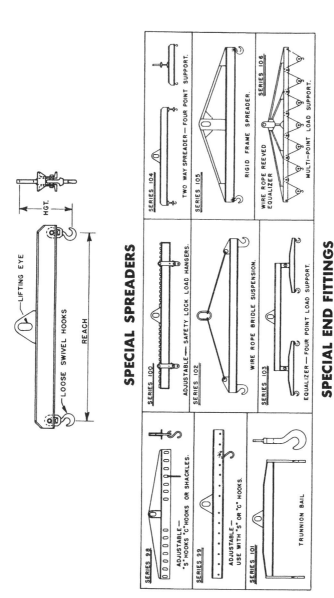

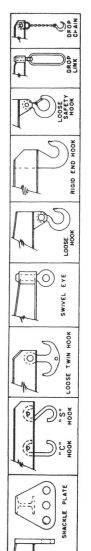

**Figure 155** Special spreaders and end fittings.

fibers (hard vegetable and synthetic) or steel. A steel core consists of a strand or an independent wire rope.

### Spreader Beams

Load spreaders are used when loads to be lifted on a single hoist must be picked up and supported at two or more suspension points. Load spreaders can be furnished in a large number of practical designs to suit any lifting or handling condition.

> **UVA F.A.C.T.**
> Spray oil or talcum powder on dolly wheels as you roll the dolly up and down the track. This transfers the lubricant to the needed area while making less of a mess.

### Sling Types

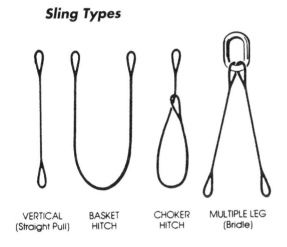

| VERTICAL (Straight Pull) | BASKET HITCH | CHOKER HITCH | MULTIPLE LEG (Bridle) |

**Figure 156a**   Hitches.

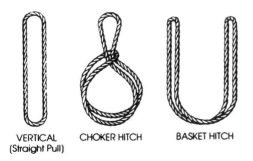

| VERTICAL (Straight Pull) | CHOKER HITCH | BASKET HITCH |

**Figure 156b**   Hitches, continued.

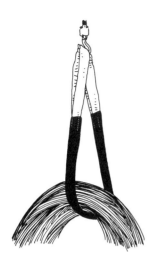

**Figure 156c**   Sling.

**Figure 156d**   Sling.

**Figure 156e**   Traveling choker hook.

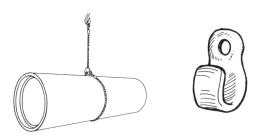

**Figure 156f**   Standard choker hook.

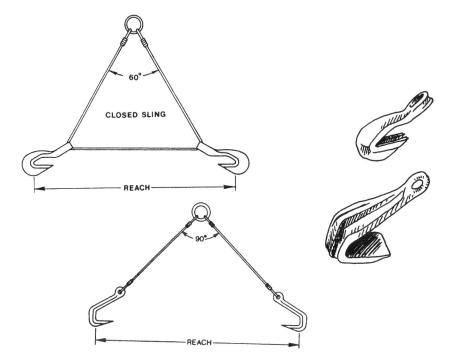

**Figure 156g**   Barrel hook.

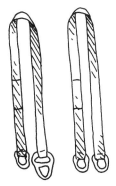

**Figure 156h**   Slings.

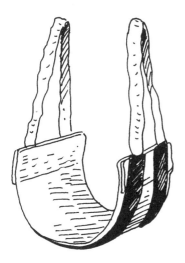

**Figure 156i**   Basket sling.

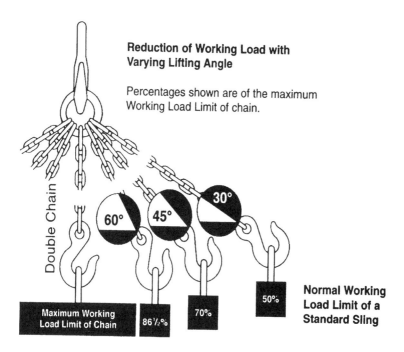

**Figure 156j**   Working load limit of standard sling.

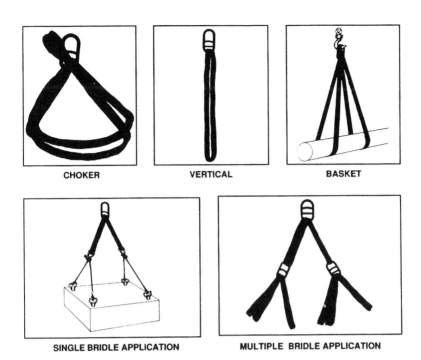

CHOKER VERTICAL BASKET

SINGLE BRIDLE APPLICATION MULTIPLE BRIDLE APPLICATION

**Figure 156k**  Slings

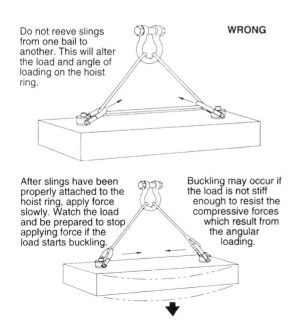

Do not reeve slings from one bail to another. This will alter the load and angle of loading on the hoist ring.

WRONG

After slings have been properly attached to the hoist ring, apply force slowly. Watch the load and be prepared to stop applying force if the load starts buckling.

Buckling may occur if the load is not stiff enough to resist the compressive forces which result from the angular loading.

**Figure 156l**  Correct and incorrect ways to attach a sling.

**193**

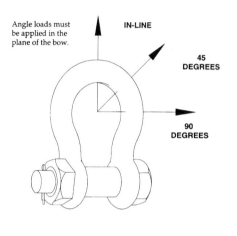

Angle loads must be applied in the plane of the bow.

IN-LINE

45 DEGREES

90 DEGREES

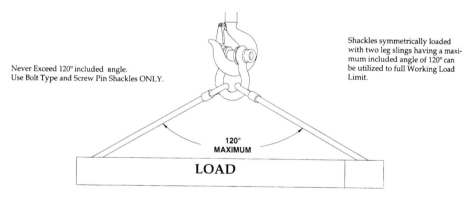

Never Exceed 120° included angle.
Use Bolt Type and Screw Pin Shackles ONLY.

Shackles symmetrically loaded with two leg slings having a maximum included angle of 120° can be utilized to full Working Load Limit.

120° MAXIMUM

LOAD

**Figure 156m**   Correct way to load a shackle.

| NAME | CODE | ILLUSTRATION | NAME | CODE | ILLUSTRATION |
|------|------|--------------|------|------|--------------|
| Clamp, Horizontal Plate | HPC |  | Socket, Open Swaged | OSS | 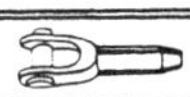 |
| Clamp, Merrill Plate | MPC |  | Socket, Closed Swaged | CSS |  |
| Hook, Barrel | BH | | Thimble, Open Boom Pendant | OBT | 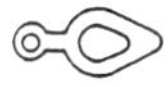 |
| Hook, Eye Hoist | H |  | Thimble, Closed Boom Pendant | CBT |  |
| Hook, Ferrule Choker | FCH | | Thimble, Heavy Wire Rope | T |  |
| Hook, Plate & Beam | PBH |  | Thimble, Crescent | CT | |
| Hook, Standard Choker | SCH | | Thimble, Equalizer | ET |  |
| Hook, Travelling Choker | TCH |  | Thimble, Slip-Through | ST | |
| Shackle, Round Pin Anchor | RPA |  | Turnbuckle, Eye & Eye | EE |  |
| Shackle, Screw Pin Anchor | SPA |  | Turnbuckle, Jaw & Eye | JE |  |
| Shackle, Round Pin Chain | RPC |  | Turnbuckle, Jaw & Jaw | JJ |  |
| Shackle, Screw Pin Chain | SPC | 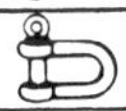 | | | |
| Socket, Open Spelter | OZS | 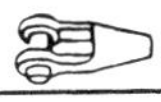 | | | |
| Socket, Closed Spelter | CZS |  | | | |

**Figure 156n**   Code identifiers for fittings and terminals.

**Figure 157**    Dynafor MWX Miniweigher.

The grip hoist Dynafor MWX Miniweigher is a new method of check-weighing and load measurement. Dynafor MWX Miniweighers work by means of micro-processor-based electronics with new standard functions and systems.

### Features of the Dynafor MWX Miniweigher

Operation set up by means of three push-button controls: on-off, 100% tare with return to total load applied, and peak hold to show the maximum load applied.

Up to 700 hours of operation before battery charge; low-battery indicator; and automatic shutdown after 20 minutes to save battery power.

Choice of unit measurement—kilograms, tons, pounds, short tons, daN, or kN—displayed on the LCD.

Overload displayed to help prevent overloading the equipment and systems. Automatic zero when switched on.

Output connection to handheld display and controls, to personal computer, or interface for processing or printing the information.

Variable response rate to save battery power.

## Glossary of Cables and Slings

**Alloy steel chain**    The only chain recommended for overhead lifting.

**Angle of lift**    Angle between horizontal surface of load and lift chain measured in degrees. Should never be less than 30 degrees.

**Elongation**    The effect on the chain of severe overload or exposure to shock load.

**Grade 30**    Proof coil chain. A general utility chain of low-carbon-steel used for many everyday applications. Grade 30 is not to be used for lifting or hoisting applications.

**Grade 40**   High test chain. A higher-carbon steel chain that is considerably stronger than grade 30, meaning that a lighter chain can often do similar work. Grade 40 is not to be used for lifting or hoisting applications.

**Grade 70**   Transport tie-down or binding chain. A high-strength, lightweight boron manganese steel chain designed for load binding applications. Grade 70 is not to be used for lifting or hoisting applications.

**Grade 80**   High strength alloy chain. A chain with a high strength-to-weight ratio. Grade 80 is used predominantly for lifting and hoisting applications. It is the only chain recommended for lifting and hoisting.

## Staging Systems

### Ferrellels

The features of the Ferrellel system are a scissors lift and a variable height feature that allows the deck to change height in seconds with no loose legs. The operator reaches under each end, squeezes the lock-pin lever, and raises or lowers the deck to 16, 24, 32, or 40 inches. Quick lock extrusions connect decks together fast with no bolts or screws. One end can be locked higher than the other to produce a ramp. Strong and solid, Ferrellels are engineered to support 160 pounds live load per square foot. The understructure is all-aluminum with no welded joints. The enclosed base provides exceptional stability and distributes weight over a large footprint.

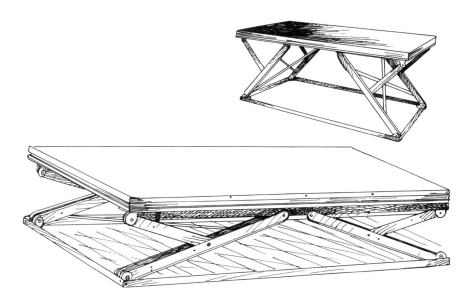

**Figure 158**   Ferrellel.

**UVA F.A.C.T.**
When pushing the dolly, watch the actor with your peripheral vision. Look at your stop marks and watch the camera operator.

I have used Ferrellels since I first learned of their existence. It is the Swiss Army knife of tables, platforms, and portable stages. It is super quick to assemble, relatively inexpensive if you consider the time, material, and personnel it takes to build a riser or stage from scratch. If you are smart, and I know you are, use Ferrellels. You will look like a million-dollar technician. It's the top gun for fast location work.

## Steeldeck

The combination of features in Steeldeck, as with all systems, represents a compromise between the properties we want a unit to possess—strength, ease of use, portability, versatility—and what is possible in light of constraints such as material and cost. What follows is a list of the main features required of a modular staging system and examples of the advantages of Steeldeck in each area. Priority among these features often depends on the requirements of the customer, so this is not intended to be a definitive order. Some features are relevant to most users most of the time.

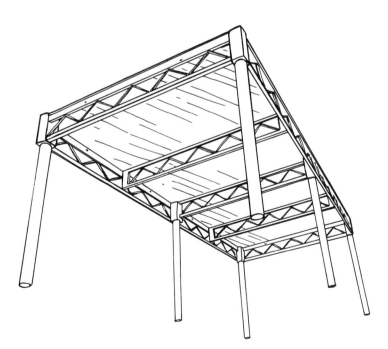

**Figure 159**   Steeldeck.

**UVA F.A.C.T.**
Have production put ice in actors' mouths before they speak; it prevents steam from coming from the mouth for a few moments.

## FEATURES OF STEELDECK

### Price

Unit prices are very competitive.
4′ × 8′ Steeldeck is less expensive than metric-size decks.

### Strength and Weight

Steeldeck achieves a very good strength-to-weight ratio.
A 4′ × 8′ deck weighs only 140 pounds (63 kilograms) and supports an evenly distributed load of more than 6,000 pounds (2,700 kilograms)

### Ease of Use

To set up a Steeldeck all the operator has to do is insert the legs, tighten the bolts, and stand the deck up.
The only tool needed is a wrench.
Simple assembly means lower set up and tear down times and costs.
For example, a 40′ × 80′ stage can be set up by four workers in 4 hours.

### Versatility

Modular design means stages can be erected in a variety of shapes and sizes.
Stage height can be changed by means of simply changing legs.
Flat platforms, tiers, or ramps can be made from the same standard units.

It is common for customers to ask about alternative deck styles or features as part of their assessment of products. Most such questions are easy to answer. What follow are a few points about alternatives and their relation to Steeldeck. Steeldeck is not suitable in every case.

Steel or aluminum? Steel is less expensive than aluminum. Steel is far stronger than aluminum, but it is heavier. Because the frame constitutes only half the weight of the Steeldeck (the other half is plywood), the difference is less than might be imagined. Aluminum is much weaker than steel. To build an aluminum structure of reasonable strength, one must increase the volume of material used, in the frame or with braces. This erodes the weight advantage and leads to higher costs. Steel is extremely durable, but aluminum deforms easily. Steel is easier and therefore less expensive to weld. A deck made from steel is less likely to be damaged than one made from aluminum. Even if it is damaged, a steel deck is relatively inexpensive to repair.

Which legs? Steeldeck has legs of standard 1$\frac{1}{2}$-inch schedule 40 pipe. This has several benefits. Because they are made from standard products, the legs are less expensive than proprietary-brand legs, are stronger, and are readily available.

The steel construction means Steeldecks have a very long life. The no-nonsense design leaves almost nothing to break or give out with wear. Because Steeldeck is durable, maintenance costs are extremely low. Because they are made from standard materials, tops and legs are easy and economical to replace or change. The use of steel rather than aluminum for the frame allows inexpensive repair should damage occur.

Accessories include stair units, handrails, soft and hard fascias, and a range of casters, couplers, and other accessories. Special items can be manufactured to order.

Steeldecks stack conveniently, and are easy to move with a forklift. They can be stored flat or on edge. The legs can be stored easily. Customized leg racks are available with or without casters. Casters can quickly transform a deck into a trolley. A ratchet strap holds the stack tight, and one person can push them into position.

Triangles, curves, and other shapes can be made to order. Tops are sold with a plain plywood finish, but almost anything is possible, such as flat or nonslip floor paint, phenol resin carpet, vinyl, clear sealant, or even steel mesh in place of plywood.

MIKE'S NOTE: *Two words*—almost bullet proof—*well, three words.*

## Lifts
### Condors and Cherry Pickers

We are shooting on a rooftop. Thirty feet up. We need to have a moonlight fling and an eye-level shooting platform. What do we need? Easy, right? Well, you knew it wasn't. What are the factors to consider?

1. Where is the building?
2. What is the ground access?
3. Are there high-tension wires overhead?
4. What size mood (how big a light) do we need?
5. Will a body have to ride the basket? At what angle?
6. Does it have to be a four-wheel-drive unit?
7. Are we on a hill?
8. Can I use the outriggers?

These are a few, but not all, of the factors you have to think about and ask questions about. Here are a few more:

1. What size shooting crew (just camera, DP, a few or many) do we need?
2. Will there be any light on the shooting basket, and will it require an electrician?
3. Are we shooting level, below level, or an above look-down?
4. Does the camera crew know how to work the lift?

These are not dumb questions; they must be answered before you do any-thing. Do not assume. First let's talk about a Condor. This is a company name that has come to be synonymous with the name of the device. Condors also are called cherry pickers, high lifts, and other names. A cherry picker or Condor usually has two-wheel drive unless you ask for a four-wheel drive. It is white or brightly col-ored and bears the name of the rental company. This would be fantastic if we were shooting a spot for that company. I usually request a cherry picker with a black arm. This reduces reflection problems, and the lift almost disappears at night. Most cherry picker or Condors have an elliptical tail travel. This means the lift is very slender when it is lined up straight with the base. Once you rotate the base section, the tail extends past the sides of the wheel base. Sometimes this blocks access. If needed, there is a Condor that has zero tail swing. This means nothing extends past the wheel base. Use this type in a tight area. I don't always call for that type because they aren't readily available with longer arms. I'm not saying that they aren't ever made. For the most part, however, that's what you'll find. Know what is available and how to use it.

Some cherry pickers have an articulating arm. These are terrific pieces of equipment and take up less room than conventional devices. As with all pieces of equipment, however, there is a price to pay—usually in lift capacity. The angle and the length of an arm determine the weight capacity and use of the arm. Look over the charts. Call and ask or even go and see for yourself. Cherry pickers come with black arms if requested. The arms usually are painted flat black, which re-duces reflection problems. If you don't remember to order an arm that's painted black and a problem arises, you can always use a long piece of Duvatyne cloth. It was one of the ways we would black out an arm before manufacturers started paint-ing the arms. My advice is always order a black arm. Sometimes day shoots end up as night shoots.

Use the right tool for the job. Don't guess or try to make do. Cherry pickers and Condors come in a wide base or narrow base. If I have the room, I usually ask for a wide base for stability. Don't get me wrong. They are all very stable, but it usually gives me and other crew members (who don't normally ride these things) a visual sense of confidence. All things being the same cost, I opt for the wider base.

### Scissors Lifts

Scissors lifts frighten me. I have used narrow ones to go high. They are safe, but this old guy doesn't like them. There are narrow and wide models with and with-out outriggers. I prefer outriggers, but sometimes you just can't use the outrigger type. There are also gas engine types and propane types and even electric ones. You certainly don't want to use a gas engine lift on a small enclosed stage. Some lifts have a platform that extends on one end; these are helpful for maneuvering over obstacles. When ordering a scissors lift, be as specific as you can be. Consider as many factors as you can to ascertain the proper piece of equipment. Do not use, move, or operate any piece of equipment until you are fully trained and fully confident that you can operate it safely.

## Suppliers

When you use any lift, know the physical weight of the unit fully loaded with persons, material, and equipment. Then determine whether you need to put double sheets of ³/₄-inch (1.9 cm) plywood under each wheel. This distributes the weight over a larger area. I always have at least eight sheets of plywood ordered for a Condor or cherry picker shoot. Here's why. Say we start shooting at 7 A.M. on a city street. Around noon the asphalt softens, and the wheels of the cherry picker slowly settle into the softened asphalt. Large ruts will be left behind if you don't use double-sheet plywood. Trust me on this. This is not to say that the plywood won't leave a ridge, but it shows you have planned ahead as well as you can. As with any piece of equipment, call the supplier with any questions you might have. Suppliers are very knowledgeable about their equipment. They don't want anyone hurt either. Don't try to figure it out. Ask questions.

### Genie Industries

Single-person Genie lifts need leveling jacks on all legs to get four green lights before the lift will operate. (See Figures 160–162.)

### Eagle High Reach

Eagle High Reach is committed to offering state-of-the-art telescoping boom material handlers. Eagle ensures that each customer receives only highly maintained, clean equipment in excellent running condition. Eagle High Reach features equipment by Grove, K-D Manitou, and Lull International. Eagle provides rental, sales, and service for all high-reach needs, including scissors lifts, boom lifts, telescoping boom forklifts, hoists and suspended scaffolding. Eagle High Reach is the authorized dealer of Grove Manlift®, scissors, and boom lifts from 16 feet to 131 feet (4.8 to 39.3 meters); Lull Industries telescoping boom forklifts and accessories; and Power Climber® hoists and products for suspended scaffolding. Eagle High Reach offers radio-dispatched field service and repair by factory-trained mechanics. Safety orientation seminars are available for all products.

Lull rough terrain telescoping boom material handlers and Lull telescoping boom forklifts have full hydraulic controls, four-heel drive, four-heel crab steering, frame leveling, and rear axle stabilization. A truss boom, loose material bucket, side tilt fork carriage, 100-degree swing carriage, and other quick attach accessories are available. (See Figures 163–187.)

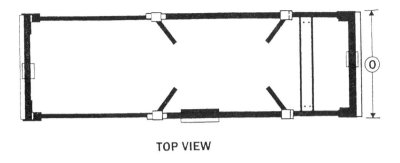

**TOP VIEW**

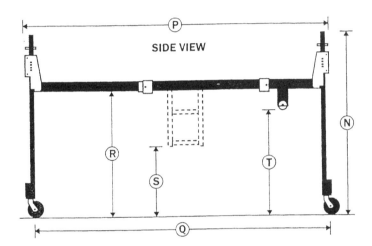

# The Genie
# Super Straddle

The perfect tool for working over fixed seating in places such as auditoriums and convention, manufacturing and auto maintenance centers. The Super Straddle is easy to use and assembles without tools. It provides up to 40 in (102 cm) of vertical clearance. End frames adjust for leveling on floors sloping up to 6 degrees.

**Figure 160**    Genie options and accessories.

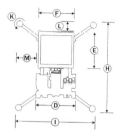

## Specifications continued on back cover

**Platform Dimensions** (l x w x h) (E x F x G)

| | US | Metric | | US | Metric |
|---|---|---|---|---|---|
| Standard Platform | 27 x 26 x 44 3/4 in | 69 x 66 x 114 cm | Gated Narrow Platform | 26 x 20 x 44 3/4 in | 66 x 51 x 114 cm |
| Gated Standard Platform | 27 x 26 x 44 3/4 in | 69 x 66 x 114 cm | Front Entry Gated Narrow Platform | 20 x 26 x 44 3/4 in | 51 x 66 x 114 cm |
| Standard Fiberglass Platform | 29 x 26 1/2 x 43 1/2 in | 74 x 67 x 110 cm | Gated Ultra-Narrow Platform | 22 x 18 x 44 3/4 in | 56 x 46 x 114 cm |
| Narrow Fiberglass Platform | 26 x 22 x 43 1/2 in | 66 x 56 x 110 cm | Front and Side Entry Extra-Large Platform | 30 x 28 x 44 3/4 in | 76 x 71 x 114 cm |

| Models | AWP-15S | | AWP-20S | | AWP-25S | | AWP-30S | |
|---|---|---|---|---|---|---|---|---|
| | US | Metric | US | Metric | US | Metric | US | Metric |
| **Rough Terrain Base** | | | | | | | | |
| Machine weight (DC/AC models) | 715/625 lbs | 325/284 kg | 750/660 lbs | 340/299 kg | 784/694 lbs | 355/315 kg | 819/729 lbs | 371/330 kg |
| (A) Height, stowed | 79 in | 201 cm | 79 in | 201 cm | 79 in | 201 cm | 79 in | 201 cm |
| (C)x(D) Length x Width | 58/30 in | 147/75 cm | 58/30 in | 147/75 cm | 58/30 in | 147/75 cm | 58/30 in | 147/75 cm |
| **Narrow Base[4]** | | | | | | | | |
| Machine weight (DC/AC models) | 711/621 lbs | 322/282 kg | 745/655 lbs | 338/297 kg | 780/690 lbs | 353/313 kg | 814/724 lbs | 369/328 kg |
| (A) Height, stowed | 78 in | 198 cm | 78 in | 198 cm | 78 in | 198 cm | 78 in | 198 cm |
| (C)x(D) Length x Width | 50/22 in | 126/56 cm | 50/22 in | 126/56 cm | 52/22 in | 132/56 cm | 55/22 in | 140/56 cm |
| **Rough Terrain and Narrow Bases** | | | | | | | | |
| (H)x(I) Outrigger footprint (l x w) ANSI | 64 x 48 in | 163 x 123 cm | 64 x 48 in | 163 x 123 cm | 64 x 48 in | 163 x 123 cm | 72 x 58 in | 182 x 147 cm |
| (H)x(I) Outrigger footprint (l x w) CSA[1] | 72 x 58 in | 182 x 147 cm | 75 x 66 in | 189 x 166 cm | 83 x 74 in | 211 x 188 cm | 95 x 90 in | 242 x 228 cm |
| (H)x(I) Outrigger footprint (l x w) CE Indoor[2] | 64 x 48 1/3 in | 163 x 123 cm | 71 x 58 in | 182 x 147 cm | 71 x 58 in | 182 x 147 cm | 83 x 74 in | 211 x 188 cm |
| (H)x(I) Outrigger footprint (l x w) CE Outdoor[2] | 95 x 90 in | 242 x 228 cm | 112 x 112 in | 284 x 284 cm | 112 x 112 in | 284 x 284 cm | 130 x 136 in | 330 x 345 cm |
| (K) Corner access[3] ANSI | 16 in | 41 cm | 14 in | 36 cm | 13 in | 33 cm | 19 in | 47 cm |
| (K) Corner access[3] CSA[1] | 23 in | 57 cm | 25 in | 62 cm | 29 in | 73 cm | 38 in | 95 cm |
| (K) Corner access[3] CE indoor[2] | 16 in | 41 cm | 21 in | 53 cm | 20 in | 50 cm | 27 1/2 in | 70 cm |
| (K) Corner access[3] CE outdoor[2] | 42 in | 107 cm | 54 in | 137 cm | 52 in | 132 cm | 61 in | 165 cm |
| (L)/(M) Wall access front/side ANSI | 11/12 in | 28/29 cm | 9/12 in | 22/29 cm | 6/12 in | 15/29 cm | 7/17 in | 19/43 cm |
| (L)/(M) Wall access front/side CSA[1] | 15/17 in | 38/43 cm | 14/20 in | 36/51 cm | 15/25 in | 38/62 cm | 19/33 in | 47/83 cm |
| (L)/(M) Wall access front/side CE indoor[2] | 11/12 in | 28/29 cm | 12/17 in | 31/43 cm | 10/17 in | 25/43 cm | 9/20 in | 23/51 cm |
| (L)/(M) Wall access front/side CE outdoor[2] | 26/133 in | 66/84 cm | 32/44 in | 81/112 cm | 29/44 in | 74/112 cm | 35/55 in | 84/140 cm |

[1]Canadian Standards Association, [2]European Community, [3]Corner of platform top rail to corner of wall with ability to rotate leveling jack handle. [4]On Narrow Base models only Gated Narrow, Gated Ultra-Narrow and Narrow Fiberglass Platforms are available.

**Super Straddle Specifications**

| | US | Metric |
|---|---|---|
| (N) Height | 70 in | 177.8 cm |
| (O) Width | 40 in | 101.6 cm |
| (P) Length | 9 ft 1 in - 10 ft 8 in | 2.8 - 3.3 m |
| (Q) Wheelbase | 8 ft 8 in - 10 ft 8 in | 2.6 - 3.3 m |
| (R) Straddle clearance | 4 ft | 1.2 m |
| (S) Height to ladder | 27 in | 68.6 cm |
| (T) Height to fixed wheel | 40 in | 101.6 cm |
| Storage dimensions | 80 x 37 x 24 in | 203.2 x 94 x 61 cm |
| Weight | 455 lb | 206 kg |

**Airmotor Specifications**

| | US | Metric |
|---|---|---|
| Power | 1.5 hp | 1.1 kw |
| Required air supply flow | 80 cfm | 2.27 m³/m |
| Required air supply pressure | 80 psi | 5.5 bar |

**Figure 161** Genie specifications.

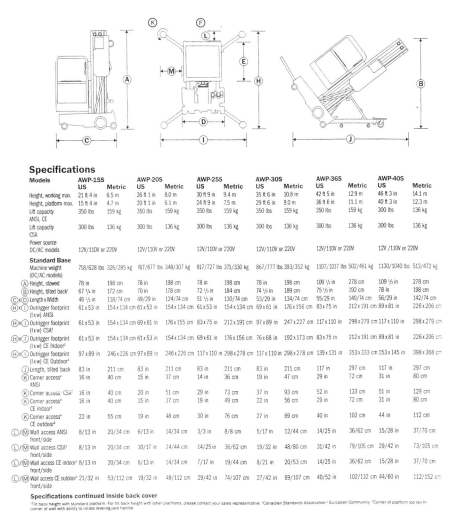

## Specifications

| Models | AWP-15S US | Metric | AWP-20S US | Metric | AWP-25S US | Metric | AWP-30S US | Metric | AWP-36S US | Metric | AWP-40S US | Metric |
|---|---|---|---|---|---|---|---|---|---|---|---|---|
| Height, working max. | 21 ft 4 in | 6.5 m | 26 ft 1 in | 8.0 m | 30 ft 9 in | 9.4 m | 35 ft 6 in | 10.8 m | 42 ft 5 in | 12.9 m | 46 ft 3 in | 14.1 m |
| Height, platform max. | 15 ft 4 in | 4.7 m | 20 ft 1 in | 6.1 m | 24 ft 9 in | 7.5 m | 29 ft 6 in | 9.0 m | 36 ft 6 in | 11.1 m | 40 ft 3 in | 12.3 m |
| Lift capacity ANSI, CE | 350 lbs | 159 kg | 350 lbs | 159 kg | 350 lbs | 159 kg | 350 lbs | 159 kg | 350 lbs | 159 kg | 300 lbs | 136 kg |
| Lift capacity CSA | 300 lbs | 136 kg | 300 lbs | 136 kg | 300 lbs | 136 kg | 300 lbs | 136 kg | 300 lbs | 136 kg | 300 lbs | 136 kg |
| Power source DC/AC models | 12V/110V or 220V | | 12V/110V or 220V | | 12V/110V or 220V | | 12V/110V or 220V | | 12V/110V or 220V | | 12V /110V or 220V | |

**Standard Base**

| | AWP-15S US | Metric | AWP-20S US | Metric | AWP-25S US | Metric | AWP-30S US | Metric | AWP-36S US | Metric | AWP-40S US | Metric |
|---|---|---|---|---|---|---|---|---|---|---|---|---|
| Machine weight (DC/AC models) | 718/628 lbs | 326/285 kg | 767/677 lbs | 348/307 kg | 817/727 lbs | 371/330 kg | 867/777 lbs | 393/352 kg | 1107/1017 lbs | 502/461 kg | 1130/1040 lbs | 513/472 kg |
| (A) Height, stowed | 78 in | 198 cm | 78 in | 198 cm | 78 in | 198 cm | 78 in | 198 cm | 109 ½ in | 278 cm | 109 ½ in | 278 cm |
| (B) Height, tilted back[1] | 67 ¾ in | 172 cm | 70 in | 178 cm | 72 ½ in | 184 cm | 74 ½ in | 189 cm | 75 ½ in | 192 cm | 78 in | 198 cm |
| (C)x(D) Length x Width | 46 ½ in | 118/74 cm | 49/29 in | 124/74 cm | 51 ½ in | 130/74 cm | 53/29 in | 134/74 cm | 55/29 in | 140/74 cm | 56/29 in | 142/74 cm |
| (H)x(I) Outrigger footprint (l x w) ANSI | 61 x 53 in | 154 x 134 cm | 61 x 53 in | 154 x 134 cm | 61 x 53 in | 154 x 134 cm | 69 x 61 in | 176 x 156 cm | 83 x 75 in | 212 x 191 cm | 89 x 81 in | 226 x 206 cm |
| (H)x(I) Outrigger footprint (l x w) CSA[2] | 61 x 53 in | 154 x 134 cm | 69 x 61 in | 176 x 155 cm | 83 x 75 in | 212 x 191 cm | 97 x 89 in | 247 x 227 cm | 117 x 110 in | 298 x 279 cm | 117 x 110 in | 298 x 279 cm |
| (H)x(I) Outrigger footprint (l x w) CE Indoor[3] | 61 x 53 in | 154 x 134 cm | 61 x 53 in | 154 x 134 cm | 69 x 61 in | 176 x 156 cm | 76 x 68 in | 192 x 173 cm | 83 x 75 in | 212 x 191 cm | 89 x 81 in | 226 x 206 cm |
| (H)x(I) Outrigger footprint (l x w) CE Outdoor[3] | 97 x 89 in | 246 x 226 cm | 97 x 89 in | 246 x 226 cm | 117 x 110 in | 298 x 278 cm | 117 x 110 in | 298 x 278 cm | 139 x 131 in | 353 x 333 cm | 153 x 145 in | 398 x 368 cm |
| (J) Length, tilted back | 83 in | 211 cm | 83 in | 211 cm | 83 in | 211 cm | 83 in | 211 cm | 117 in | 297 cm | 117 in | 297 cm |
| (K) Corner access[4] ANSI | 16 in | 40 cm | 15 in | 37 cm | 14 in | 36 cm | 19 in | 47 cm | 29 in | 72 cm | 31 in | 80 cm |
| (K) Corner access CSA[2] | 16 in | 40 cm | 20 in | 51 cm | 29 in | 73 cm | 37 in | 93 cm | 52 in | 133 cm | 51 in | 129 cm |
| (K) Corner access[4] CE indoor[3] | 16 in | 40 cm | 15 in | 37 cm | 19 in | 49 cm | 22 in | 56 cm | 29 in | 72 cm | 31 in | 80 cm |
| (K) Corner access[4] CE outdoor[3] | 22 in | 55 cm | 19 in | 48 cm | 30 in | 76 cm | 27 in | 69 cm | 40 in | 102 cm | 44 in | 112 cm |
| (L)/(M) Wall access ANSI front/side | 8/13 in | 20/34 cm | 6/13 in | 14/34 cm | 3/3 in | 8/8 cm | 5/17 in | 12/44 cm | 14/25 in | 36/62 cm | 15/28 in | 37/70 cm |
| (L)/(M) Wall access CSA[2] front/side | 8/13 in | 20/34 cm | 10/17 in | 24/44 cm | 14/25 in | 36/62 cm | 19/32 in | 48/80 cm | 31/42 in | 79/105 cm | 29/42 in | 73/105 cm |
| (L)/(M) Wall access CE indoor[3] front/side | 8/13 in | 20/34 cm | 6/13 in | 14/34 cm | 7/17 in | 19/44 cm | 8/21 in | 20/53 cm | 14/25 in | 36/62 cm | 15/28 in | 37/70 cm |
| (L)/(M) Wall access CE outdoor[3] front/side | 21/32 in | 53/112 cm | 19/32 in | 48/112 cm | 29/42 in | 74/107 cm | 27/42 in | 69/107 cm | 40/52 in | 102/132 cm | 44/60 in | 112/152 cm |

Specifications continued inside back cover

[1]Tilt back height with standard platform. For tilt back height with other platfroms, please contact your sales representative. [2]Canadian Standards Association [3] European Community [4]Corner of platform top rail to corner of wall with ability to rotate leveling jack handle.

**Figure 162** Genie specifications.

| *Specifications* | AMZ39NE |
|---|---|
| **Platform:** | |
| Working Height | 39 ft. (11.9 m) |
| Platform Height | 33 ft. (10.1 m) |
| Horizontal Reach | 21 ft. (6.4 m) |
| Riser Height | 15 ft. (4.57 m) |
| Capacity | 500 lbs. (227 kg) |
| **Dimensions:** | |
| Platform Size | 30 x 48 in. (0.76 x 1.2 m) |
| Overall Height | 6 ft. 7 in. (2.0 m) |
| Overall Length (Travel) | 17 ft. 2 in. (5.23 m) |
| Overall Length (Stowed) | 12 ft. 2 in. (3.7 m) |
| Overall Width | 4 ft. (1.21 m) |
| Wheelbase | 64 in. (1.62 m) |
| Inside Turning Radius | 5 ft. 6 in. (1.67 m) |
| Ground Clearance | 5-1/2 in. (138 mm) |
| Tailswing | Zero |
| **Performance:** | |
| Maximum Drive Speed | 3.0 mph (4.82 km/h) |
| Gradeability (Theoretical)* | 25% |
| Tire Size | 26 x 8-22PR |
| Tire Fill | Solid |
| Machine Rotation | 359° (non-continuous) |
| Weight (Standard Unit) | 14,500 lbs. (6577 kg) |
| **Power Source:** | |
| **Upper:** | |
| Motor Horsepower | 4.25 hp (3.17 kW) |
| Pump | 1 Section Gear |
| Reservoir Capacity | 5.5 gal. (20.82 liters) |
| **Lower:** | |
| Drive System | Direct drive w/axle |
| Motor | 7 hp (5.22 kW) |
| Batteries | (8) 6 V |
| Battery Amps | 370 |
| Charger | 21 amp automatic |

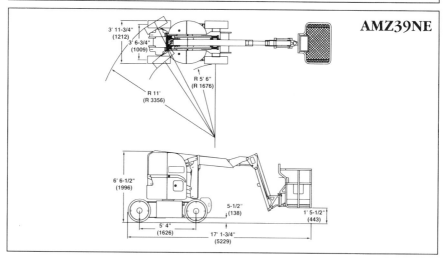

AMZ39NE

*Published machine gradeability is theoretical. Machine to be in a stowed driving position.
Always operate machine on a firm, level surface when elevated.

**Figure 163**  Lift diagram and specifications.

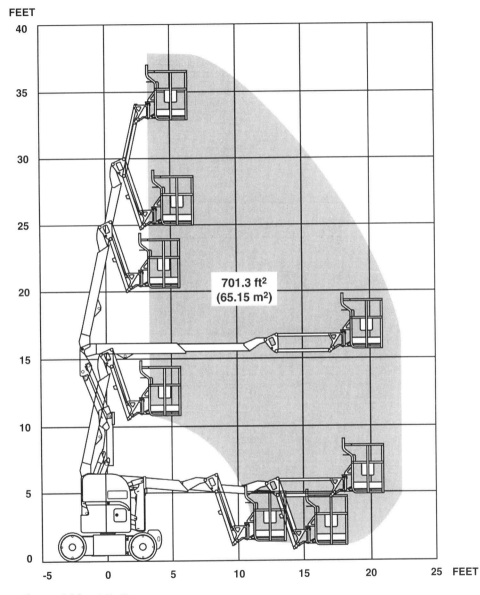

**Figure 164** Lift diagram.

## *Specifications*

| | AMZ36E | AMZ46E | AMZ46NE | AMZ51E |
|---|---|---|---|---|
| **Platform** | | | | |
| Working Height | 36 ft. 10 in. (11.23 m) | 46 ft. 3 in. (14.1 m) | 46 ft. 3 in. (14.1 m) | 51 ft. (15.55 m) |
| Platform Height | 30 ft. 10 in. (9.4 m) | 40 ft. 3 in. (12.27 m) | 40 ft. 3 in. (12.27 m) | 45 ft. (13.71 m) |
| Horizontal Reach | 20 ft. 6 in. (6.25 m) | 21 ft. 11 in. (6.68 m) | 21 ft. 11 in. (6.68 m) | 25 ft. 5 in. (7.8 m) |
| Riser Height | 15 ft. (4.57 m) | 23 ft. 4 in. (7.11 m) | 23 ft. 4 in. (7.11 m) | 23 ft. 4 in. (7.11 m) |
| Capacity | 500 lbs. (227 kg) | 500 lbs. (227 kg) | 500 lbs. (227 kg) | 500 lbs. (227 kg) |
| **Dimensions** | | | | |
| Platform Size | 30 x 48 in. | 30 x 48 in. | 30 x 48 in. | 30 x 48 in. |
| | (0.76 x 1.22 m) | (0.76 x 1.22 m) | (0.76 x 1.22 m) | (0.76 x 1.22 m) |
| Overall Height | 6 ft. 7 in. (2.0 m) | 6 ft. 7 in. (2.0 m) | 6 ft. 7 in. (2.0 m) | 6 ft. 7 in. (2.0 m) |
| Overall Length | 16 ft. 5 in. (5.0 m) | 18 ft. 8 in. (5.69 m) | 18 ft. 8 in. (5.69 m) | 19 ft. 10 in. (6.05 m) |
| Overall Width | 5 ft. 9 in. (1.75 m) | 5 ft. 9 in. (1.75 m) | 4 ft. 11 in. (1.5 m) | 5 ft. 9 in. (1.75 m) |
| Track | 5 ft. 1 in. (1.55 m) | 5 ft. 1 in. (1.55 m) | 4 ft. 4 in. (1.32 m) | 5 ft. 1 in. (1.55 m) |
| Wheelbase | 6 ft. 4 in. (1.93 m) | 6 ft. 4 in. (1.93 m) | 6 ft. 4 in. (1.93 m) | 6 ft. 4 in. (1.93 m) |
| Inside Turning Radius | 51 in. (1.3 m) | 51 in. (1.3 m) | 63 in. (1.6 m) | 51 in. (1.3 m) |
| Ground Clearance | 6 in. (0.15 m) | 6 in. (0.15 m) | 6 in. (0.15 m) | 6 in. (0.15 m) |
| Tailswing | Zero | Zero | 5 in. (0.13 m) | Zero |
| **Performance** | | | | |
| Maximum Drive Speed | 3 mph (4.8 km/h) | 3 mph (4.8 km/h) | 3 mph (4.8 km/h) | 3 mph (4.8 km/h) |
| Gradeability* (Theoretical) | 30% | 30% | 30% | 30% |
| Tire Size | 7.00 x 15 NHS 12 PR | 7.00 x 15 NHS 12 PR | 22 x 7 - 16 Solid | 7.00 x 15 NHS 12 PR |
| Tire Fill | Air | Air | N/A | Air |
| Weight | 10,200 lbs. | 11,600 lbs. | 13,100 lbs. | 14,300 lbs. |
| | (4627 kg) | (5262 kg) | (5942 kg) | (6486 kg) |
| **Power Source** | | | | |
| **Upper:** | | | | |
| Motor Horsepower | 4.6 hp | 4.6 hp | 4.6 hp | 4.6 hp |
| Pump | 1 Section Gear | 2 Section Gear | 2 Section Gear | 2 Section Gear |
| Reservoir Capacity | 5 gal. (18.9 L) | 5 gal. (18.9 L) | 5 gal. (18.9 L) | 5 gal. (18.9 L) |
| **Lower:** | | | | |
| Drive System | Direct drive | Direct drive | Direct drive | Direct drive |
| | w/wheel drive | w/axle | w/axle | w/axle |
| Motor | (2) 1.75 hp | 7 hp | 7 hp | 7 hp |
| Batteries | (8) 6 V | (8) 6 V | (8) 6 V | (8) 6 V |
| Battery Amps | 370 | 370 | 370 | 370 |
| Charger | 21 amp automatic | 21 amp automatic | 21 amp automatic | 21 amp automatic |

*Published machine gradeability is theoretical. Machine to be in a stowed driving position.
Always operate machine on a firm, level surface when elevated.

**Figure 165** Lift specifications.

## AMZ46E & AMZ46NE Working Range Diagram & Dimensions

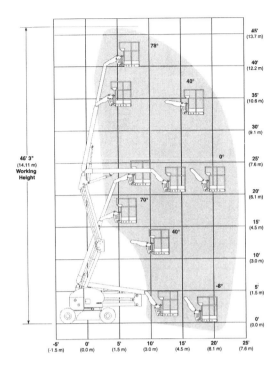

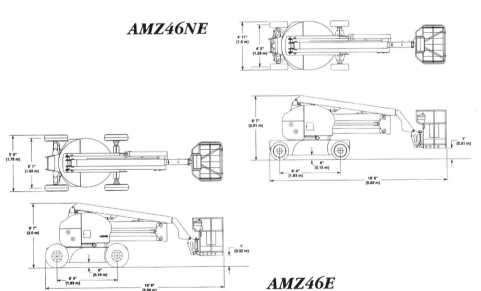

AMZ46NE

AMZ46E

**Figure 166**   Lift diagram.

# AMZ51E
# Working Range
# Diagram &
# Dimensions

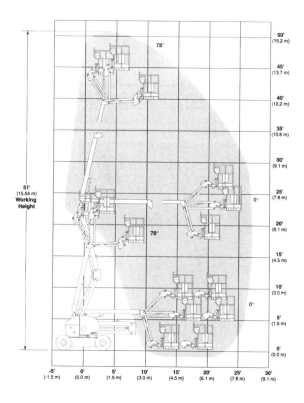

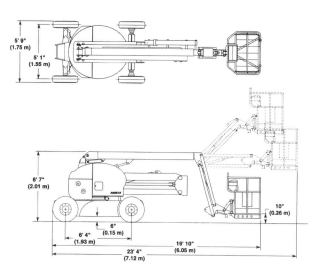

**Figure 167** Lift diagram.

## *Specifications*

| | AMZ51 | AMZ51XT |
|---|---|---|
| **Platform** | | |
| Working Height | 51 ft. (15.54 m) | 51 ft. (15.54 m) |
| Platform Height | 45 ft. (13.71 m) | 45 ft. (13.71 m) |
| Platform Capacity | 500 lbs. (227 kg) | 500 lbs. (227 kg) |
| Horizontal Reach (w/Riser Elevated) | 24 ft. 6 in. (7.5 m) | 24 ft. 6 in. (7.5 m) |
| | | |
| **Dimensions** | | |
| Platform Size (steel) | 30 x 60 in. (0.76 x 1.5 m) | 30 x 60 in. (0.76 x 1.5 m) |
| Overall Height (stowed) | 6 ft. 7 in. (2.01 m) | 6 ft. 7 in. (2.01 m) |
| Overall Length | 20 ft. (6.10 m) | 20 ft. (6.10 m) |
| Overall Width | 5 ft. 10.5 in. (1.79 m) | 6 ft. 7 in. (2.0 m)** |
| Wheelbase | 6 ft. 6 in. (1.98 m) | 6 ft. 6 in. (1.98 m) |
| Outside Turning Radius | 14 ft. 6 in. (4.4 m) | 14 ft. 6 in. (4.4 m) |
| Ground Clearance | 8 in. (0.2 m) | 8 in. (0.2 m) |
| Tailswing (Elevated) | Zero | Zero |
| | | |
| **Performance** | | |
| Maximum Drive Speed | 4.0 mph (6.4 km/h) | 3.5 mph (5.6 km/h) |
| Gradeability (Theoretical)* | 30% | 50% |
| Tire Size | 7.00 x 15  12 pr | 12.00 x 16.5  8 pr loader lug |
| Tire Fill | Air | Air |
| | | |
| **Power Source** | | |
| Standard Engine | Ford LRG425 Dual/fuel | Ford LRG425 Dual/fuel |
| Engine Horsepower | 65 hp (48.5 kW) | 65 hp (48.5 kW) |
| Optional Diesel Engine | Deutz F4L-1011F | Deutz F4L-1011F |
| Fuel Tank Capacity | 14 gal. (53 litres) | 14 gal. (53 litres) |
| | | |
| **Hydraulics** | | |
| Reservoir Capacity | 20 gal (75.7 litres) | 20 gal (75.7 litres) |
| Pump Type | Axial Piston | Axial Piston |
| Auxiliary Power | Std. | Std. |
| | | |
| **Shipping Information** | | |
| Weight | 14,400 lbs. (6523 kg) | 14,600 lbs. (6623 kg) |
| Shipping Cube | 1524 cu. ft. (43 m³) | 863 cu. ft. (24.43 m³) |

*Published machine gradeability is theoretical. Machine to be in a stowed position. Always operate machine on a firm, level surface when elevated.

**XT models available with optional 5' 10.5" (1.79 m) chassis.

**Figure 168**   Lift specifications.

# AMZ51/AMZ51XT

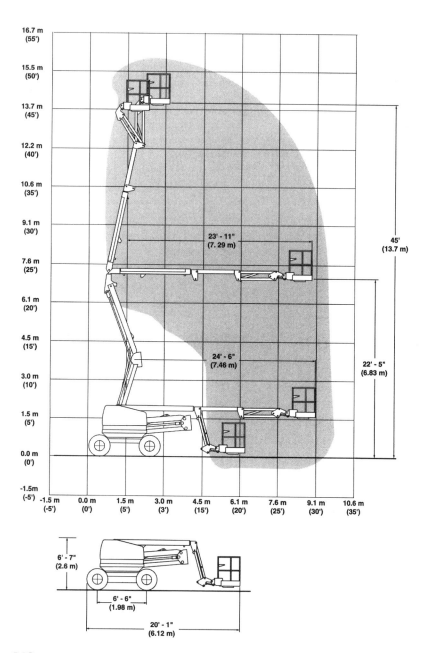

**Figure 169** Lift diagram.

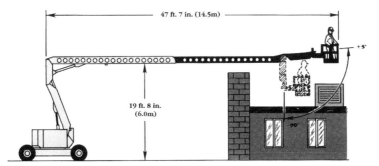

*Three dimensional articulating boom on the AMZ68 and AMZ68XT lets you reach up, over and around obstacles.*

Riser is an all steel fabricated mechanical parallelogram with integrally pinned mast.

Double-acting lift cylinder with integral load-holding valve provides boom elevation. Articulating jib with double-acting lift cylinder and integral holding valve.

Ball bearing swing circle with 360° continuous rotation. Planetary double reduction gearbox with hydraulic motor and spring-applied hydraulically released brake. Plunger-type mechanical house lock.

**Power Plant**

Ford LRG 423 4-cylinder water cooled gasoline engine with 63 hp (47 kw) @ 2,800 rpm.

60 amp alternator.

12-V DC with 700 CCA.

25 gal. (95 L) steel fuel tank with sight gauge.

**Hydraulic System**

Pressure/flow compensated, variable displacement axial piston hydraulic pump with 43 gpm (163 lpm) capacity. Maximum system operating pressure of 3,750 psi (259 bar).

Electrically activated, consolidated proportional and non-proportional valve bank provides simultaneous functioning of drive, steer, lift, telescope, swing, platform rotate and platform level.

45 gal. (170 lpm) steel hydraulic reservoir with sight gauge.

10 micron hydraulic pressure filter, 10 micron return filter, fill strainer and magnet plug in the reservoir.

**Chassis**

Two speed drive motors. Front wheel drive on the AMZ68, and four-wheel drive on the AMZ68XT.

Counterbalance valve provides dynamic braking. Automatic spring-applied hydraulically released disc type parking brakes on the drive wheels.

Tilt alarm, all motion alarm.

*Options*

- Ford LRG 423 4-cylinder water cooled dual fuel engine with 63 hp (47 kw) @ 2,800 rpm.
- Deutz F4L-1011F 4-cylinder air cooled diesel engine with 60 hp (44.7 kw) @ 3,000 rpm.
- 96 in. (2.4 m) aluminum platform.
- Enclosed upper control box cover.
- 2,000 watt self-contained generator.
- 120 psi (8.27 bar) air line to platform.
- Platform worklights.
- Travel lights.
- Amber strobe lights.
- Foam-filled tires.
- Hostile Environment Protection Package.

*\*Patented Grove feature.*

**Figure 170**   Lift diagram and specifications.

## Specifications                                    AMZ68/AMZ68XT

**Platform**

Working Height ...........................68 ft. (20.73 m)
Platform Height............................62 ft. (18.89 m)
Horizontal Reach
w/ Riser Elevated...............47 ft. 7 in. (14.5 m)
Riser Height..............................19 ft. 8 in. (6.0 m)
Platform Capacity ...................500 lbs. (227 kg)

**Dimensions**

Platform Size
Standard ................36 x 72 in. (0.91 x 1.83 m)
Optional .................36 x 96 in. (0.91 x 2.44 m)
Overall Height (stowed) .......8 ft. 11 in. (2.72 m)
Overall Length......................30 ft. 7 in. (9.32 m)
Overall Width .................................8 ft. (2.44 m)
Track......................................6 ft. 6.5 in. (1.99 m)
Turning Radius
(outside)........................... 14 ft. 10 in. (4.52 m)
Tailswing
Riser Up...............................................0
Riser Down ..........................5 ft. 1 in. (1.55 m)
Wheelbase..............................9 ft. (2.74 m)
Ground Clearance.......................12 in. (0.30 m)

**Performance**

Drive/Steer
AMZ68 ..........Front wheel drive, 4 wheel steer
AMZ68XT ............4 wheel drive, 4 wheel steer
Maximum Drive Speed
AMZ68 ...............................3.0 mph (4.8 km/h)
AMZ68XT........................3.0 mph (4.8 km/h)
Gradeability (Theoretical)
AMZ68 .......................................................27%
AMZ68XT....................................................40%
Tire Size ..................................................15x19.5
Tire Fill ...............................................Pneumatic
Swing Speed ...........................................0.5 rpm

**Power Source**

Engine .....................Ford LRG 42.3 water cooled
Engine Horsepower......................63 hp (47 kw)
Fuel Tank Capacity ........................25 gal. (95 L)

**Hydraulics**

Reservoir Capacity..........................24 gal. (91 L)
Hydraulic Pump Type...............................Piston
Filtration...............................................10 micron

**Shipping Information**

Weight
AMZ68 ...........................26,500 lbs. (12020 kg)
AMZ68XT......................26,800 lbs. (12157 kg)
Shipping Cube ................2,202 cu. ft. (62.35 m³)

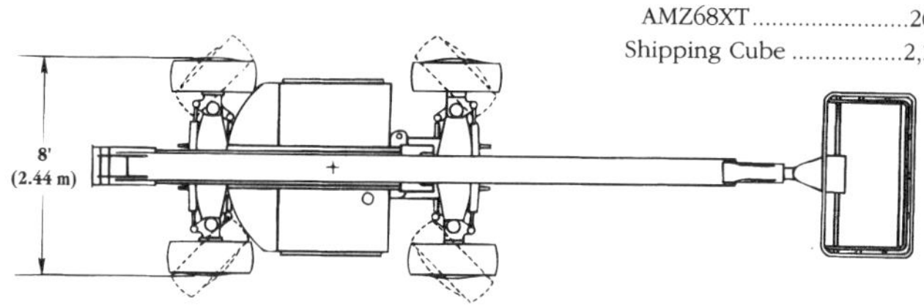

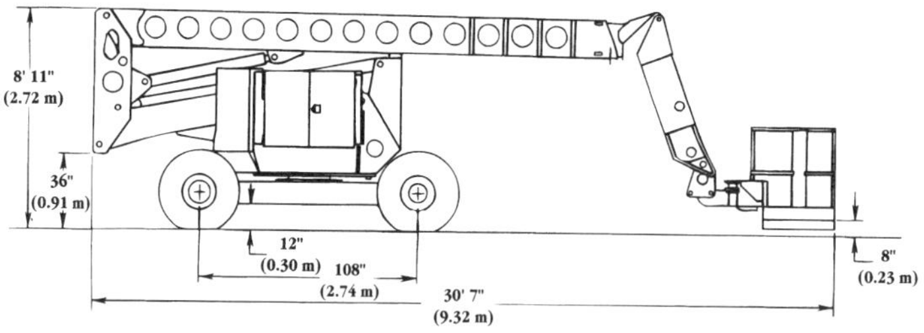

**Figure 171**   Lift diagram and specifications.

# AMZ68/AMZ68XT

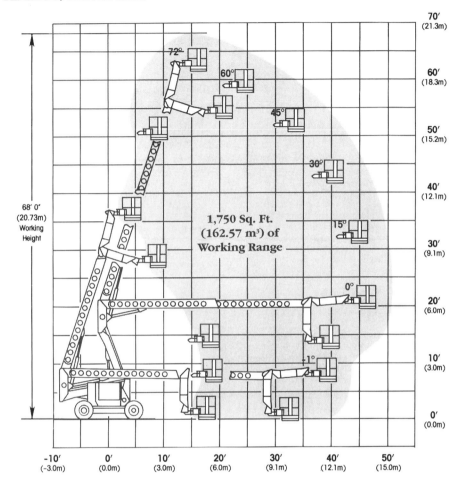

**Figure 172** Lift diagram.

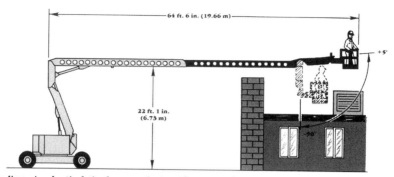

*Three dimensional articulating boom on the AMZ86 and AMZ86XT lets you reach up, over and around obstacles.*

Lower control panel features non-proportional control switches for drive, steer, lift, telescope, swing and platform level. Selection switches for lower/ upper controls, boom/riser/jib/lift, and auxiliary power unit. Also included are a voltmeter, hourmeter, and ignition switch.

All-steel, 2-section Vierendeel-embossed trapezoidal boom with articulating jib attached to fly section. Telescoping boom sections supported by adjustable Nylatron wear pads. Internal power guide routes hydraulic and electric lines to platform.

Triple cell** riser with patented centerline design.

Double-acting lift cylinder with integral holding valves provides boom elevation from -1.3° to +75° above horizontal. Articulating jib with double-acting lift cylinder and integral holding valve provides elevation from +5° to -90° relative to horizontal boom.

Double-acting boom telescope cylinder with integral holding valve.

Ball bearing swing circle with 360° continuous rotation. Planetary double reduction gear box with hydraulic motor and spring-applied hydraulically released brake. Plunger-type mechanical house lock.

Pressure/flow compensated, variable displacement axial piston hydraulic pump with 43 gpm (163 lpm) capacity. Maximum system operating pressure of 3,750 psi (259 bar).

Electrically-activated, consolidated proportional and nonproportional valve bank provides simultaneous functioning of drive, steer, lift, telescope, swing, platform rotate, and platform level.

10 micron hydraulic pressure filter, 10 micron return filter, fill strainer and magnetic plug in reservoir. 50 gal. (189 liter) hydraulic reservoir with sight gauge.

Ford CSG-649 6-cylinder water-cooled gasoline engine with 110 hp (82 kw) at 2500 rpm and 60 amp alternator.

45 gal. (170 liter) steel fuel tank with gauge.

12-volt DC negative ground battery with 750 CCA @ 0° F (-17° C).

*Options*

36 x 96 in. (0.91 x 2.44m) platform.

110-volt AC wiring to platform with plug and junction box on turntable and two outlets on platform, 15-amp resettable circuit breaker, and ground fault interrupter.

2000-watt 110-volt AC generator with two outlets on platform.

120 psi (8.27 bar) 3/4 in. I.D. air hose to platform with quick disconnect on turntable.

Halogen worklights on platform.

Ford CSG-649 6-cylinder water-cooled dual fuel engine with 110 hp (82 kw) at 2500 rpm and 60 amp alternator.

Cummins 4BT3.9 4-cylinder turbo-charged water-cooled diesel engine with 100 hp (75 kw) at 2500 rpm and 60 amp alternator.

18R-19.5 foam-filled flotation tires (increases overall width to 8 ft. 6 in. [2.6m]).

Amber strobe lights.

Halogen travel lights.

Fire extinguisher.

In-plant tow package.

Hostile Environment Protection Package.

Special paint.

**Figure 173**  Lift diagram and specifications.

## Specifications                                        AMZ86/AMZ86XT

### Platform

Working Height..............................86 ft. (26.21m)
Platform Height..............................80 ft. (24.38m)
Horizontal Reach
w/ Riser Elevated..............64 ft. 6 in. (19.66m)
Riser Height............................22 ft. 1 in. (6.73m)
Platform Capacity
500 lbs. (227 kg) with standard tires and either
36 x 72, 96 in. (0.91 x 1.83, 2.44m) platform.
600 lbs. (272 kg) with optional tires and standard
36 x 72 in. (0.91 x 1.83m) platform.
500 lbs. (227 kg) with optional tires and optional
36 x 96 in. (0.91 x 2.44m) platform.

### Dimensions

Platform Size
Standard....................36 x 72 in. (0.91 x 1.83m)
Optional....................36 x 96 in. (0.91 x 2.44m)
Overall Height (stowed)..........9 ft. 8 in. (2.95m)
Overall Length......................36 ft. 6 in. (11.13m)
Overall Width....................................8 ft. (2.44m)
Track..........................................6 ft. 6 in. (1.98m)
Turning Radius
(outside)............................ 17 ft. 6 in. (5.33m)
Tailswing
Riser Up .......................................12 in. (0.30m)
Riser Down..........................5 ft. 5.5 in. (1.66m)
Wheelbase........................................12 ft. (3.66m)
Ground Clearance.........................12 in. (0.30m)

### Performance

Drive/Steer
AMZ86 ..........Front wheel drive, 4 wheel steer
AMZ86XT ............4 wheel drive, 4 wheel steer
Maximum Drive Speed
AMZ86 ................................3.5 mph (5.6 km/h)
AMZ86XT............................2.5 mph (4.0 km/h)
Gradeability
AMZ86 ........................................................30%
AMZ86XT......................................................50%
Tire Size ..................................................13.00R20
Tire Fill .........................................................Foam
Swing Speed ...........................................0.5 rpm

### Power Source

Engine ......................Ford CSG-649 Water-Cooled
Engine Horsepower....................110 hp (82 kw)
Fuel Tank Capacity ................45 gal. (170 liters)

### Hydraulics

Reservoir Capacity...................50 gal. (189 liters)
Hydraulic Pump Type...............................Piston
Filtration .................................................10 micron

### Shipping Information

Weight
AMZ86 ..........................42,300 lbs. (19190 kg)
AMZ86XT......................42,800 lbs. (19415 kg)
Shipping Cube .................2,774 cu. ft. (78.5 m$^3$)

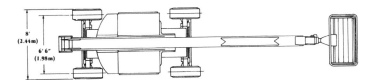

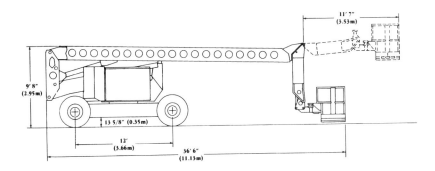

**Figure 174**    Lift diagram and specifications.

# Riser Lowered

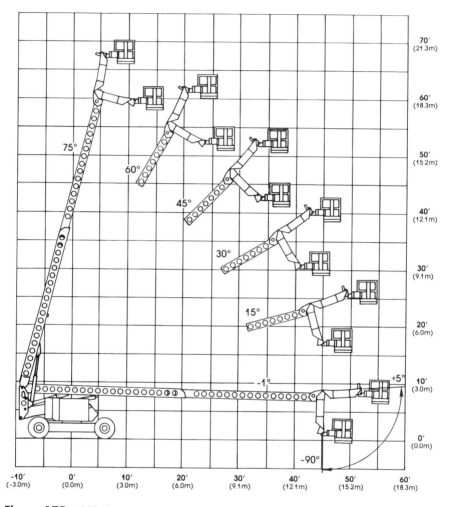

**Figure 175**   Lift diagram.

# Riser Elevated

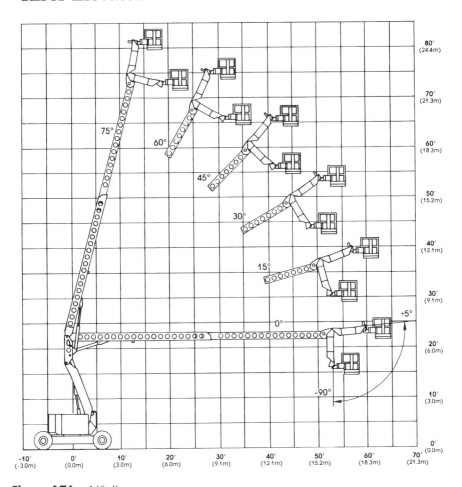

**Figure 176**  Lift diagram.

## Specifications

### AMZ131XT

**Platform**

Working Height . . . . . . . . . . . . . . . . . . 131 ft. (39.9 m)
Platform Height . . . . . . . . . . . . . . . . . . 125 ft. (38.1 m)
Riser Height:
  Retracted . . . . . . . . . . . . . . . . . . 34 ft. 4 in. (10.5 m)
  Extended . . . . . . . . . . . . 61 ft. 9 in. (18.8 m)
Horizontal Reach:
  Riser Retracted . . . . . . . . . . . . . . 69 ft. 8 in. (21.2 m)
  Riser Extended . . . . . . . . . . . . . . 62 ft. 7 in. (19.1 m)
Platform Capacity . . . . . . . . . . . . . . . . 600 lbs. (272 kg)

**Dimensions**

Platform Size . . . . . . . . . . . . 36 x 72 in. (0.92 x 1.83 m)
Overall Height (stowed) . . . . . . . . . . 9 ft. 10 in. (3.0 m)
Overall Length . . . . . . . . . . . . . . . 39 ft. 4 in.(11.99 m)
Overall Width:
  Axles Retracted . . . . . . . . . . . . . . . . 8 ft. 6 in. (2.6 m)
  Axles Extended . . . . . . . . . . . . . . . . . . 12 ft. (3.7 m)
Turning Radius (inside):
  Axles Retracted . . . . . . . . . . 15 ft. 3-1/2 in. (4.66 m)
  Axles Extended . . . . . . . . . . . . . . 14 ft. 6 in. (4.42 m)
Turning Radius (outside):
  Axles Retracted . . . . . . . . . . . . . . 24 ft. 11 in. (7.59 m)
  Axles Extended . . . . . . . . . . . . . . 28 ft. 6 in. (8.69 m)

Wheel base . . . . . . . . . . . . . . . . . . . . . . . . 14 ft. (4.27 m)
Tailswing (beyond tires):
  Riser Extended . . . . . . . . . . . . . . . . 3 ft. 8 in. (1.1 m)
  Riser Retracted . . . . . . . . . . . . . . . . . . . . . . . . . . . Zero

**Performance**

Maximum Drive Speed . . . . . . . . . . . 2.5 mph (4.0 km/h)
Gradeability (theoretical) . . . . . . . . . . . . . . . . . . . . . 50%
Tires . . . . . . . . . . . . . . . . . . . . 14.75/80R20 Foam Filled
Swing Speed . . . . . . . . . . . . . . . . . . . . . . . . . . . . 0.5 RPM

**Power Source**

Engine Make/Model . . . . . . . . . . . . . . . . . . Ford CSG-649
Engine Horsepower . . . . . . . . . . . . . . . . 110 hp (82 kw)
Fuel Tank Capacity . . . . . . . . . . . . 45 gallons (170 liters)

**Hydraulics**

Reservoir Capacity . . . . . . . . . . . 102 gallons (386 liters)
Hydraulic Pump Type . . . . . . . . . . . . . . . . . . Axial Piston
Auxiliary Power . . . . . . . . . . . . . . . . . . . . . . . . . . . . . Yes

**Shipping Information**

Weight . . . . . . . . . . . . . . . . . . . . 47,900 lbs. (21727 kg)
Shipping Cube . . . . . . . . . . . . . . . . 3,274 cu. ft. (92.7 m³)

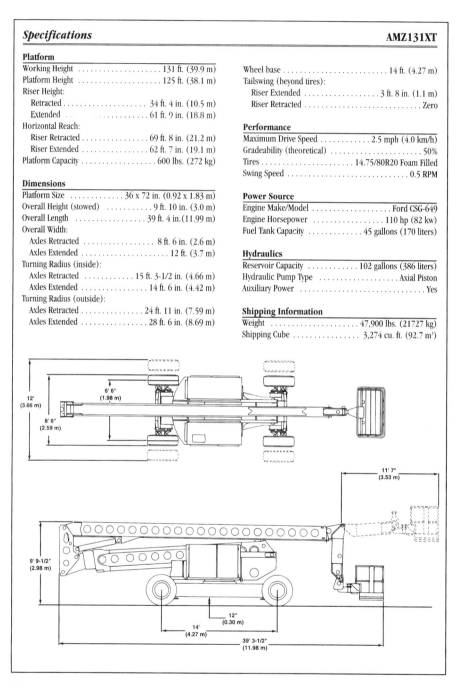

**Figure 177**   Lift diagram and specifications.

# Range Diagram AMZ131XT

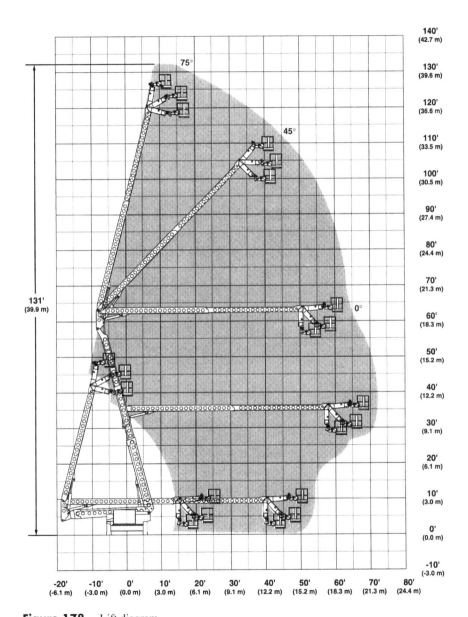

**Figure 178**  Lift diagram.

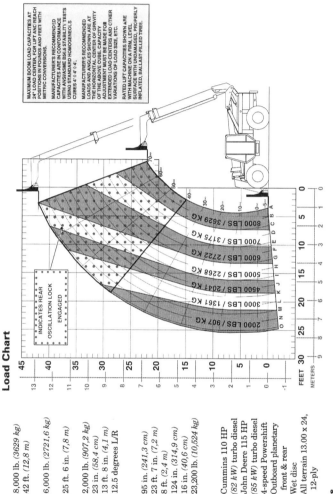

## Load Chart

MAXIMUM BOOM LOAD CAPACITIES AT 24" LOAD CENTER, FOR LIFT ANC REACH POSITIONS IN POUNDS AND FEET WITH METRIC CONVERSIONS.

MANUFACTURER'S RECOMMENDED CAPACITIES ARE IN CONFORMANCE WITH ANSI/ASME B56.6 STABILITY TESTS USING STANDARD HOMOGENEOLS CUBES 4' 0' 4'.

MANUFACTURER'S RECOMMEND LOADS AND ANGLES SHOWN ARE AT THE HORIZONTAL CENTER OF GRAVITY OF THE ABOVE CUBE. CAPACITY ADJUSTMENT MUST BE MADE FOR EXTENDED LOAD CENTERS AND OTHER VARIATIONS OF LOAD SIZE, ETC.

RATED LIFT CAPACITIES SHOWN ARE WITH MACHINE ON A FIRM, LEVEL SURFACE WITH UNDAMAGED, PROPERLY INFLATED, BALLAST-FILLED TIRES.

INDICATES REAR OSCILLATION LOCK ENGAGED

8000 LBS / 3629 KG
7000 LBS / 3175 KG
6000 LBS / 2722 KG
5000 LBS / 2268 KG
4500 LBS / 2041 KG
3000 LBS / 1361 KG
2000 LBS / 907 KG

## Performance

Max. Capacity ...........8,000 lb. *(3629 kg)*
Lift height ................42 ft. *(12,8 m)*
Max. Capacity @
full height ..............6,000 lb. *(2721,6 kg)*
Max. forward
reach ......................25 ft. 6 in. *(7,8 m)*
Capacity @ max.
forward reach .........2,000 lb. *(907,2 kg)*
Reach below grade ....23 in. *(58,4 cm)*
Outside turn radius ...13 ft. 8 in. *(4,1 m)*
Frame leveling .........12.5 degrees L/R

## Dimensions

Height .....................95 in. *(241,3 cm)*
Length (w/ 42 in. forks)..23 ft. 7 in. *(7,2 m)*
Width.......................8 ft. *(2,4 m)*
Wheelbase .............124 in. *(314,9 cm)*
Ground clearance .....16 in. *(40,6 cm)*
Weight ...................23,200 lb. *(10,524 kg)*

## Drive Train

Engine ....................Cummins 110 HP
*(82 kW)* turbo diesel
John Deere 115 HP
*(85 kW)* turbo diesel
Transmission...........4-speed Powershift
Outboard planetary
front & rear
Axles ......................Wet disc
Brakes ....................All terrain 13.00 x 24,
Tires .......................12-ply

## Standard Features

4 wheel drive ...........................................Yes
4 wheel round, 2 wheel front
& 4 wheel crab ........................................Yes
Automatic fork leveling ............................Yes
Multi-function joystick control ..............Yes
Number of boom sections ..........................3
Rear axle stabilizer system ....................Yes

## Options

• 1st Auxiliary hydraulics
• Multiple tire options
• Cab enclosure options
• Suspension seat
• Light packages
• Engine block heaters

## Attachments

• Standard fork carriages
• Side-tilt carriages
• Hydraulic fork position carriage
• Lumber forks
• Truss boom with or without winch
• Sweeper broom with bucket
• Concrete hoppers
• Framers carriages
• Swing carriages
• Pallet forks
• Cubing forks
• Augers
• 1¼ cu. yd. (,96 cu. m) light material bucket

**Figure 179** 8K-42 telescopic handler specifications.

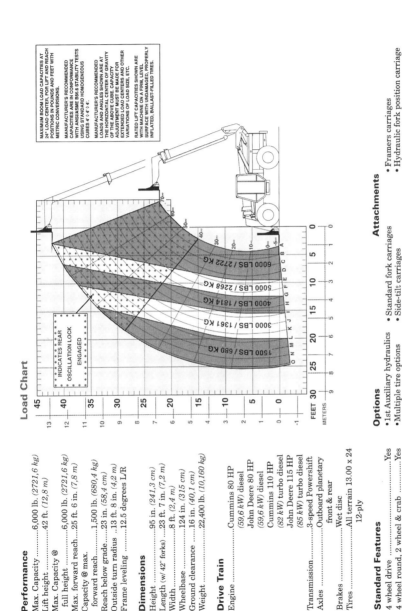

MAXIMUM BOOM LOAD CAPACITIES AT 24" LOAD CENTER, FOR LIFT AND REACH POSITIONS IN POUNDS AND FEET WITH METRIC CONVERSIONS.

MANUFACTURER'S RECOMMENDED CAPACITIES ARE IN CONFORMANCE WITH ANSI/ASME B56.6 STABILITY TESTS USING STANDARD HOMOGENEOUS CUBES 4' 4' 4'.

MANUFACTURER'S RECOMMENDED LOADS AND ANGLES SHOWN ARE AT THE HORIZONTAL CENTER OF GRAVITY OF THE ABOVE CUBE. CAPACITY ADJUSTMENT MUST BE MADE FOR EXTENDED LOAD CENTERS AND OTHER VARIATIONS OF LOAD SIZE, ETC.

RATED LIFT CAPACITIES SHOWN ARE WITH MACHINE ON A FIRM, LEVEL SURFACE WITH UNDAMAGED, PROPERLY INFLATED, BALLAST-FILLED TIRES.

**Load Chart**

INDICATES REAR OSCILLATION LOCK ENGAGED

6000 LBS / 2722 KG
5000 LBS / 2268 KG
4000 LBS / 1814 KG
3000 LBS / 1361 KG
1500 LBS / 680 KG

## Performance
Max. Capacity ..............6,000 lb. *(2721,6 kg)*
Lift height .................42 ft. *(12,8 m)*
Max. Capacity @
full height ...............6,000 lb. *(2721,6 kg)*
Max. forward reach ....25 ft. 6 in. *(7,8 m)*
Capacity @ max.
forward reach...........1,500 lb. *(680,4 kg)*
Reach below grade.....23 in. *(58,4 cm)*
Outside turn radius ...13 ft. 8 in. *(4,2 m)*
Frame leveling .........12.5 degrees L/R

## Dimensions
Height .......................95 in. *(241,3 cm)*
Length (w/ 42" forks) ..23 ft. 7 in. *(7,2 m)*
Width........................8 ft. *(2,4 m)*
Wheelbase ................124 in. *(315 cm)*
Ground clearance .....16 in. *(40,1 cm)*
Weight .....................22,400 lb. *(10,160 kg)*

## Drive Train
Engine ......................Cummins 80 HP
*(59,6 kW)* diesel
John Deere 80 HP
*(59,6 kW)* diesel
Cummins 110 HP
*(82 kW)* turbo diesel
John Deere 115 HP
*(85 kW)* turbo diesel
Transmission.............3-speed Powershift
Axles .......................Outboard planetary
front & rear
Brakes ......................Wet disc
Tires ........................All terrain 13.00 x 24
12-ply

## Standard Features
4 wheel drive ....................................Yes
4 wheel round, 2 wheel & crab ..........Yes
Automatic fork leveling ......................Yes
Multi-function joystick control ............Yes
Number of boom sections ...................3

## Options
• 1st Auxiliary hydraulics
• Multiple tire options
• Cab enclosure options
• Suspension seat
• Light packages
• Engine block heaters

## Attachments
• Standard fork carriages
• Side-tilt carriages
• Pallet forks
• Cubing forks
• Truss boom with or without winch
• Sweeper broom with bucket
• Framers carriages
• Hydraulic fork position carriage
• Lumber forks
• Augers
• Concrete hoppers
• 1¼ cu. yd. (.96 cu. m) light material bucket

**Figure 180**   6K-42 telescopic handler specifications.

EAGLE SUSPENDED PLATFORM, AND SCAFFOLD EQUIPMENT FEATURING:
- *35ft. per minute high-speed hoists*
- *Same hoist operates on either 110v & 220v*
- *Self-threading and breach-loading hoists*
- *Powerless controlled descent for emergencies*
- *Air-powered and manual hoists*

WE ALSO OFFER THE FOLLOWING SUPPORT EQUIPMENT & SERVICES
- *Rolling roof rigs*
- *Parapet clamps & hooks*
- *Professional engineering & design services*
- *Beams & weights*
- *Davits & sockets*
- *Experienced installation crews*

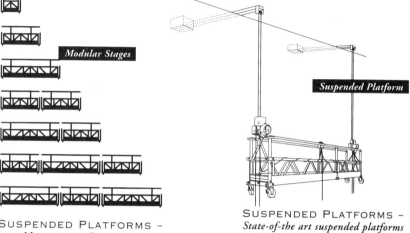

**Suspended Platform**

*Modular Stages*

**SUSPENDED PLATFORMS –
MODULAR STAGES**
*Available in varying lengths
from 4' to 62',
30°, 45°, 60° & 90° corners
allow greater versatility*

**SUSPENDED PLATFORMS –**
*State-of-the art suspended platforms
with load capacities up to 2,000 lbs.*

**Work Cages**

**Bosun Chairs**

**Safety Equipment**

**FALL ARREST EQUIPMENT**
*Sale of safety Harnesses, Lanyards,
Rope Grabs and Confined
Space Apparatus.*

**WORK CAGES**
*Economical, efficient
1 or 2 person platform*

**BOSUN CHAIRS**
*For working in
tight spaces*

**Figure 181**   Scaffolding.

### LULL ROUGH TERRAIN TELESCOPING BOOM MATERIAL HANDLERS

*All Lull Telescoping Boom Forklifts have full hydraulic controls, four wheel drive, four wheel crab steering, frame leveling, and rear axle stabilization. Truss Boom, Loose Material Bucket, Side Tilt Fork Carriage, 100° Swing Carriage and other Quick Attach Accessories are available.*

| MODEL | MAXIMUM LIFT HEIGHT | MAXIMUM LANDING HEIGHT | MAXIMUM LOAD | MAXIMUM HORIZONTAL REACH @ 24" LOAD CENTER | STOWED HEIGHT | MACHINE WIDTH | MACHINE LENGTH (42" FORKS W/O OUTRIGGERS) | MACHINE WEIGHT (W/O OUTRIGGERS) | AVAILABLE WITH OUTRIGGERS |
|---|---|---|---|---|---|---|---|---|---|
| 6K-42 | 42' | 38' | 6,000 | 25.5' | 95" | 96" | 23'7" | 22,300 | No |
| 644B-42* | 42' | 42' | 6,000 | 32' | 95" | 96" | 23'7" | 22,700 | No |
| 8K-42 | 42' | 38' | 8,000 | 25.5' | 95" | 96" | 23'7" | 23,160 | Yes |
| 844C-42* | 42' | 42' | 8,000 | 32' | 95" | 96" | 23'7" | 22,320 | Yes |
| 1044C-54* | 54' | 54' | 10,000 | 45' | 95" | 100" | 24'10" | 29,200 | Yes |

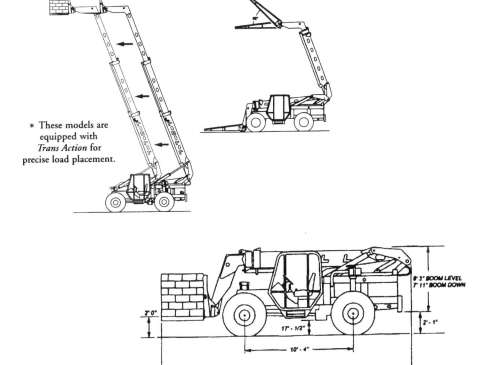

\* These models are equipped with *Trans Action* for precise load placement.

**Figure 182**   Lift specifications.

### SCISSOR LIFTS
*All Scissor Lifts come with extension decks and generators.*

| MODEL | WORK HEIGHT | PLATFORM HEIGHT | PLATFORM SIZE | STOWED HT W/ RAILS | OVERALL WIDTH | MACHINE WEIGHT | LIFT CAPACITY |
|---|---|---|---|---|---|---|---|
| SM 2232 E | 22' | 16' | 32" X 63" | 76" | 32" | 2,280 lbs | 500 lbs |
| SM 2632 E | 26' | 20' | 32" X 88" | 77 1/2" | 33" | 3,750 lbs | 750 lbs |
| SM 2646 E | 26' | 20' | 42" X 92' | 72" | 46' | 3,880 lbs | 1,250 lbs |
| SM 3146 E | 31' | 25' | 42" X 92" | 78" | 46" | 4,220 lbs | 650 lbs |
| SM 3160 E | 31' | 25' | 56" X 92" | 78" | 60" | 4,320 lbs | 1,000 lbs |
| MEC 2558 DF | 31' | 25' | 56" X 100" | 78 1/2" | 64" | 4,550 lbs | 1,250 lbs |
| SM 3184 | 31' | 25' | 74" X 140" | 96" | 84" | 6,900 lbs | 1,500 lbs |
| SJ 6832 E | 38' | 32' | 57" X 80" | 78 1/2" | 68" | 5,480 lbs | 1,000 lbs |
| SM 3884 E | 38' | 32' | 74" X 140" | 103" | 84" | 10,600 lbs | 1,250 lbs |
| SM 3884 XT 4WD | 38' | 32' | 74" X 140" | 103" | 84" | 8,800 lbs | 1,250 lbs |
| SM 4688 XT 4WD | 46' | 40' | 74" X 140" | 113" | 88" | 10,000 lbs | 1,000 lbs |

### ARTICULATED BOOMS
*All Articulated Booms come with rotating platforms, generators and fuel options of gas, propane or diesel.*
*\* Denotes also available electric powered.*

| MODEL | WORK HEIGHT | PLATFORM HEIGHT | PLATFORM SIZE | STOWED HT W/ RAILS | OVERALL WIDTH | MACHINE WEIGHT | LIFT CAPACITY |
|---|---|---|---|---|---|---|---|
| AMZ 40 B* 4W Steer | 40' | 34' | 5' | 6'7" | 6' | 9,900 lbs | 500 lbs |
| AMZ 46 NE* | 46' | 40' | 4' | 6'7" | 4'11" | 13,100 lbs | 500 lbs |
| AMZ 50* 4W Steer | 50' | 44' | 6' | 6'8" | 6' | 14,600 lbs | 500 lbs |
| AMZ 50XT 4WD/Steer | 50' | 44' | 6' | 6'8" | 6'6" | 15,400 lbs | 500 lbs |
| AMZ 51E* | 51' | 45' | 4' | 6'7" | 5'9" | 14,300 lbs | 500 lbs |
| AMZ 68 XT 4WD/Steer | 68' | 62' | 8' | 8'11" | 8' | 26,800 lbs | 500 lbs |
| AMZ 86 XT 4WD/Steer | 86' | 80' | 8' | 9'8" | 8' | 42,800 lbs | 500 lbs |
| AMZ 131 XT 4WD/Steer | 131' | 125' | 8' | 9'10" | 8'6"/12' | 47,700 lbs | 500 lbs |

### STRAIGHT MAST BOOMS
*All Straight Mast Booms come with rotating platforms, generators and fuel options of gas, propane or diesel.*

| MODEL | WORK HEIGHT | PLATFORM HEIGHT | PLATFORM SIZE | STOWED HT W/ RAILS | OVERALL WIDTH | MACHINE WEIGHT | LIFT CAPACITY |
|---|---|---|---|---|---|---|---|
| MZ 48 B 2WD/4WD | 48' | 42' | 8' | 7'7" | 7'11" | 11,500 lbs | 500 lbs |
| MZ 66 B 2WD/4WD | 66' | 60' | 8' | 7'11" | 7'11" | 20,500 lbs | 500 lbs |
| MZ 116 D 4WD/Steer | 116' | 110' | 8' | 8'8" | 8'6"/12' | 40,000 lbs | 500 lbs |
| JLG 120 HX 4WD/Steer | 126' | 120' | 6' | 10'4" | 8'6"/10'10" | 43,500 lbs | 500 lbs |

**Figure 183**   Lift specifications.

LULL ROUGH TERRAIN TELESCOPING BOOM MATERIAL HANDLERS

*All Lull Telescoping Boom Forklifts have full hydraulic controls, four wheel drive, four wheel crab steering, frame leveling, and rear axle stabilization. Truss Boom, Loose Material Bucket, Side Tilt Fork Carriage, 100° Swing Carriage and other Quick Attach Accessories are available.*

| MODEL | MAXIMUM LIFT HEIGHT | MAXIMUM LANDING HEIGHT | MAXIMUM LOAD | MAXIMUM HORIZONTAL REACH @ 24" LOAD CENTER | STOWED HEIGHT | MACHINE WIDTH | MACHINE LENGTH (42" FORKS W/O OUTRIGGERS) | MACHINE WEIGHT (W/O OUTRIGGERS) | AVAILABLE WITH OUTRIGGERS |
|---|---|---|---|---|---|---|---|---|---|
| 6K-42 | 42' | 38' | 6,000 | 25.5' | 95" | 96" | 23'7" | 22,300 | No |
| 644B-42* | 42' | 42' | 6,000 | 32' | 95" | 96" | 23'7" | 22,700 | No |
| 8K-42 | 42' | 38' | 8,000 | 25.5' | 95" | 96" | 23'7" | 23,160 | Yes |
| 844C-42* | 42' | 42' | 8,000 | 32' | 95" | 96" | 23'7" | 22,320 | Yes |
| 1044C-54* | 54' | 54' | 10,000 | 45' | 95" | 100" | 24'10" | 29,200 | Yes |

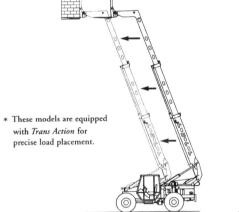

* These models are equipped with *Trans Action* for precise load placement.

**Figure 184**   Lift specifications.

## MVT 1340 L

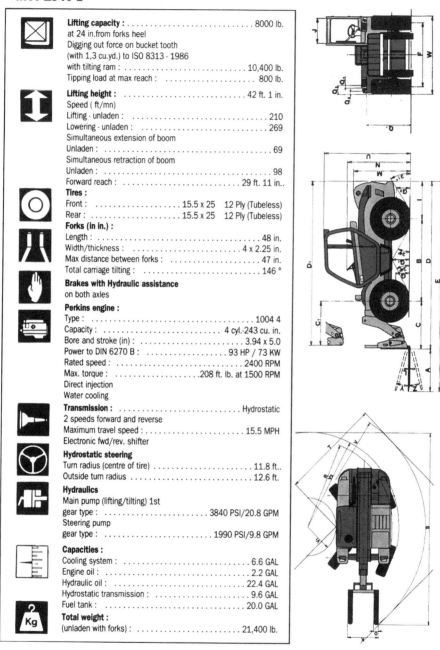

**Lifting capacity :** .......................... 8000 lb.
at 24 in.from forks heel
Digging out force on bucket tooth
(with 1,3 cu.yd.) to ISO 8313 - 1986
with tilting ram : .......................... 10,400 lb.
Tipping load at max reach : .................... 800 lb.

**Lifting height :** .......................... 42 ft. 1 in.
Speed ( ft/mn)
Lifting - unladen : ............................ 210
Lowering - unladen : .......................... 269
Simultaneous extension of boom
Unladen : ..................................... 69
Simultaneous retraction of boom
Unladen : ..................................... 98
Forward reach : .......................... 29 ft. 11 in..

**Tires :**
Front : .................. 15.5 x 25    12 Ply (Tubeless)
Rear : .................. 15.5 x 25    12 Ply (Tubeless)

**Forks (in in.) :**
Length : ..................................... 48 in.
Width/thickness : .................... 4 x 2.25 in.
Max distance between forks : .................... 47 in.
Total carriage tilting : .................... 146 °

**Brakes with Hydraulic assistance**
on both axles

**Perkins engine :**
Type : ..................................... 1004 4
Capacity : .......................... 4 cyl.-243 cu. in.
Bore and stroke (in) : .................... 3.94 x 5.0
Power to DIN 6270 B : .................. 93 HP / 73 KW
Rated speed : .......................... 2400 RPM
Max. torque : .................. 208 ft. lb. at 1500 RPM
Direct injection
Water cooling

**Transmission :** .......................... Hydrostatic
2 speeds forward and reverse
Maximum travel speed : .................... 15.5 MPH
Electronic fwd./rev. shifter

**Hydrostatic steering**
Turn radius (centre of tire) .................... 11.8 ft..
Outside turn radius .......................... 12.6 ft.

**Hydraulics**
Main pump (lifting/tilting) 1st
gear type : .................... 3840 PSI/20.8 GPM
Steering pump
gear type : .................... 1990 PSI/9.8 GPM

**Capacities :**
Cooling system : .......................... 6.6 GAL
Engine oil : .................................. 2.2 GAL
Hydraulic oil : .......................... 22.4 GAL
Hydrostatic transmission : .................... 9.6 GAL
Fuel tank : .................................. 20.0 GAL

**Total weight :**
(unladen with forks) : .................... 21,400 lb.

**Figure 185**    Lift diagram and specifications.

## MVT 1340 L LOAD CAPACITY CHART
### EQUIPPED WITH FORK CARRIAGE ATTACHMENT

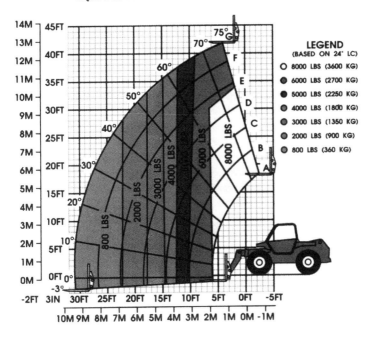

Boom angle and reach indicators on the above chart correspond to the indicators provided on the boom of the truck. Capacities shown in pounds/feet and kilograms/meters are the maximum recommended load limits at the indicated angles and extensions of the boom. Capacity ratings are based on a 48" homogeneous cube and are in accordance with ANSI/ASME B56.6 stability standards. Capacity reductions must be made for extended load centers and when used with various other attachments; contact KD MANITOU INC.

| | INCHES | | INCHES |
|---|---|---|---|
| A | 48.0 | L | 2.25 |
| B | 104.3 | M | 71.2 |
| C | 76.7 | N | 74.8 |
| C¹ | 73.2 | O | 4.0 |
| D | 234.1 | R | 134.4 |
| D¹ | 230.6 | S | 327.2 |
| E | 282.1 | T | 180.6 |
| F | 78 | U | 95 |
| G | 18.1 | V | 206.8 |
| G¹ | 14.6 | V¹ | 34.6 |
| G² | 18.1 | V² | 151 |
| I | 53.1 | Y | 12° |
| J | 28.5 | Z | 134 |
| K | 53 | W | 93.7 |

### STANDARD EQUIPMENT:
- Full Time Power Steering
- Engine Hour Meter
- Alternator
- Adjustable Cushioned Ride Seat
- Warning Lights for High Oil Temperatures
- Air Cleaner Service Indicator
- Hydraulic Oil Filter Restriction Gauge
- Tow Pin
- Horn
- 3 Hydraulic Circuits
- Headlights & Turn Signals
- Neutral Start Switch
- Keyed Ignition Switch
- Instrument Cluster with Engine Oil Pressure, Water Temperature, Ammeter & Fuel Level Gauge
- Transmission and Hydraulic Oil Level Sight Gauges

### OPTIONAL EQUIPMENT:
Tilting Carriage
1.25 cu. yd. Bucket
Enclosed Cab
Jib Extention
Multi-Purpose Bucket (4 in 1)

**Figure 185** Lift diagram and specifications, continued.

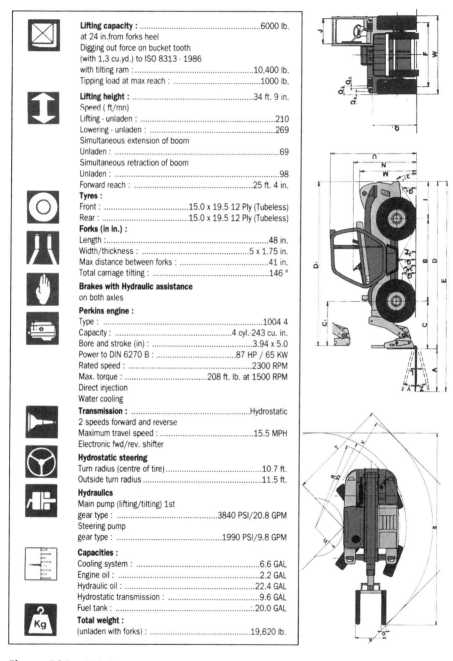

Lifting capacity : ....................................................6000 lb.
at 24 in.from forks heel
Digging out force on bucket tooth
(with 1,3 cu.yd.) to ISO 8313 - 1986
with tilting ram : ..................................................10,400 lb.
Tipping load at max reach : ......................................1000 lb.

Lifting height : .................................................34 ft. 9 in.
Speed ( ft/mn)
Lifting - unladen : .......................................................210
Lowering - unladen : ....................................................269
Simultaneous extension of boom
Unladen : ..................................................................69
Simultaneous retraction of boom
Unladen : ..................................................................98
Forward reach : ...................................................25 ft. 4 in.

Tyres :
Front : ....................................15.0 x 19.5 12 Ply (Tubeless)
Rear : .....................................15.0 x 19.5 12 Ply (Tubeless)

Forks (in in.) :
Length : .................................................................48 in.
Width/thickness : ...............................................5 x 1.75 in.
Max distance between forks : ....................................41 in.
Total carriage tilting : ..............................................146 °

Brakes with Hydraulic assistance
on both axles

Perkins engine :
Type : ....................................................................1004 4
Capacity : ...................................................4 cyl.-243 cu. in.
Bore and stroke (in) : .........................................3.94 x 5.0
Power to DIN 6270 B : ...............................87 HP / 65 KW
Rated speed : .....................................................2300 RPM
Max. torque : ......................208 ft. lb. at 1500 RPM
Direct injection
Water cooling

Transmission : ...................................................Hydrostatic
2 speeds forward and reverse
Maximum travel speed : ......................................15.5 MPH
Electronic fwd/rev. shifter

Hydrostatic steering
Turn radius (centre of tire)........................................10.7 ft.
Outside turn radius ..................................................11.5 ft.

Hydraulics
Main pump (lifting/tilting) 1st
gear type : .................................................3840 PSI/20.8 GPM
Steering pump
gear type : .............................................1990 PSI/9.8 GPM

Capacities :
Cooling system : ....................................................6.6 GAL
Engine oil : .............................................................2.2 GAL
Hydraulic oil : .......................................................22.4 GAL
Hydrostatic transmission : ......................................9.6 GAL
Fuel tank : ...........................................................20.0 GAL

Total weight :
(unladen with forks) : .........................................19,620 lb.

**Figure 186**   Lift diagram and specifications.

## MVT 1130 L LOAD CAPACITY CHART
### EQUIPPED WITH FORK CARRIAGE ATTACHMENT

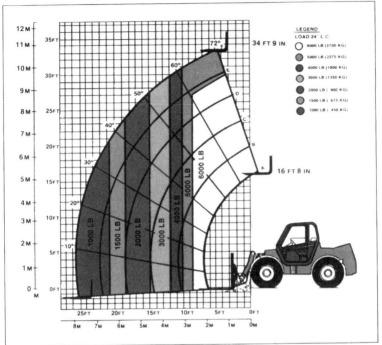

Boom angle and reach indicators on the above chart correspond to the indicators provided on the boom of the truck. Capacities shown in pounds/feet and kilograms/meters are the maximum recommended load limits at the indicated angles and extensions of the boom. Capacity ratings are based on a 48" homogeneous cube and are in accordance with ANSI/ASME B56.6 stability standards. Capacity reductions must be made for extended load centers and when used with various other attachments; contact KD MANITOU INC.

| | INCHES | | INCHES |
|---|---|---|---|
| A | 48.0 | L | 1.75 |
| B | 92.5 | M | 61.5 |
| C | 70.5 | N | 71.8 |
| C¹ | 67.0 | O | 5.0 |
| D | 204.7 | R | 128 |
| D¹ | 201.2 | S | 299 |
| E | 252.7 | T | 165 |
| F | 76.1 | U | 93.5 |
| G | 13.3 | V | 189 |
| G¹ | 17.0 | V¹ | 33.4 |
| G² | 13.3 | V² | 138 |
| I | 41.7 | Y | 12° |
| J | 28.5 | Z | 134 |
| K | 51.0 | W | 91.5 |

### STANDARD EQUIPMENT:

- Full Time Power Steering
- Engine Hour Meter
- Alternator
- Adjustable Cushioned Ride Seat
- Warning Lights for High Oil Temperatures
- Air Cleaner Service Indicator
- Hydraulic Oil Filter Restriction Gauge
- Tow Pin
- Horn
- 3 Hydraulic Circuits
- Headlights & Turn Signals
- Neutral Start Switch
- Keyed Ignition Switch
- Instrument Cluster with Engine Oil Pressure, Water Temperature, Ammeter & Fuel Level Gauge
- Transmission and Hydraulic Oil Level Sight Gauges

### OPTIONAL EQUIPMENT:

Tilting Carriage
1.25 cu. yd. Bucket
Enclosed Cab
Jib Extention
Multi-Purpose Bucket (4 in 1)

**Figure 186**   Lift diagram and specifications, continued.

## "M" SERIES VERTICAL MAST FORKLIFT

**Capacity:** (at 24 in. load center)
M230/M430 ......................................6,000 lb.
M240/M440 ......................................8,000 lb.
M250/M450 ....................................10,000 lb.

**Lift**
Standard Lift Height: ........................ 12'0"
Lifting Speed (ft/mn.):
Empty/Loaded: ..................................... 96/80
Lowering Speed (ft./mn.):
Empty/Loaded: ..................................... 79/81

**Tires**
M230 - Front : ................. 16.9 x 24 10 PR R4
Rear : ......................... 12 x 16.5 10PR
M240 - Front : ...................... 19.5LR x 24
Rear : ......................... 12 x 16.5 10PR
M250 - Front : ........................... 17.5 x 25 SGL
Rear : ......................... 12.5 x 16.5 SGL
4 WD - Rear : ....................14 x 17.5 N.H.S.

**Forks**
Length : ...................................... 48"
Thickness/Width (M230) : ............... 1.75" x 5"
Thickness/Width (M240) : .................... 2" x 6"
Thickness/Width (M250) : ............... 2.25" x 6"

**Brakes:**
Service Brake: ............. Fully Enclosed Wet Disc
Park Brake: ........... Over Center Hand Operated

**Perkins Engine**
Bore and Stroke: .........................3.87" x 5"
Cylinders: ...........................4 cyl. - 236 cu. in.
Rated Speed: ...........................2200 RPM
Horsepower (Gross): .......................80 (54 kw)
Maximum Torque : ....... 195 ft. lb. @ 1200 RPM
Injection: .................................. Direct
Cooling: .................................. Water

**Transmission**
Type: ........................... Full Syncro Four Speed
with Torque Converter and "Soft Shift"
Power Reversing
Maximum Travel Speed: ...........................18 MPH

**Hydraulics**
Main Pump: ...................................... Gear Type
Pressure/Flow: ...........2400 PSI/25.5 gal./min.
Steering Pump: ............................... Gear Type
Pressure: ........................1700 PSI/7 gal./min.

**Capacities:**
Cooling System: ...............................4.2 Gal.
Motor Oil: ...................................2.0 Gal.
Hydraulic Oil: ...............................24.8 Gal.
Transmission Oil: ...............................2.3 Gal.
Fuel Tank: ...................................24.8 Gal.

**Weight with forks:** (Add 400 lb. for 4 WD)
M230 (11'11"): ...............................12,970 lb.
M240 (12'4"): ...............................14,985 lb.
M250 (12'4"): ...............................18,060 lb.

### STANDARD EQUIPMENT
• Full Time Power Steering
• Engine Hour Meter
• Seat Belt
• Keyed Ignition Switch
• Adjustable Seat
• Forward Tilt Cab for Service
• Hydraulic Load Accumulator
• Differential Lock
• Side Shift Mast
• Air Cleaner Service Indicator
• Overhead Guard
• Three Hydraulic Circuits
• Neutral Start Switch
• Cold Weather Start Aid
• Rubber Mounted Operator's Cab
• Hydraulic Oil Level Sight Gauge
• Gauges for Engine Temp. and
  Fuel Level
• Warning Lights for Eng. Oil Press.
  Torque Converter Temp., Alternator
• Horn

### OPTIONAL EQUIPMENT
• Enclosed Cab with Heater/Defrost
• Fourth and Fifth Hyd. Circuits
• Stop, Tail, Turn Lights
• Turbo II Precleaner
• Engine Block Heater
• 45° Mast Tilt
• Anti Vandalism Kit
• Four Wheel Drive

### DIMENSIONS:

|  | M230 M430 | M240 M440 | M250 M450 |
|---|---|---|---|
|  | INCHES | INCHES | INCHES |
| A | 48.0 | 48.0 | 48.0 |
| B | 34.25 | 34.25 | 34.25 |
| C | 81.5 | 81.5 | 81.5 |
| D | 31.5 | 36 | 39.75 |
| E | 147.25 | 150.75 | 155.25 |
| F | 195.25 | 198.75 | 203.25 |
| G¹ | 12 | 12 | 12 |
| G² | 18 | 18 | 18 |
| G³ | 12.5 | 12.5 | 12.5 |
| J | 95 | 95 | 95 |
| K | 20° | 20° | 20° |
| L | 15° | 15° | 15° |
| N | 70.5 | 73.5 | 70.75 |
| O | 87.5 | 94 | 89.5 |
| P | 40.5 | 40.5 | 40.5 |
| R | 64.0 | 64.0 | 64.0 |
| S | 160 | 160 | 160 |
| T | 125 | 129 | 134 |
| U | 48 | 48 | 48 |
| W | 5.0 | 6.0 | 6.0 |
| X | 1.75 | 2.0 | 2.25 |
| Y | 170 | 173 | 178 |

**Figure 187** Lift diagram and specifications.

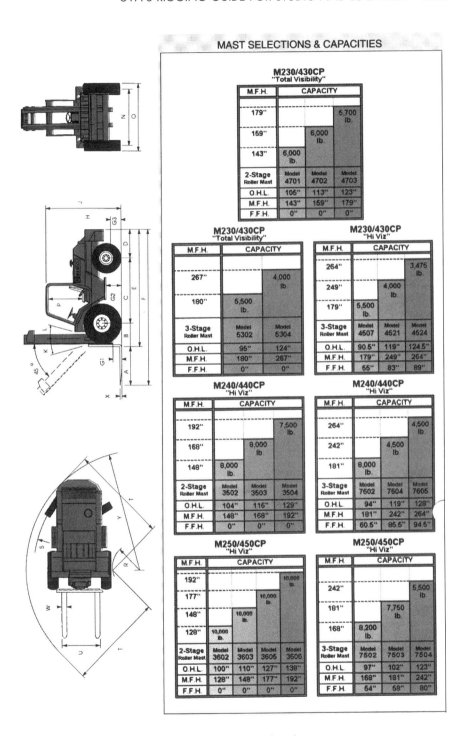

## MAST SELECTIONS & CAPACITIES

### M230/430CP
"Total Visibility"

| M.F.H. | CAPACITY | | |
|---|---|---|---|
| 179" | | | 5,700 lb. |
| 159" | | 6,000 lb. | |
| 143" | 6,000 lb. | | |
| 2-Stage Roller Mast | Model 4701 | Model 4702 | Model 4703 |
| O.H.L. | 105" | 113" | 123" |
| M.F.H. | 143" | 159" | 179" |
| F.F.H. | 0" | 0" | 0" |

### M230/430CP
"Total Visibility"

| M.F.H. | CAPACITY | |
|---|---|---|
| 267" | | 4,000 lb. |
| 180" | 5,500 lb. | |
| 3-Stage Roller Mast | Model 5302 | Model 5304 |
| O.H.L. | 95" | 124" |
| M.F.H. | 180" | 267" |
| F.F.H. | 0" | 0" |

### M230/430CP
"Hi Viz"

| M.F.H. | CAPACITY | | |
|---|---|---|---|
| 264" | | | 3,475 lb. |
| 249" | | 4,000 lb. | |
| 179" | 5,500 lb. | | |
| 3-Stage Roller Mast | Model 4507 | Model 4621 | Model 4624 |
| O.H.L. | 90.5" | 119" | 124.5" |
| M.F.H. | 179" | 249" | 264" |
| F.F.H. | 55" | 83" | 89" |

### M240/440CP
"Hi Viz"

| M.F.H. | CAPACITY | | |
|---|---|---|---|
| 192" | | | 7,500 lb. |
| 168" | | 8,000 lb | |
| 148" | 8,000 lb. | | |
| 2-Stage Roller Mast | Model 3502 | Model 3503 | Model 3504 |
| O.H.L. | 104" | 116" | 129" |
| M.F.H. | 148" | 168" | 192" |
| F.F.H. | 0" | 0" | 0" |

### M240/440CP
"Hi Viz"

| M.F.H. | CAPACITY | | |
|---|---|---|---|
| 264" | | | 4,500 lb. |
| 242" | | 4,500 lb. | |
| 181" | 8,000 lb. | | |
| 3-Stage Roller Mast | Model 7602 | Model 7604 | Model 7605 |
| O.H.L. | 94" | 119" | 128" |
| M.F.H. | 181" | 242" | 264" |
| F.F.H. | 60.5" | 85.5" | 94.5" |

### M250/450CP
"Hi Viz"

| M.F.H. | CAPACITY | | | |
|---|---|---|---|---|
| 192" | | | | 10,000 lb. |
| 177" | | | 10,000 lb. | |
| 148" | | 10,000 lb. | | |
| 128" | 10,000 lb. | | | |
| 2-Stage Roller Mast | Model 3602 | Model 3603 | Model 3605 | Model 3606 |
| O.H.L. | 100" | 110" | 127" | 138" |
| M.F.H. | 128" | 148" | 177" | 192" |
| F.F.H. | 0" | 0" | 0" | 0" |

### M250/450CP
"Hi Viz"

| M.F.H. | CAPACITY | | |
|---|---|---|---|
| 242" | | | 5,500 lb. |
| 181" | | 7,750 lb. | |
| 168" | 8,200 lb. | | |
| 3-Stage Roller Mast | Model 7502 | Model 7503 | Model 7504 |
| O.H.L. | 97" | 102" | 123" |
| M.F.H. | 168" | 181" | 242" |
| F.F.H. | 64" | 69" | 80" |

**Figure 187** Lift diagram and specifications, continued.

### JLG Industries, Inc.
JLG lifts and booms can be ordered through NES Equipment Services.

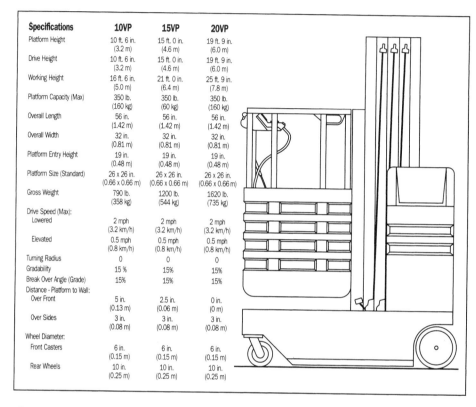

| Specifications | 10VP | 15VP | 20VP |
|---|---|---|---|
| Platform Height | 10 ft. 6 in. (3.2 m) | 15 ft. 0 in. (4.6 m) | 19 ft. 9 in. (6.0 m) |
| Drive Height | 10 ft. 6 in. (3.2 m) | 15 ft. 0 in. (4.6 m) | 19 ft. 9 in. (6.0 m) |
| Working Height | 16 ft. 6 in. (5.0 m) | 21 ft. 0 in. (6.4 m) | 25 ft. 9 in. (7.8 m) |
| Platform Capacity (Max) | 350 lb. (160 kg) | 350 lb. (60 kg) | 350 lb. (160 kg) |
| Overall Length | 56 in. (1.42 m) | 56 in. (1.42 m) | 56 in. (1.42 m) |
| Overall Width | 32 in. (0.81 m) | 32 in. (0.81 m) | 32 in. (0.81 m) |
| Platform Entry Height | 19 in. (0.48 m) | 19 in. (0.48 m) | 19 in. (0.48 m) |
| Platform Size (Standard) | 26 x 26 in. (0.66 x 0.66 m) | 26 x 26 in. (0.66 x 0.66 m) | 26 x 26 in. (0.66 x 0.66 m) |
| Gross Weight | 790 lb. (358 kg) | 1200 lb. (544 kg) | 1620 lb. (735 kg) |
| Drive Speed (Max): | | | |
| Lowered | 2 mph (3.2 km/h) | 2 mph (3.2 km/h) | 2 mph (3.2 km/h) |
| Elevated | 0.5 mph (0.8 km/h) | 0.5 mph (0.8 km/h) | 0.5 mph (0.8 km/h) |
| Turning Radius | 0 | 0 | 0 |
| Gradability | 15 % | 15% | 15% |
| Break Over Angle (Grade) | 15% | 15% | 15% |
| Distance - Platform to Wall: | | | |
| Over Front | 5 in. (0.13 m) | 2.5 in. (0.06 m) | 0 in. (0 m) |
| Over Sides | 3 in. (0.08 m) | 3 in. (0.08 m) | 3 in. (0.08 m) |
| Wheel Diameter: | | | |
| Front Casters | 6 in. (0.15 m) | 6 in. (0.15 m) | 6 in. (0.15 m) |
| Rear Wheels | 10 in. (0.25 m) | 10 in. (0.25 m) | 10 in. (0.25 m) |

**Figure 188**   Lift specifications.

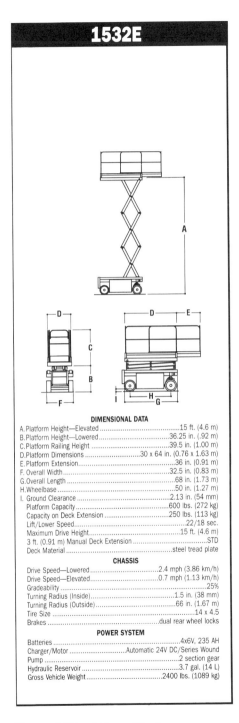

**1532E**

**DIMENSIONAL DATA**

A. Platform Height—Elevated .........................................15 ft. (4.6 m)
B. Platform Height—Lowered ....................................36.25 in. (.92 m)
C. Platform Railing Height .....................................39.5 in. (1.00 m)
D. Platform Dimensions ...........................30 x 64 in. (0.76 x 1.63 m)
E. Platform Extension..................................................36 in. (0.91 m)
F. Overall Width.....................................................32.5 in. (0.83 m)
G. Overall Length ........................................................68 in. (1.73 m)
H. Wheelbase.............................................................50 in. (1.27 m)
I. Ground Clearance ...............................................2.13 in. (54 mm)
Platform Capacity .................................................600 lbs. (272 kg)
Capacity on Deck Extension .................................250 lbs. (113 kg)
Lift/Lower Speed.......................................................22/18 sec.
Maximum Drive Height..........................................15 ft. (4.6 m)
3 ft. (0.91 m) Manual Deck Extension .......................................STD
Deck Material .........................................................steel tread plate

**CHASSIS**

Drive Speed—Lowered .....................................2.4 mph (3.86 km/h)
Drive Speed—Elevated..................................0.7 mph (1.13 km/h)
Gradeability .................................................................................25%
Turning Radius (Inside)...........................................1.5 in. (38 mm)
Turning Radius (Outside) .........................................66 in. (1.67 m)
Tire Size ......................................................................14 x 4.5
Brakes .......................................................dual rear wheel locks

**POWER SYSTEM**

Batteries .............................................................4x6V, 235 AH
Charger/Motor ..............................Automatic 24V DC/Series Wound
Pump .................................................................2 section gear
Hydraulic Reservoir ....................................................3.7 gal. (14 L)
Gross Vehicle Weight........................................2400 lbs. (1089 kg)

**Figure 189**  Lift specifications.

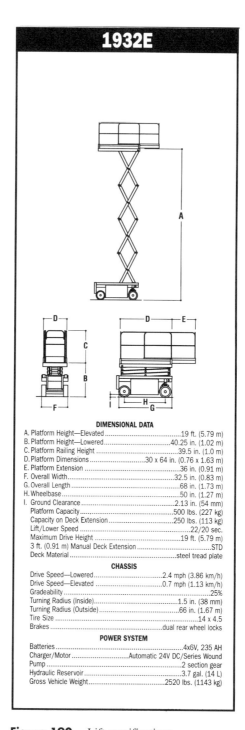

**DIMENSIONAL DATA**

A. Platform Height—Elevated .........................................19 ft. (5.79 m)
B. Platform Height—Lowered.................................40.25 in. (1.02 m)
C. Platform Railing Height .........................................39.5 in. (1.0 m)
D. Platform Dimensions ............................30 x 64 in. (0.76 x 1.63 m)
E. Platform Extension .................................................36 in. (0.91 m)
F. Overall Width.........................................................32.5 in. (0.83 m)
G. Overall Length .........................................................68 in. (1.73 m)
H. Wheelbase...............................................................50 in. (1.27 m)
I. Ground Clearance .................................................2.13 in. (54 mm)
Platform Capacity ...............................................500 lbs. (227 kg)
Capacity on Deck Extension .................................250 lbs. (113 kg)
Lift/Lower Speed ...........................................................22/20 sec.
Maximum Drive Height ..............................................19 ft. (5.79 m)
3 ft. (0.91 m) Manual Deck Extension .......................................STD
Deck Material .........................................................steel tread plate

**CHASSIS**

Drive Speed—Lowered....................................2.4 mph (3.86 km/h)
Drive Speed—Elevated ..................................0.7 mph (1.13 km/h)
Gradeability.........................................................................25%
Turning Radius (Inside)................................................1.5 in. (38 mm)
Turning Radius (Outside).........................................66 in. (1.67 m)
Tire Size ..........................................................................14 x 4.5
Brakes .........................................................dual rear wheel locks

**POWER SYSTEM**

Batteries.................................................................4x6V, 235 AH
Charger/Motor .............................Automatic 24V DC/Series Wound
Pump .......................................................................2 section gear
Hydraulic Reservoir .................................................3.7 gal. (14 L)
Gross Vehicle Weight........................................2520 lbs. (1143 kg)

**Figure 190**   Lift specifications.

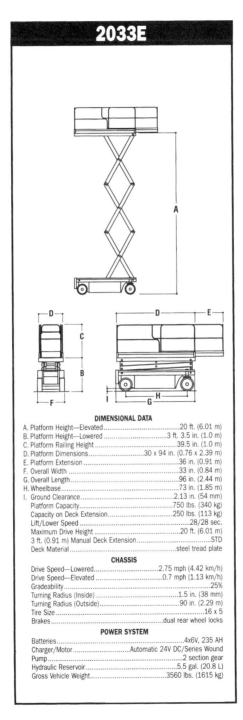

## 2033E

### DIMENSIONAL DATA

A. Platform Height—Elevated ....................................... 20 ft. (6.01 m)
B. Platform Height—Lowered ................................. 3 ft. 3.5 in. (1.0 m)
C. Platform Railing Height ........................................... 39.5 in. (1.0 m)
D. Platform Dimensions ........................... 30 x 94 in. (0.76 x 2.39 m)
E. Platform Extension ................................................ 36 in. (0.91 m)
F. Overall Width ....................................................... 33 in. (0.84 m)
G. Overall Length ....................................................... 96 in. (2.44 m)
H. Wheelbase ............................................................ 73 in. (1.85 m)
I. Ground Clearance .................................................. 2.13 in. (54 mm)
Platform Capacity ................................................. 750 lbs. (340 kg)
Capacity on Deck Extension .................................. 250 lbs. (113 kg)
Lift/Lower Speed .......................................................... 28/28 sec.
Maximum Drive Height .......................................... 20 ft. (6.01 m)
3 ft. (0.91 m) Manual Deck Extension ..................................... STD
Deck Material ...................................................... steel tread plate

### CHASSIS

Drive Speed—Lowered ................................. 2.75 mph (4.42 km/h)
Drive Speed—Elevated ................................ 0.7 mph (1.13 km/h)
Gradeability ................................................................................ 25%
Turning Radius (Inside) ............................................ 1.5 in. (38 mm)
Turning Radius (Outside) ......................................... 90 in. (2.29 m)
Tire Size ................................................................................ 16 x 5
Brakes .......................................................... dual rear wheel locks

### POWER SYSTEM

Batteries ............................................................... 4x6V, 235 AH
Charger/Motor .............................. Automatic 24V DC/Series Wound
Pump ................................................................... 2 section gear
Hydraulic Reservoir ............................................... 5.5 gal. (20.8 L)
Gross Vehicle Weight ...................................... 3560 lbs. (1615 kg)

**Figure 191**   Lift specifications.

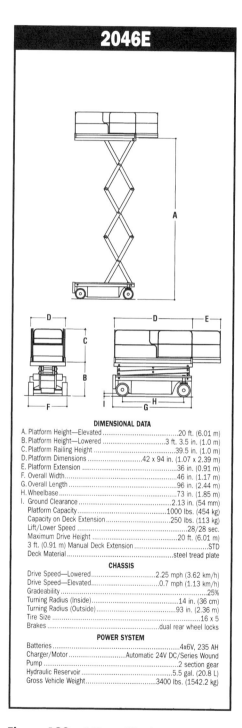

## 2046E

### DIMENSIONAL DATA

A. Platform Height—Elevated .......................................20 ft. (6.01 m)
B. Platform Height—Lowered ...............................3 ft. 3.5 in. (1.0 m)
C. Platform Railing Height ..........................................39.5 in. (1.0 m)
D. Platform Dimensions ...........................42 x 94 in. (1.07 x 2.39 m)
E. Platform Extension ...............................................36 in. (0.91 m)
F. Overall Width........................................................46 in. (1.17 m)
G. Overall Length .......................................................96 in. (2.44 m)
H. Wheelbase ............................................................73 in. (1.85 m)
I. Ground Clearance .............................................2.13 in. (54 mm)
Platform Capacity..............................................1000 lbs. (454 kg)
Capacity on Deck Extension ...............................250 lbs. (113 kg)
Lift/Lower Speed ...................................................28/28 sec.
Maximum Drive Height ...........................................20 ft. (6.01 m)
3 ft. (0.91 m) Manual Deck Extension .......................................STD
Deck Material ....................................................steel tread plate

### CHASSIS

Drive Speed—Lowered...............................2.25 mph (3.62 km/h)
Drive Speed—Elevated.................................0.7 mph (1.13 km/h)
Gradeability .........................................................................25%
Turning Radius (Inside).............................................14 in. (36 cm)
Turning Radius (Outside).........................................93 in. (2.36 m)
Tire Size ...............................................................................16 x 5
Brakes ..............................................dual rear wheel locks

### POWER SYSTEM

Batteries.................................................................4x6V, 235 AH
Charger/Motor ..............................Automatic 24V DC/Series Wound
Pump ..................................................................2 section gear
Hydraulic Reservoir ................................................5.5 gal. (20.8 L)
Gross Vehicle Weight....................................3400 lbs. (1542.2 kg)

**Figure 192**   Lift specifications.

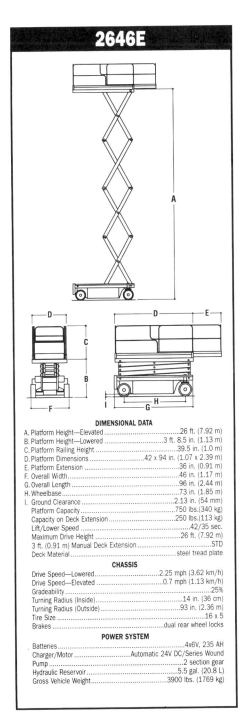

### 2646E

**DIMENSIONAL DATA**

A. Platform Height—Elevated ........................................26 ft. (7.92 m)
B. Platform Height—Lowered ...............................3 ft. 8.5 in. (1.13 m)
C. Platform Railing Height ...........................................39.5 in. (1.0 m)
D. Platform Dimensions ...........................42 x 94 in. (1.07 x 2.39 m)
E. Platform Extension ................................................36 in. (0.91 m)
F. Overall Width.......................................................46 in. (1.17 m)
G. Overall Length .....................................................96 in. (2.44 m)
H. Wheelbase ..........................................................73 in. (1.85 m)
I. Ground Clearance ................................................2.13 in. (54 mm)
    Platform Capacity ..............................................750 lbs.(340 kg)
    Capacity on Deck Extension ..................................250 lbs.(113 kg)
    Lift/Lower Speed .....................................................42/35 sec.
    Maximum Drive Height ..........................................26 ft. (7.92 m)
    3 ft. (0.91 m) Manual Deck Extension ...................................STD
    Deck Material .....................................................steel tread plate

**CHASSIS**

Drive Speed—Lowered...................................2.25 mph (3.62 km/h)
Drive Speed—Elevated ..................................0.7 mph (1.13 km/h)
Gradeability ................................................................................25%
Turning Radius (Inside)............................................14 in. (36 cm)
Turning Radius (Outside)..........................................93 in. (2.36 m)
Tire Size ........................................................................16 x 5
Brakes .....................................................dual rear wheel locks

**POWER SYSTEM**

Batteries...........................................................4x6V, 235 AH
Charger/Motor ............................Automatic 24V DC/Series Wound
Pump .........................................................2 section gear
Hydraulic Reservoir ...............................................5.5 gal. (20.8 L)
Gross Vehicle Weight.........................................3900 lbs. (1769 kg)

**Figure 193**   Lift specifications.

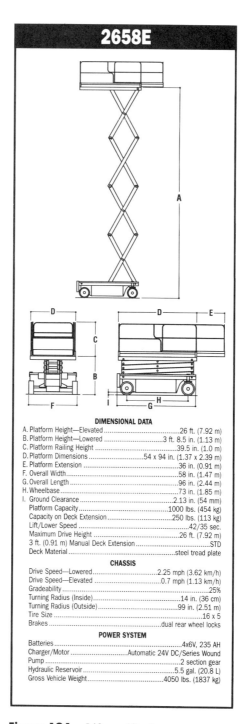

## 2658E

**DIMENSIONAL DATA**

A. Platform Height—Elevated ........................................26 ft. (7.92 m)
B. Platform Height—Lowered ..............................3 ft. 8.5 in. (1.13 m)
C. Platform Railing Height ..........................................39.5 in. (1.0 m)
D. Platform Dimensions ..........................54 x 94 in. (1.37 x 2.39 m)
E. Platform Extension ................................................36 in. (0.91 m)
F. Overall Width...........................................................58 in. (1.47 m)
G. Overall Length ......................................................96 in. (2.44 m)
H. Wheelbase ...............................................................73 in. (1.85 m)
I. Ground Clearance ................................................2.13 in. (54 mm)
   Platform Capacity..............................................1000 lbs. (454 kg)
   Capacity on Deck Extension.................................250 lbs. (113 kg)
   Lift/Lower Speed .......................................................42/35 sec.
   Maximum Drive Height .........................................26 ft. (7.92 m)
   3 ft. (0.91 m) Manual Deck Extension ......................................STD
   Deck Material ....................................................steel tread plate

**CHASSIS**

   Drive Speed—Lowered..................................2.25 mph (3.62 km/h)
   Drive Speed—Elevated ...................................0.7 mph (1.13 km/h)
   Gradeability ....................................................................................25%
   Turning Radius (Inside)..................................................14 in. (36 cm)
   Turning Radius (Outside)..........................................99 in. (2.51 m)
   Tire Size ........................................................................16 x 5
   Brakes ..........................................................dual rear wheel locks

**POWER SYSTEM**

   Batteries.................................................................4x6V, 235 AH
   Charger/Motor ...........................Automatic 24V DC/Series Wound
   Pump .......................................................................2 section gear
   Hydraulic Reservoir .................................................5.5 gal. (20.8 L)
   Gross Vehicle Weight.......................................4050 lbs. (1837 kg)

**Figure 194**   Lift specifications.

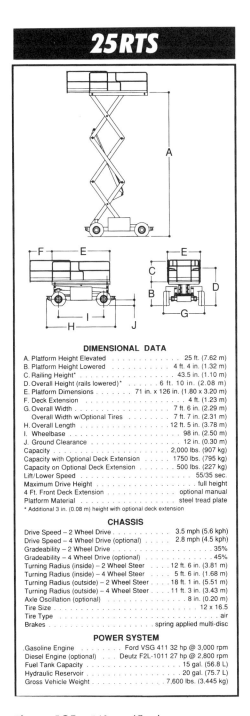

## 25RTS

### DIMENSIONAL DATA

A. Platform Height Elevated . . . . . . . . . . . . . 25 ft. (7.62 m)
B. Platform Height Lowered . . . . . . . . . . . 4 ft. 4 in. (1.32 m)
C. Railing Height* . . . . . . . . . . . . . . . . . 43.5 in. (1.10 m)
D. Overall Height (rails lowered)* . . . . . . 6 ft. 10 in. (2.08 m)
E. Platform Dimensions . . . . . . . 71 in. x 126 in. (1.80 x 3.20 m)
F. Deck Extension . . . . . . . . . . . . . . . . . 4 ft. (1.23 m)
G. Overall Width . . . . . . . . . . . . . . . . . 7 ft. 6 in. (2.29 m)
   Overall Width w/Optional Tires . . . . . . . 7 ft. 7 in. (2.31 m)
H. Overall Length . . . . . . . . . . . . . . . . 12 ft. 5 in. (3.78 m)
I. Wheelbase . . . . . . . . . . . . . . . . . . . 98 in. (2.50 m)
J. Ground Clearance . . . . . . . . . . . . . . . . 12 in. (0.30 m)
Capacity . . . . . . . . . . . . . . . . . . . . . 2,000 lbs. (907 kg)
Capacity with Optional Deck Extension . . . . . 1750 lbs. (795 kg)
Capacity on Optional Deck Extension . . . . . . . 500 lbs. (227 kg)
Lift/Lower Speed . . . . . . . . . . . . . . . . . . . . 55/35 sec.
Maximum Drive Height . . . . . . . . . . . . . . . . . . full height
4 Ft. Front Deck Extension . . . . . . . . . . . . . optional manual
Platform Material . . . . . . . . . . . . . . . . . steel tread plate
* Additional 3 in. (0.08 m) height with optional deck extension

### CHASSIS

Drive Speed – 2 Wheel Drive . . . . . . . . . . . 3.5 mph (5.6 kph)
Drive Speed – 4 Wheel Drive (optional) . . . . . 2.8 mph (4.5 kph)
Gradeability – 2 Wheel Drive . . . . . . . . . . . . . . . . . . 35%
Gradeability – 4 Wheel Drive (optional) . . . . . . . . . . . . . 45%
Turning Radius (inside) – 2 Wheel Steer . . . . 12 ft. 6 in. (3.81 m)
Turning Radius (inside) – 4 Wheel Steer . . . . 5 ft. 6 in. (1.68 m)
Turning Radius (outside) – 2 Wheel Steer . . . . 18 ft. 1 in. (5.51 m)
Turning Radius (outside) – 4 Wheel Steer . . . . 11 ft. 3 in. (3.43 m)
Axle Oscillation (optional) . . . . . . . . . . . . . 8 in. (0.20 m)
Tire Size . . . . . . . . . . . . . . . . . . . . . . . . . 12 x 16.5
Tire Type . . . . . . . . . . . . . . . . . . . . . . . . . . . . air
Brakes . . . . . . . . . . . . . . . . . . spring applied multi-disc

### POWER SYSTEM

.Gasoline Engine . . . . . . . . Ford VSG 411 32 hp @ 3,000 rpm
Diesel Engine (optional) . . . Deutz F2L-1011 27 hp @ 2,800 rpm
Fuel Tank Capacity . . . . . . . . . . . . . . . . . 15 gal. (56.8 L)
Hydraulic Reservoir . . . . . . . . . . . . . . . . . 20 gal. (75.7 L)
Gross Vehicle Weight . . . . . . . . . . . . . 7,600 lbs. (3.445 kg)

**Figure 195**   Lift specifications.

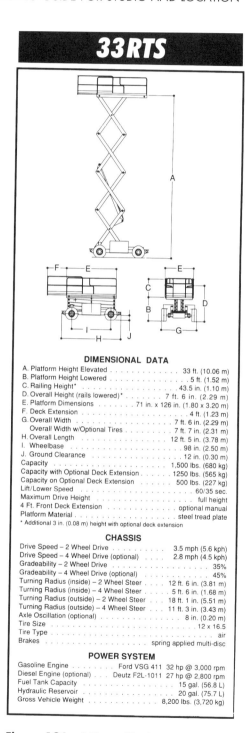

## 33RTS

### DIMENSIONAL DATA

A. Platform Height Elevated . . . . . . . . . . . . . 33 ft. (10.06 m)
B. Platform Height Lowered . . . . . . . . . . . . . . 5 ft. (1.52 m)
C. Railing Height* . . . . . . . . . . . . . . . . . . 43.5 in. (1.10 m)
D. Overall Height (rails lowered)* . . . . . . . 7 ft. 6 in. (2.29 m)
E. Platform Dimensions . . . . . . . 71 in. x 126 in. (1.80 x 3.20 m)
F. Deck Extension . . . . . . . . . . . . . . . . . . 4 ft. (1.23 m)
G. Overall Width . . . . . . . . . . . . . . . . . 7 ft. 6 in. (2.29 m)
   Overall Width w/Optional Tires . . . . . . . . 7 ft. 7 in. (2.31 m)
H. Overall Length . . . . . . . . . . . . . . . 12 ft. 5 in. (3.78 m)
I. Wheelbase . . . . . . . . . . . . . . . . . . . . 98 in. (2.50 m)
J. Ground Clearance . . . . . . . . . . . . . . . 12 in. (0.30 m)
Capacity . . . . . . . . . . . . . . . . . . . . 1,500 lbs. (680 kg)
Capacity with Optional Deck Extension . . . . . . 1250 lbs. (565 kg)
Capacity on Optional Deck Extension . . . . . . . 500 lbs. (227 kg)
Lift/Lower Speed . . . . . . . . . . . . . . . . . . . . 60/35 sec.
Maximum Drive Height . . . . . . . . . . . . . . . . . . full height
4 Ft. Front Deck Extension . . . . . . . . . . . . . optional manual
Platform Material . . . . . . . . . . . . . . . . . . steel tread plate
* Additional 3 in. (0.08 m) height with optional deck extension

### CHASSIS

Drive Speed – 2 Wheel Drive . . . . . . . . . .   3.5 mph (5.6 kph)
Drive Speed – 4 Wheel Drive (optional) . . . .   2.8 mph (4.5 kph)
Gradeability – 2 Wheel Drive . . . . . . . . . . . . . . . . . . 35%
Gradeability – 4 Wheel Drive (optional) . . . . . . . . . . . . 45%
Turning Radius (inside) – 2 Wheel Steer . . . . 12 ft. 6 in. (3.81 m)
Turning Radius (inside) – 4 Wheel Steer . . . . . 5 ft. 6 in. (1.68 m)
Turning Radius (outside) – 2 Wheel Steer . . . . 18 ft. 1 in. (5.51 m)
Turning Radius (outside) – 4 Wheel Steer . . . . 11 ft. 3 in. (3.43 m)
Axle Oscillation (optional) . . . . . . . . . . . . . . 8 in. (0.20 m)
Tire Size . . . . . . . . . . . . . . . . . . . . . . . . . 12 x 16.5
Tire Type . . . . . . . . . . . . . . . . . . . . . . . . . . . . air
Brakes . . . . . . . . . . . . . . . . . . spring applied multi-disc

### POWER SYSTEM

Gasoline Engine . . . . . . . . Ford VSG 411  32 hp @ 3,000 rpm
Diesel Engine (optional) . . . Deutz F2L-1011  27 hp @ 2,800 rpm
Fuel Tank Capacity . . . . . . . . . . . . . . . . . 15 gal. (56.8 L)
Hydraulic Reservoir . . . . . . . . . . . . . . . . 20 gal. (75.7 L)
Gross Vehicle Weight . . . . . . . . . . . . . 8,200 lbs. (3,720 kg)

**Figure 196**   Lift specifications.

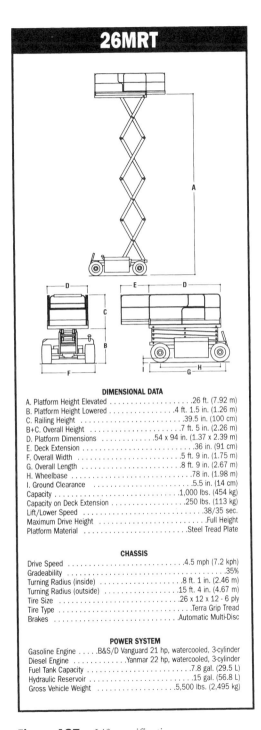

## 26MRT

### DIMENSIONAL DATA

A. Platform Height Elevated . . . . . . . . . . . . . . . . . . .26 ft. (7.92 m)
B. Platform Height Lowered . . . . . . . . . . . . . . .4 ft. 1.5 in. (1.26 m)
C. Railing Height . . . . . . . . . . . . . . . . . . . . . . . .39.5 in. (100 cm)
B+C. Overall Height . . . . . . . . . . . . . . . . . . . . .7 ft. 5 in. (2.26 m)
D. Platform Dimensions . . . . . . . . . . . .54 x 94 in. (1.37 x 2.39 m)
E. Deck Extension . . . . . . . . . . . . . . . . . . . . . . . . .36 in. (91 cm)
F. Overall Width . . . . . . . . . . . . . . . . . . . . . .5 ft. 9 in. (1.75 m)
G. Overall Length . . . . . . . . . . . . . . . . . . . . . .8 ft. 9 in. (2.67 m)
H. Wheelbase . . . . . . . . . . . . . . . . . . . . . . . . . . .78 in. (1.98 m)
I. Ground Clearance . . . . . . . . . . . . . . . . . . . . . . .5.5 in. (14 cm)
Capacity . . . . . . . . . . . . . . . . . . . . . . . . . . . .1,000 lbs. (454 kg)
Capacity on Deck Extension . . . . . . . . . . . . . . . . .250 lbs. (113 kg)
Lift/Lower Speed . . . . . . . . . . . . . . . . . . . . . . . . . . .38/35 sec.
Maximum Drive Height . . . . . . . . . . . . . . . . . . . . . . . .Full Height
Platform Material . . . . . . . . . . . . . . . . . . . . . . .Steel Tread Plate

### CHASSIS

Drive Speed . . . . . . . . . . . . . . . . . . . . . . . . . . .4.5 mph (7.2 kph)
Gradeability . . . . . . . . . . . . . . . . . . . . . . . . . . . . . . . . . . . . .35%
Turning Radius (inside) . . . . . . . . . . . . . . . . . . .8 ft. 1 in. (2.46 m)
Turning Radius (outside) . . . . . . . . . . . . . . . . .15 ft. 4 in. (4.67 m)
Tire Size . . . . . . . . . . . . . . . . . . . . . . . . .26 x 12 x 12 - 6 ply
Tire Type . . . . . . . . . . . . . . . . . . . . . . . . . . . . . .Terra Grip Tread
Brakes . . . . . . . . . . . . . . . . . . . . . . . . . . . .Automatic Multi-Disc

### POWER SYSTEM

Gasoline Engine . . . . .B&S/D Vanguard 21 hp, watercooled, 3-cylinder
Diesel Engine . . . . . . . . . . . .Yanmar 22 hp, watercooled, 3-cylinder
Fuel Tank Capacity . . . . . . . . . . . . . . . . . . . . . . .7.8 gal. (29.5 L)
Hydraulic Reservoir . . . . . . . . . . . . . . . . . . . . . . . .15 gal. (56.8 L)
Gross Vehicle Weight . . . . . . . . . . . . . . . . . .5,500 lbs. (2,495 kg)

**Figure 197**   Lift specifications.

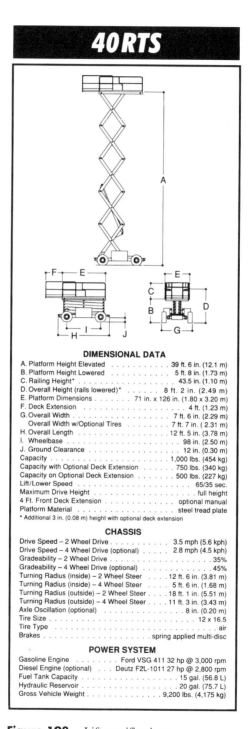

**DIMENSIONAL DATA**

A. Platform Height Elevated . . . . . . . . . . . 39 ft. 6 in. (12.1 m)
B. Platform Height Lowered . . . . . . . . . . . 5 ft. 8 in. (1.73 m)
C. Railing Height* . . . . . . . . . . . . . . . . . . 43.5 in. (1.10 m)
D. Overall Height (rails lowered)* . . . . . . 8 ft. 2 in. (2.49 m)
E. Platform Dimensions . . . . . . 71 in. x 126 in. (1.80 x 3.20 m)
F. Deck Extension . . . . . . . . . . . . . . . . . . . 4 ft. (1.23 m)
G. Overall Width . . . . . . . . . . . . . . . . . . 7 ft. 6 in. (2.29 m)
　　Overall Width w/Optional Tires . . . . . . . 7 ft. 7 in. ( 2.31 m)
H. Overall Length . . . . . . . . . . . . . . . . 12 ft. 5 in. (3.78 m)
I. Wheelbase . . . . . . . . . . . . . . . . . . . . 98 in. (2.50 m)
J. Ground Clearance . . . . . . . . . . . . . . . 12 in. (0.30 m)
Capacity . . . . . . . . . . . . . . . . . . . . . 1,000 lbs. (454 kg)
Capacity with Optional Deck Extension . . . . . . 750 lbs. (340 kg)
Capacity on Optional Deck Extension . . . . . . . 500 lbs. (227 kg)
Lift/Lower Speed . . . . . . . . . . . . . . . . . . . 65/35 sec.
Maximum Drive Height . . . . . . . . . . . . . . . . . full height
4 Ft. Front Deck Extension . . . . . . . . . . . . optional manual
Platform Material . . . . . . . . . . . . . . . . . steel tread plate
* Additional 3 in. (0.08 m) height with optional deck extension

**CHASSIS**

Drive Speed – 2 Wheel Drive . . . . . . . . . . . 3.5 mph (5.6 kph)
Drive Speed – 4 Wheel Drive (optional) . . . . . 2.8 mph (4.5 kph)
Gradeability – 2 Wheel Drive . . . . . . . . . . . . . . . . . . . 35%
Gradeability – 4 Wheel Drive (optional) . . . . . . . . . . . . . 45%
Turning Radius (inside) – 2 Wheel Steer . . . . 12 ft. 6 in. (3.81 m)
Turning Radius (inside) – 4 Wheel Steer . . . . 5 ft. 6 in. (1.68 m)
Turning Radius (outside) – 2 Wheel Steer . . . . 18 ft. 1 in. (5.51 m)
Turning Radius (outside) – 4 Wheel Steer . . . . 11 ft. 3 in. (3.43 m)
Axle Oscillation (optional) . . . . . . . . . . . . . . 8 in. (0.20 m)
Tire Size . . . . . . . . . . . . . . . . . . . . . . . . . 12 x 16.5
Tire Type . . . . . . . . . . . . . . . . . . . . . . . . . . . . . air
Brakes . . . . . . . . . . . . . . . . . . . . spring applied multi-disc

**POWER SYSTEM**

Gasoline Engine . . . . . . . . Ford VSG 411 32 hp @ 3,000 rpm
Diesel Engine (optional) . . . Deutz F2L-1011 27 hp @ 2,800 rpm
Fuel Tank Capacity . . . . . . . . . . . . . . . . . 15 gal. (56.8 L)
Hydraulic Reservoir . . . . . . . . . . . . . . . . 20 gal. (75.7 L)
Gross Vehicle Weight . . . . . . . . . . . . . 9,200 lbs. (4,175 kg)

**Figure 198** Lift specifications.

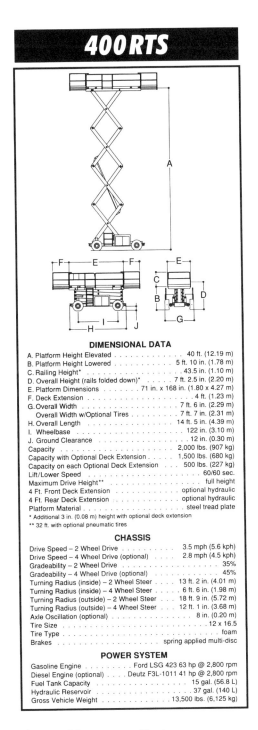

## 400 RTS

### DIMENSIONAL DATA

A. Platform Height Elevated . . . . . . . . . . . . . 40 ft. (12.19 m)
B. Platform Height Lowered . . . . . . . . . . 5 ft. 10 in. (1.78 m)
C. Railing Height* . . . . . . . . . . . . . . . . . . 43.5 in. (1.10 m)
D. Overall Height (rails folded down)* . . . . . 7 ft. 2.5 in. (2.20 m)
E. Platform Dimensions . . . . . . . 71 in. x 168 in. (1.80 x 4.27 m)
F. Deck Extension . . . . . . . . . . . . . . . . . . . 4 ft. (1.23 m)
G. Overall Width . . . . . . . . . . . . . . . . . 7 ft. 6 in. (2.29 m)
  Overall Width w/Optional Tires . . . . . . . . 7 ft. 7 in. (2.31 m)
H. Overall Length . . . . . . . . . . . . . . . 14 ft. 5 in. (4.39 m)
I. Wheelbase . . . . . . . . . . . . . . . . . . . 122 in. (3.10 m)
J. Ground Clearance . . . . . . . . . . . . . . . . 12 in. (0.30 m)
Capacity . . . . . . . . . . . . . . . . . . . . 2,000 lbs. (907 kg)
Capacity with Optional Deck Extension . . . . . 1,500 lbs. (680 kg)
Capacity on each Optional Deck Extension . . . 500 lbs. (227 kg)
Lift/Lower Speed . . . . . . . . . . . . . . . . . . 60/60 sec.
Maximum Drive Height** . . . . . . . . . . . . . . . full height
4 Ft. Front Deck Extension . . . . . . . . . . . . optional hydraulic
4 Ft. Rear Deck Extension . . . . . . . . . . . . . optional hydraulic
Platform Material . . . . . . . . . . . . . . . . steel tread plate
* Additional 3 in. (0.08 m) height with optional deck extension
** 32 ft. with optional pneumatic tires

### CHASSIS

Drive Speed – 2 Wheel Drive . . . . . . . . . . 3.5 mph (5.6 kph)
Drive Speed – 4 Wheel Drive (optional) . . . . 2.8 mph (4.5 kph)
Gradeability – 2 Wheel Drive . . . . . . . . . . . . . . 35%
Gradeability – 4 Wheel Drive (optional) . . . . . . . . 45%
Turning Radius (inside) – 2 Wheel Steer . . . . 13 ft. 2 in. (4.01 m)
Turning Radius (inside) – 4 Wheel Steer . . . . . 6 ft. 6 in. (1.98 m)
Turning Radius (outside) – 2 Wheel Steer . . . 18 ft. 9 in. (5.72 m)
Turning Radius (outside) – 4 Wheel Steer . . . 12 ft. 1 in. (3.68 m)
Axle Oscillation (optional) . . . . . . . . . . . . . . 8 in. (0.20 m)
Tire Size . . . . . . . . . . . . . . . . . . . . . . . . 12 x 16.5
Tire Type . . . . . . . . . . . . . . . . . . . . . . . . . . foam
Brakes . . . . . . . . . . . . . . . . . . . . spring applied multi-disc

### POWER SYSTEM

Gasoline Engine . . . . . . . . . Ford LSG 423 63 hp @ 2,800 rpm
Diesel Engine (optional) . . . . Deutz F3L-1011 41 hp @ 2,800 rpm
Fuel Tank Capacity . . . . . . . . . . . . . . . . 15 gal. (56.8 L)
Hydraulic Reservoir . . . . . . . . . . . . . . . . 37 gal. (140 L)
Gross Vehicle Weight . . . . . . . . . . . . 13,500 lbs. (6,125 kg)

**Figure 199**  Lift specifications.

## 500 RTS

### DIMENSIONAL DATA

A. Platform Height Elevated . . . . . . . . . . . . . 50 ft. (15.24 m)
B. Platform Height Lowered . . . . . . . . . . . 6 ft. 8 in. (2.03 m)
C. Railing Height* . . . . . . . . . . . . . . . . . . . 43.5 in. (1.10 m)
D. Overall Height (rails folded down)* . . . . . 8 ft. 0.5 in. (2.45 m)
E. Platform Dimensions . . . . . . . 71 in. x 168 in. (1.80 x 4.27 m)
F. Deck Extension . . . . . . . . . . . . . . . . . . 4 ft. (1.23 m)
G. Overall Width . . . . . . . . . . . . . . . . . . . . 7 ft 6 in. (2.29 m)
   Overall Width w/Optional Tires . . . . . . . . 7 ft. 7 in. (2.31 m)
H. Overall Length . . . . . . . . . . . . . . . . . 15 ft. 5 in. (4.70 m)
I. Wheelbase . . . . . . . . . . . . . . . . . . . . 122 in. (3.10 m)
J. Ground Clearance . . . . . . . . . . . . . . . . 12 in. (0.30 m)
Capacity . . . . . . . . . . . . . . . . . . . 2,500 lbs. (1,134 kg)
Capacity with Optional Deck Extension . . . . . 2,000 lbs. (907 kg)
Capacity on each Optional Deck Extension . . . . 500 lbs. (227 kg)
Lift/Lower Speed . . . . . . . . . . . . . . . . . . . . . 72/72 sec.
Maximum Drive Height . . . . . . . . . . . . . . . 22 ft. (6.71 m)
4 Ft. Front Deck Extension . . . . . . . . . . . . optional hydraulic
4 Ft. Rear Deck Extension . . . . . . . . . . . . optional hydraulic
Platform Material . . . . . . . . . . . . . . . . . . steel tread plate
\* Additional 3 in. (0.08 m) height with optional deck extension

### CHASSIS

Drive Speed – 2 Wheel Drive . . . . . . . . . . . 3.5 mph (5.6 kph)
Drive Speed – 4 Wheel Drive (optional) . . . . . 2.8 mph (4.5 kph)
Gradeability – 2 Wheel . . . . . . . . . . . . . . . . . . . . . 35%
Gradeability – 4 Wheel (optional) . . . . . . . . . . . . . . . . 45%
Turning Radius (inside) – 2 Wheel Steer . . . . 13 ft. 2 in. (3.99 m)
Turning Radius (inside) – 4 Wheel Steer . . . . 6 ft. 6 in. (2.98 m)
Turning Radius (outside) – 2 Wheel Steer . . . . 18 ft. 9 in. (5.72 m)
Turning Radius (outside) – 4 Wheel Steer . . . . 12 ft. 1 in. (3.68 m)
Axle Oscillation (optional) . . . . . . . . . . . . . . 8 in. (0.20 m)
Tire Size . . . . . . . . . . . . . . . . . . . . . . . . . . 12 x 16.5
Tire Type . . . . . . . . . . . . . . . . . . . . . . . . . . . . . air
Brakes . . . . . . . . . . . . . . . . . . . . spring applied multi-disc

### POWER SYSTEM

Gasoline Engine . . . . . . . Ford LSG 423 63 hp @ 2,800 rpm
Diesel Engine (optional) . . . Deutz F3L-1011 41 hp @ 2,800 rpm
Fuel Tank Capacity . . . . . . . . . . . . . . . . . 15 gal. (56.8 L)
Hydraulic Reservoir . . . . . . . . . . . . . . . . . 37 gal. (140 L)
Gross Vehicle Weight . . . . . . . . . . . . . 15,300 lbs. (6,940 kg)

**Figure 200** Lift specifications.

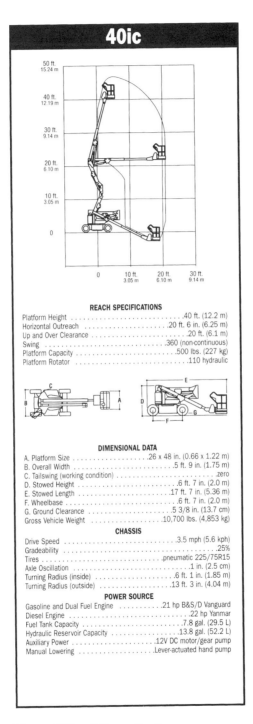

## 40ic

### REACH SPECIFICATIONS

Platform Height . . . . . . . . . . . . . . . . . . . . . . . . . . . .40 ft. (12.2 m)
Horizontal Outreach . . . . . . . . . . . . . . . . . . . . .20 ft. 6 in. (6.25 m)
Up and Over Clearance . . . . . . . . . . . . . . . . . . . . . . .20 ft. (6.1 m)
Swing . . . . . . . . . . . . . . . . . . . . . . . . . . . . . .360 (non-continuous)
Platform Capacity . . . . . . . . . . . . . . . . . . . . . . . . .500 lbs. (227 kg)
Platform Rotator . . . . . . . . . . . . . . . . . . . . . . . . . . .110 hydraulic

### DIMENSIONAL DATA

A. Platform Size . . . . . . . . . . . . . . . . . .26 x 48 in. (0.66 x 1.22 m)
B. Overall Width . . . . . . . . . . . . . . . . . . . . . . . . .5 ft. 9 in. (1.75 m)
C. Tailswing (working condition) . . . . . . . . . . . . . . . . . . . . . .zero
D. Stowed Height . . . . . . . . . . . . . . . . . . . . . . . .6 ft. 7 in. (2.0 m)
E. Stowed Length . . . . . . . . . . . . . . . . . . . . . .17 ft. 7 in. (5.36 m)
F. Wheelbase . . . . . . . . . . . . . . . . . . . . . . . . . .6 ft. 7 in. (2.0 m)
G. Ground Clearance . . . . . . . . . . . . . . . . . . . .5 3/8 in. (13.7 cm)
Gross Vehicle Weight . . . . . . . . . . . . . . . .10,700 lbs. (4,853 kg)

### CHASSIS

Drive Speed . . . . . . . . . . . . . . . . . . . . . . . . . . . .3.5 mph (5.6 kph)
Gradeability . . . . . . . . . . . . . . . . . . . . . . . . . . . . . . . . . . . . . .25%
Tires . . . . . . . . . . . . . . . . . . . . . . . . . . . . . .pneumatic 225/75R15
Axle Oscillation . . . . . . . . . . . . . . . . . . . . . . . . . . . .1 in. (2.5 cm)
Turning Radius (inside) . . . . . . . . . . . . . . . . . . . .6 ft. 1 in. (1.85 m)
Turning Radius (outside) . . . . . . . . . . . . . . . . . .13 ft. 3 in. (4.04 m)

### POWER SOURCE

Gasoline and Dual Fuel Engine . . . . . . . . . . .21 hp B&S/D Vanguard
Diesel Engine . . . . . . . . . . . . . . . . . . . . . . . . . . . . . .22 hp Yanmar
Fuel Tank Capacity . . . . . . . . . . . . . . . . . . . . . . . .7.8 gal. (29.5 L)
Hydraulic Reservoir Capacity . . . . . . . . . . . . . . . .13.8 gal. (52.2 L)
Auxiliary Power . . . . . . . . . . . . . . . . . . . . .12V DC motor/gear pump
Manual Lowering . . . . . . . . . . . . . . . . . . . .Lever-actuated hand pump

**Figure 201**    Lift specifications.

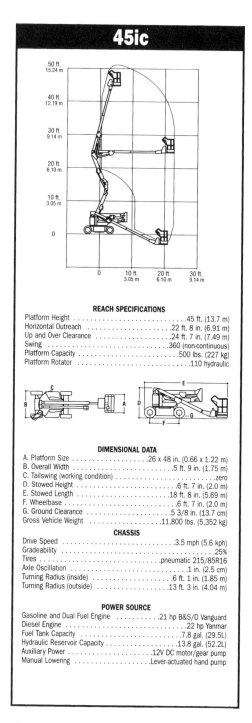

**Figure 202** Lift specifications.

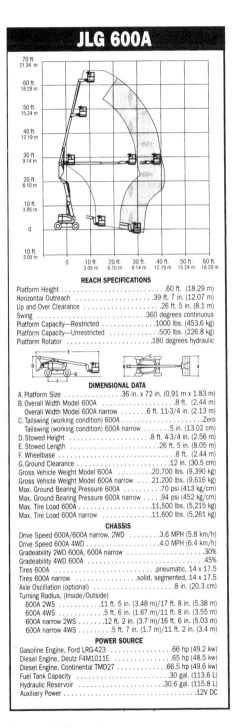

**JLG 600A**

**REACH SPECIFICATIONS**

Platform Height . . . . . . . . . . . . . . . . . . . . . . . . . . .60 ft. (18.29 m)
Horizontal Outreach . . . . . . . . . . . . . . . . . . .39 ft. 7 in. (12.07 m)
Up and Over Clearance . . . . . . . . . . . . . . . . . .26 ft. 5 in. (8.1 m)
Swing . . . . . . . . . . . . . . . . . . . . . . . . . . . .360 degrees continuous
Platform Capacity—Restricted . . . . . . . . . . . . . .1000 lbs. (453.6 kg)
Platform Capacity—Unrestricted . . . . . . . . . . . .500 lbs. (226.8 kg)
Platform Rotator . . . . . . . . . . . . . . . . . . . . . .180 degrees hydraulic

**DIMENSIONAL DATA**

A. Platform Size . . . . . . . . . . . . . . .36 in. x 72 in. (0.91 m x 1.83 m)
B. Overall Width Model 600A . . . . . . . . . . . . . . . . . . .8 ft. (2.44 m)
   Overall Width Model 600A narrow . . . . . . .6 ft. 11-3/4 in. (2.13 m)
C. Tailswing (working condition) 600A . . . . . . . . . . . . . . . . . . . .Zero
   Tailswing (working condition) 600A narrow . . . . . . .5 in. (13.02 cm)
D. Stowed Height . . . . . . . . . . . . . . . . . . . .8 ft. 4-3/4 in. (2.56 m)
E. Stowed Length . . . . . . . . . . . . . . . . . . . . . .26 ft. 5 in. (8.05 m)
F. Wheelbase . . . . . . . . . . . . . . . . . . . . . . . . . . . . .8 ft. (2.44 m)
G. Ground Clearance . . . . . . . . . . . . . . . . . . . . . .12 in. (30.5 cm)
Gross Vehicle Weight Model 600A . . . . . . . .20,700 lbs. (9,390 kg)
Gross Vehicle Weight Model 600A narrow . . . .21,200 lbs. (9,616 kg)
Max. Ground Bearing Pressure 600A . . . . . . . . . .70 psi (413 kg/cm)
Max. Ground Bearing Pressure 600A narrow . . . . .94 psi (452 kg/cm)
Max. Tire Load 600A . . . . . . . . . . . . . . . . . .11,500 lbs. (5,215 kg)
Max. Tire Load 600A narrow . . . . . . . . . . . . .11,600 lbs. (5,261 kg)

**CHASSIS**

Drive Speed 600A/600A narrow, 2WD . . . . . . .3.6 MPH (5.8 km/h)
Drive Speed 600A 4WD . . . . . . . . . . . . . . . . .4.0 MPH (6.4 km/h)
Gradeability 2WD 600A, 600A narrow . . . . . . . . . . . . . . . . . .30%
Gradeability 4WD 600A . . . . . . . . . . . . . . . . . . . . . . . . . . . .45%
Tires 600A . . . . . . . . . . . . . . . . . . . . . . . .pneumatic, 14 x 17.5
Tires 600A narrow . . . . . . . . . . . . . . . .solid, segmented, 14 x 17.5
Axle Oscillation (optional) . . . . . . . . . . . . . . . . . . . .8 in. (20.3 cm)
Turning Radius, (Inside/Outside)
   600A 2WS . . . . . . . . . . .11 ft. 5 in. (3.48 m)/17 ft. 8 in. (5.38 m)
   600A 4WS . . . . . . . . . . .5 ft. 6 in. (1.67 m)/11 ft. 8 in. (3.55 m)
   600A narrow 2WS . . . . . .12 ft. 2 in. (3.7 m)/16 ft. 6 in. (5.03 m)
   600A narrow 4WS . . . . . . . .5 ft. 7 in. (1.7 m)/11 ft. 2 in. (3.4 m)

**POWER SOURCE**

Gasoline Engine, Ford LRG-423 . . . . . . . . . . . . . .66 hp (49.2 kw)
Diesel Engine, Deutz F4M1011E . . . . . . . . . . . . . .65 hp (48.5 kw)
Diesel Engine, Continental TMD27 . . . . . . . . . . . .66.5 hp (49.6 kw)
Fuel Tank Capacity . . . . . . . . . . . . . . . . . . . . . .30 gal. (113.6 L)
Hydraulic Reservoir . . . . . . . . . . . . . . . . . . . . .30.6 gal. (115.8 L)
Auxiliary Power . . . . . . . . . . . . . . . . . . . . . . . . . . . . . . . .12V DC

**Figure 203**   Lift specifications.

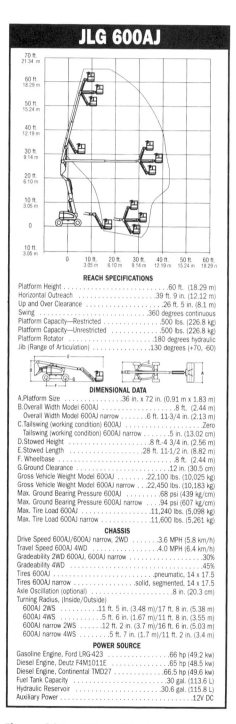

**JLG 600AJ**

**REACH SPECIFICATIONS**

Platform Height . . . . . . . . . . . . . . . . . . . . . . . . . . .60 ft. (18.29 m)
Horizontal Outreach . . . . . . . . . . . . . . . . . . . .39 ft. 9 in. (12.12 m)
Up and Over Clearance . . . . . . . . . . . . . . . . . .26 ft. 5 in. (8.1 m)
Swing . . . . . . . . . . . . . . . . . . . . . . . . . . .360 degrees continuous
Platform Capacity—Restricted . . . . . . . . . . . . .500 lbs. (226.8 kg)
Platform Capacity—Unrestricted . . . . . . . . . . .500 lbs. (226.8 kg)
Platform Rotator . . . . . . . . . . . . . . . . . . . . .180 degrees hydraulic
Jib (Range of Articulation) . . . . . . . . . . . . . .130 degrees (+70, -60)

**DIMENSIONAL DATA**

A.Platform Size . . . . . . . . . . . . . . .36 in. x 72 in. (0.91 m x 1.83 m)
B.Overall Width Model 600AJ . . . . . . . . . . . . . . . . .8 ft. (2.44 m)
Overall Width Model 600AJ narrow . . . . . . .6 ft. 11-3/4 in. (2.13 m)
C.Tailswing (working condition) 600AJ . . . . . . . . . . . . . . . . . .Zero
Tailswing (working condition) 600AJ narrow . . . . . . .5 in. (13.02 cm)
D.Stowed Height . . . . . . . . . . . . . . . . . .8 ft.-4 3/4 in. (2.56 m)
E.Stowed Length . . . . . . . . . . . . . . . . . . .28 ft. 11-1/2 in. (8.82 m)
F. Wheelbase . . . . . . . . . . . . . . . . . . . . . . . . . . . .8 ft. (2.44 m)
G.Ground Clearance . . . . . . . . . . . . . . . . . . . . . .12 in. (30.5 cm)
Gross Vehicle Weight Model 600AJ . . . . . . . .22,100 lbs. (10,025 kg)
Gross Vehicle Weight Model 600AJ narrow . . .22,450 lbs. (10,183 kg)
Max. Ground Bearing Pressure 600AJ . . . . . . . .68 psi (439 kg/cm)
Max. Ground Bearing Pressure 600AJ narrow . . . .94 psi (607 kg/cm)
Max. Tire Load 600AJ . . . . . . . . . . . . . . . .11,240 lbs. (5,098 kg)
Max. Tire Load 600AJ narrow . . . . . . . . . . . .11,600 lbs. (5,261 kg)

**CHASSIS**

Drive Speed 600AJ/600AJ narrow, 2WD . . . . . . .3.6 MPH (5.8 km/h)
Travel Speed 600AJ 4WD . . . . . . . . . . . . . . . .4.0 MPH (6.4 km/h)
Gradeability 2WD 600AJ, 600AJ narrow . . . . . . . . . . . . . . . . . .30%
Gradeability 4WD . . . . . . . . . . . . . . . . . . . . . . . . . . . . . . . .45%
Tires 600AJ . . . . . . . . . . . . . . . . . . . . . . .pneumatic, 14 x 17.5
Tires 600AJ narrow . . . . . . . . . . . . . . .solid, segmented, 14 x 17.5
Axle Oscillation (optional) . . . . . . . . . . . . . . . . . . . .8 in. (20.3 cm)
Turning Radius, (Inside/Outside)
600AJ 2WS . . . . . . . . .11 ft. 5 in. (3.48 m)/17 ft. 8 in. (5.38 m)
600AJ 4WS . . . . . . . . . .5 ft. 6 in. (1.67 m)/11 ft. 8 in. (3.55 m)
600AJ narrow 2WS . . . . . .12 ft. 2 in. (3.7 m)/16 ft. 6 in. (5.03 m)
600AJ narrow 4WS . . . . . . .5 ft. 7 in. (1.7 m)/11 ft. 2 in. (3.4 m)

**POWER SOURCE**

Gasoline Engine, Ford LRG-423 . . . . . . . . . . . . . . .66 hp (49.2 kw)
Diesel Engine, Deutz F4M1011E . . . . . . . . . . . . . .65 hp (48.5 kw)
Diesel Engine, Continental TMD27 . . . . . . . . . . . .66.5 hp (49.6 kw)
Fuel Tank Capacity . . . . . . . . . . . . . . . . . . . . . .30 gal. (113.6 L)
Hydraulic Reservoir . . . . . . . . . . . . . . . . . . . . .30.6 gal. (115.8 L)
Auxiliary Power . . . . . . . . . . . . . . . . . . . . . . . . . . . . . . . .12V DC

**Figure 204** Lift specifications.

# 150HAX ARTICULATING BOOM LIFT

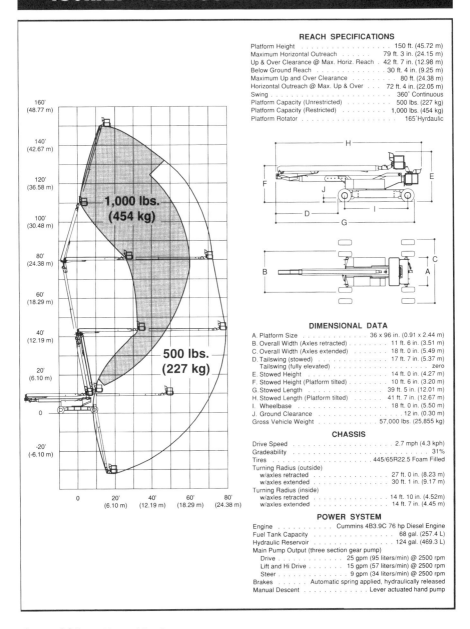

**REACH SPECIFICATIONS**

| | |
|---|---|
| Platform Height | 150 ft. (45.72 m) |
| Maximum Horizontal Outreach | 79 ft. 3 in. (24.15 m) |
| Up & Over Clearance @ Max. Horiz. Reach | 42 ft. 7 in. (12.98 m) |
| Below Ground Reach | 30 ft. 4 in. (9.25 m) |
| Maximum Up and Over Clearance | 80 ft. (24.38 m) |
| Horizontal Outreach @ Max. Up & Over | 72 ft. 4 in. (22.05 m) |
| Swing | 360° Continuous |
| Platform Capacity (Unrestricted) | 500 lbs. (227 kg) |
| Platform Capacity (Restricted) | 1,000 lbs. (454 kg) |
| Platform Rotator | 165° Hyrdaulic |

**1,000 lbs. (454 kg)**

**500 lbs. (227 kg)**

**DIMENSIONAL DATA**

| | |
|---|---|
| A. Platform Size | 36 x 96 in. (0.91 x 2.44 m) |
| B. Overall Width (Axles retracted) | 11 ft. 6 in. (3.51 m) |
| C. Overall Width (Axles extended) | 18 ft. 0 in. (5.49 m) |
| D. Tailswing (stowed) | 17 ft. 7 in. (5.37 m) |
| Tailswing (fully elevated) | zero |
| E. Stowed Height | 14 ft. 0 in. (4.27 m) |
| F. Stowed Height (Platform tilted) | 10 ft. 6 in. (3.20 m) |
| G. Stowed Length | 39 ft. 5 in. (12.01 m) |
| H. Stowed Length (Platform tilted) | 41 ft. 7 in. (12.67 m) |
| I. Wheelbase | 18 ft. 0 in. (5.50 m) |
| J. Ground Clearance | 12 in. (0.30 m) |
| Gross Vehicle Weight | 57,000 lbs. (25,855 kg) |

**CHASSIS**

| | |
|---|---|
| Drive Speed | 2.7 mph (4.3 kph) |
| Gradeability | 31% |
| Tires | 445/65R22.5 Foam Filled |
| Turning Radius (outside) | |
| w/axles retracted | 27 ft. 0 in. (8.23 m) |
| w/axles extended | 30 ft. 1 in. (9.17 m) |
| Turning Radius (inside) | |
| w/axles retracted | 14 ft. 10 in. (4.52m) |
| w/axles extended | 14 ft. 7 in. (4.45 m) |

**POWER SYSTEM**

| | |
|---|---|
| Engine | Cummins 4B3.9C 76 hp Diesel Engine |
| Fuel Tank Capacity | 68 gal. (257.4 L) |
| Hydraulic Reservoir | 124 gal. (469.3 L) |
| Main Pump Output (three section gear pump) | |
| Drive | 25 gpm (95 liters/min) @ 2500 rpm |
| Lift and Hi Drive | 15 gpm (57 liters/min) @ 2500 rpm |
| Steer | 9 gpm (34 liters/min) @ 2500 rpm |
| Brakes | Automatic spring applied, hydraulically released |
| Manual Descent | Lever actuated hand pump |

**Figure 205** Lift specifications.

MIKE'S NOTE: *Too large costs extra money. Too small costs time and money. The dispatcher asks necessary questions about details to avoid extra costs and to ensure you have the proper size crane.*

### Additional Equipment

The following pieces of equipment are helpful for work with lifts, cherry pickers, or booms:

**Figure 206**  Camera tie-down.

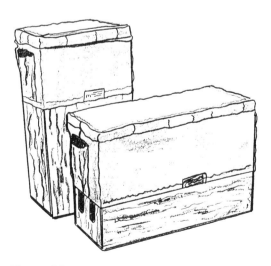

**Figure 207**  Apple boxes.

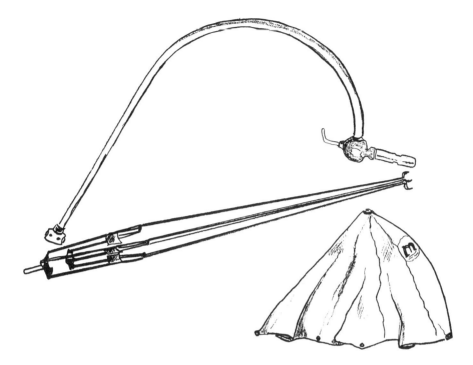

**Figure 208**    Sun umbrella.

**Figure 209**    Cherry picker, boom, scissors lift light mount.

**Figure 210a**   Full body harness.

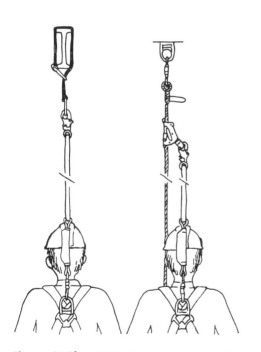

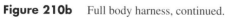

**Figure 210b**   Full body harness, continued.

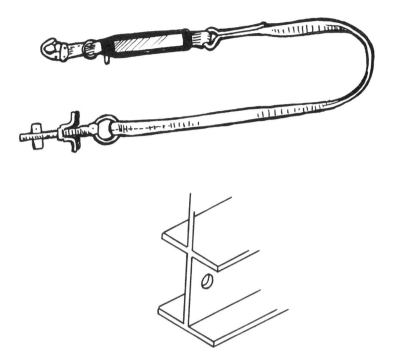

**Figure 210c**   Full body harness, continued.

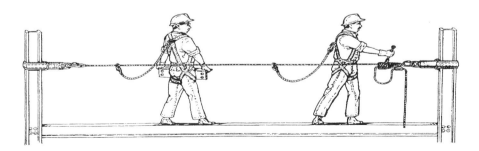

**Figure 210d**   Full body harness, continued.

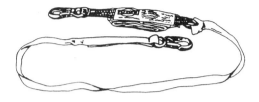

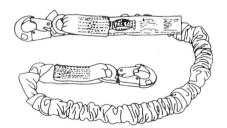

**Figure 210e**   Full body harness, continued.

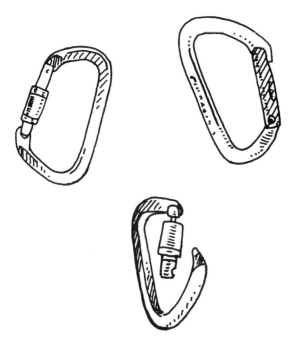

**Figure 210f**   Quick release rings for full body harness.

The body harness is great for retrieval and rescue. A retrieval safety line is attached to a D ring on the back of the harness.

# Glossary

I list some terms or words that you may hear daily in the course of your stay in the film and television business. A few of these words may be exclusive to the grip department. For the sake of giving you an overall flavor of a working set, I felt you should be aware of some general words used almost daily. Here is an example: You're a grip asked to work the *sticks* for the camera department. The assistant director (AD) yells, "Tail Slate." Or you might hear something like, "Hey, Sue, grab a Gary Coleman with a postage stamp and put an ear on the third zip light. Moveit lamp right next to the egg crate, then drop some beach on that hog trough before they pull the buck." Say what?

**Abby singer**   The shot before the last shot.

**Ambiance**   Sound recorded in the area in which filming was done. This recorded "quiet" sound is added to set the mood of a scene.

**B team**   The stand-ins used for blocking and lighting a scene.

**Baby**   A 1,000-watt lamp

**Backing**   A photographed or painted canvas background used on movie sets seen outside windows or doors.

**Bail**   The U-shaped metal arm on which a movie lamp sits. The bottom of the U has either a male pin or a female receiver for attachment to a stand or hanger device.

**Beach**   A sandbag.

**Block and fall**   A rope and pulley system that allows one to lift a heavy object with less pulling force.

**Blocking**   A rehearsal for actors and camera movement.

**Boggie wheels**   Wheels that do not usually come standard with a dolly. They are used to adapt a dolly to specialty track, such as a pipe dolly, sled dolly, or tube track. There are several types or sets of boggie wheels.

**Booties**   Surgical paper shoes worn over street shoes before walking on a dry painted surface. Prevents a mar or a scuff.

**259**

**Brownie**   Camera.

**Brute**   A carbon arc lamp that runs on 225 amperes.

**Buck**   A car that has been cut in half or the roof cut off for filming the inside of the vehicle, as to show a center console or dashboard.

**Charlie bar**   A 1- to 6-inch wide by 3-foot long strip of wood with an attached pin used to create shadows on an object (thin long flags, gobos).

**Cleat**   A point on which to tie off rope, usually an X-shaped or cross-shaped piece of wood nailed to a stage floor.

**Come-a-long**   A hand crank cable that can pull heavy objects closer together, such as a wrenching block and fall.

**Crossing**   Spoken or yelled when crossing in front of a lens. A courtesy to a camera person who is looking through the eyepiece.

**Cyc-strips**   A single lamp or several lamps in one housing fixture.

**Dailies**   Film shot the day before that is shown to the director, camera operator, and crew. A review of the day's work to ensure reshoots are not needed. Sometimes called *rushes.*

**Dapple**   Shadows made by a branch with leaves on it.

**Deal memo**   A document that describes the fee you have accepted for your service.

**Down stage**   Closer to the camera or audience.

**Dutch angle**   To lean the camera sideways to film in that position.

**Ears on**   Turn on your handheld walkie-talkie.

**Egg crate**   A soft-light control frame that directs light without it spilling off the subject. Looks like a rectangular box with several dividers spaced evenly in it.

**Fill light**   Light added opposite the key light. Used to wash out shadows.

**First team**   The talent, the heroes. The actors being filmed; also called the *A team.*

**Flare**   Unwanted light that hits the lens, causing a distortion or distracting light on film.

**Flashing**   A warning called out before someone takes a flash photo. This lets the gaffer know that one of her lights has not burned out.

**Float a flag**   To handhold a flag as the camera is moved; to float with the camera to block unwanted light flares.

**Fly it out**   Pull something out of a scene (i.e., a prop or product that is not to be filmed).

**Flying in**   Acquisition of a requested object in an extremely quick manner.

**Flying the moon**   A technique in which a bunch of lights is hung on pipes shaped into a box frame, wrapped in a muslin cover, and flown over an exterior location by a cable on a crane.

**Fresnel**   The glass piece in front of a lamp that will focus the light.

**Gary Coleman**   A nickname for a 20-inch high C stand.

**Greek it out**   To disguise a word to make a logo unrecognizable. Example: Coke might become Ooko AA Cola.

**Hemp**   Rope from $^1/_4$ to 1 inch, usually.

**Hero**   The product in a commercial, such as a perfectly prepared hamburger, a toy, or color-corrected label. Whatever it is, it is perfect (hero) for the shot.

**Highlight**   A technique to brighten an area or an object or to emphasize an interesting part with light.

**History**   Remove it from the set, lose it, only a memory, gone, vapor.

**Hog trough**   Use of nails, screws, or glue and two pieces of 1-inch by 3-inch lumber to make an L- or V-shaped brace. This process makes an otherwise flimsy piece of 1 by 3 stronger by giving it a backbone.

**Inky**   A small 200 to 500 watt lamp.

**Junior**   A 2,000 watt lamp

**Kick**   A sparkle off an object or person. May be desired or may have to be removed.

**Luan**   Plywood-like material about ¹/₈ inch thick used to make set walls.

**Make it live**   Set the object in place.

**Martini shot**   Last film shot of the day. The wrap shot is "in a glass."

**Michael Jackson**   Get out of the way; taken from his song "Beat It."

**Mickey mole**   A 1,000 watt lamp.

**Mickey Rooney**   A nickname for a little creep of the dolly; a slight, slow movement.

**Midget**   A small lamp 200 watt to 500 watt.

**Mighty mole**   A 2,000 watt lamp.

**Molelipso**   A 1,000 to 2,000 watt lamp used mainly for performances.

**Neck down**   Hired from the neck down; that is, not to think, but just for physical labor.

**NG**   "No good."

**Nodal point**   The dead center of the camera lens if the camera were to rotate in a 360-degree twisting motion.

**Nook lite**   A lamp of 650 to 2,000 watts.

**On stage**   Move toward the center of the set or stage.

**Over-cranking**   A technique to speed up the frame rate of film through a camera. When processed and projected at normal speed (24 feet per second), the action appears in slow motion.

**Pepper**   A 200 watt lamp.

**Poor man's process**   Filming a stationary vehicle by means of passing a light, shadow, or background object by it to the impression that the vehicle is in motion. Also slight shaking or using a lever under the frame to give it a small jolt.

**Postage stamp**   A 10-inch-by-12-inch framed diffusion used to block or reduce light.

**Reefing**   A way to fold a large rag, such as grifflon, black, or any material that requires folding.

**Seamless paper**   A wide roll of paper used for a background, as in a portrait shot.

**Sheave**   A wheel with a grooved rim, as in a pulley.

**Softlight**   A range from 650 watts to 4,000 watts on an average; also known as *zip light.*

**Snoot**  A device shaped like a funnel or coffee can hooked to the front of a lamp.

**Span set**  A loop of extremely strong material wrapped around a frame or beam being hoisted up by a winch or crane. Comes in 1- to 20-foot loops and can be larger on request.

**Speed**  The condition in which the camera operator or sound technician has the equipment running at the desired speed or operating revolutions per minute for filming.

**Squib**  A small explosive device activated by means of pressing the talk button on a two-way radio. Used to make a bullet hole or wound during a scene.

**Sticks**  Usually clapped together to help the editor to "merry up" the sound of a scene (aka, slate).

**Storyboards**  Cartoon-like drawings used as a representation for the shoot to indicate the camera angles or framing.

**Tag lines**  Ropes, usually $1/4$-inch hemp, tied to a lamp hanger used to pan or tie off a lamp.

**Tail slate**  To hit the camera sticks after the scene has been shot. The slate is turned upside down with wording facing the lens, then the hinged sticks are slapped together, also called *tail sticks*.

**Talent**  Actors.

**Tetons**  A sharp flat peg with a ring welded to it on which to tie off a rope. It can be hammered into small cracks in concrete or asphalt without much damage.

**Tilt**  Move camera up and down in a tilting motion.

**Tweenie**  A 650-watt lamp.

**Upstage**  To move toward the back of the set or stage (comes from older stages that were built with a higher or raked upward incline toward the rear, away from the audience).

**Waffling**  To fan out the applied atmosphere smoke with a paddle or small flag.

**Wall brace**  A metal rod flattened on each end with holes drilled through it to attach a set wall to the wood slatted floor. Also a hog trough can be used (see hog trough).

**Wall jack**  A two-wheeled brace or jack used to transport a large set wall.

**Wall sconce**  A lamp hung on a wall; a practical fixture.

**Warner Brothers**  Term used for an extreme close-up of a person that cuts the top of the head from the frame.

**Whip-pan**  A fast pan of the camera that causes a blur in the motion.

**Wild ceiling or wild wall**  Walls made to move individually from each other for filming.

**Wipe**  An image that moves across the frame during filming; used to hide a cut during editing.

**Zip light**  See *softlight*.